DEPRESSION

DEPRESSION
The way out of your prison

Dorothy Rowe

Routledge & Kegan Paul
London and New York

First published in 1983
by Routledge & Kegan Paul Ltd.
11 New Fetter Lane, London EC4P 4EE
Published in the USA by
Routledge and Kegan Paul Inc.
in association with Methuen Inc.
29 West 35th Street, New York, NY 10001
Set in Century Schoolbook, 10 on 11½pt
and printed in Great Britain by
Cox & Wyman Ltd, Reading
Reprinted in 1983, 1984, 1985 (twice) and 1987
© Dorothy Rowe 1983

Library of Congress Cataloging in Publication Data

Rowe, Dorothy.
Depression, the way out of your prison.
Bibliography: p.
Includes index.
I. Depression, Mental. 1, Title [DNLM: 1, Depressive
disorder. WM 171 R878d]
RC537.R66 1983   616.85'27   83–11074

ISBN 0–7100–9699–2
ISBN 0–7100–9586–4 (pbk.)

CONTENTS

PREFACE

Depression is as old as the human race, and rare is the person who has not felt its touch. Sometimes, suddenly, without apparent reason, we feel unbearably sad. The world turns grey, and we taste a bitterness in our mouth. We hear an echo of the bell that tolls our passing, and we reach out for a comforting hand, but find ourselves alone. For some of us this experience is no more than a fleeting moment, or something we can dispel with common-sense thoughts and practical actions. But for some of us this experience becomes a ghost whose unbidden presence mars every feast, or, worse, a prison whose walls, though invisible, are quite impenetrable.

Depression, in this century, has been called an illness and treated with pills and ECT. Some people are greatly helped by this treatment. Their depression vanishes, never to return. However, for some people, pills and ECT bring only temporary relief or no change at all. For these people something more is needed, and this is not surprising, since being depressed is something more than being ill.

If we have measles or a broken leg, we may feel miserable and inconvenienced, but, unless we feel we are so ill that we might die, we do not spend our time worrying about our sins, or contemplating the futility of existence. Yet if we are depressed this is what we do. In our own way and in our own terms we think about, agonise about, the issues of life and death – which are about what purpose life has, what faith we can live by, whether our life ends in death or whether something lies beyond death, what we have done and our feelings of shame and guilt, fear and courage, forgiveness and revenge, anger, jealousy, hate and love. For some of us, out of this period of painful turmoil comes a measure of peace and wisdom; for others, the confusion continues.

Depression is so common in all cultures and throughout history that it seems to be more than just a painful illness. It seems to be a universal experience, a period of unhappy withdrawal, an uncomfortable hibernation where the person comes to realise that something has gone wrong with his life and that something needs to be put right. Why is it, then, that some people going through this experience do discover what it is that needs to be put right, while others go on and on in miserable confusion?

Over the past twelve years I have had long conversations with people whose depression has persisted despite all the best medical treatment. I have also had long conversations with people who have had their fair share of problems but nevertheless still cope. People who cope and people who get depressed see the issues of life and death in very different terms.

Some of the depressed people I have talked with have found their way out of their depression. Others still get depressed from time to time, but they now have some idea why this happens. Depression is a prison which we build for ourselves. Just as we build it, so we can unlock the door and let ourselves out.

Dorothy Rowe
Eagle, Lincolnshire

ACKNOWLEDGMENTS

The authors and publishers are grateful to the following for their permission to reproduce cartoons: Hector Breeze and *Punch* (p. 43: 12 August 1981), reproduced by permission of *Punch*; Fiona Buckland (p. 173); Phil Evans and *Sanity* (p. 121: 1981, no. 6, December/January); Jules Feiffer and Shanks, Davis & Remer (p. 23: *Observer*, 20 February 1977), reprinted by permission of Jules Feiffer; Tony Heath and the *Guardian* (p. 132: 27 January 1982; p. 151: 14 April 1982; p. 217: 12 May 1982); A.F. Ralley and Advance Features (p. 161: *Lincolnshire Echo*, 2 January 1982). They also acknowledge permission to quote passages from copyright material as follows: Connie Bensley and Harry Chambers for extracts from *Progress Report, Poems by Connie Bensley* (Harry Chambers/Peterloo Poets, 1981, copyright Connie Bensley); Collins, Publishers, for extracts from Philip Toynbee, *Part of a Journey* (1981); Faber & Faber for quotations from T.S. Eliot, Robert Lowell and Louis MacNeice; Farrar, Straus & Giroux Inc. for quotations from 'Day by Day' by Robert Lowell and 'The Elder Statesman' by T.S. Eliot; Harcourt Brace Jovanovich Inc. for a quotation from 'Little Gidding' from *Four Quartets* by T.S. Eliot; The Hogarth Press for an extract from *Requiem and Other Poems* by R.M. Rilke, translated by J.B. Leishman (1957); Bill Lyons and Bill McLean for a poem from a BBC radio play 'The Stranger in My Head', written by Bill Lyons; MIND for an extract from an article by Jeremy Ross in *Mind Out*, no. 56, 1981; Laurence Pollinger Ltd, Viking-Penguin Inc. and the estate of Frieda Lawrence Ravagli for lines from 'The Hands of God' by D.H. Lawrence; Oxford University Press for 'Things' from *The Inner Harbour* by Fleur Adcock, © Fleur Adcock 1979, reprinted by permission of Oxford University Press; Jill Tweedie, Jonathan Cape Ltd and Pantheon Books Inc. for extracts from *In the Name of Love* (1979); Jill Tweedie and the *Guardian* for extracts from her article of 17 April 1982; John Wiley & Sons Ltd for extracts from Dorothy Rowe, *The Experience of Depression* (1978) and *The Construction of Life and Death* (1982).

Chapter 1

THE PRISON

What is the difference between being depressed and being unhappy? There is a difference, and when you have experienced both you know what this difference is.

When you are unhappy, even if you have suffered the most grievous blow, you are able to seek comfort and let that comfort come through to you to ease the pain. You can seek out and obtain another's sympathy and loving concern; you can be kind and comfort yourself. But in depression neither the sympathy and concern of others nor the gentle love of oneself is available. Other people may be there, offering all the love, sympathy and concern any person could want, but none of this compassion can pierce the wall that separates you from them, while inside the wall you not only refuse yourself the smallest ease and comfort but you also punish yourself by words and deeds. Depression is a prison where you are both the suffering prisoner and the cruel jailer.

It is this peculiar isolation which distinguishes depression from common unhappiness.[1] It is not simply loneliness, although in the prison of depression you are pitifully alone. It is an isolation which changes even your perception of your environment. Intellectually you know that you are sharing a space with other people, that you are talking to them and they are hearing you. But their words come to you as if across a bottomless chasm, and even though you can reach out and touch another person, or that person touches you, nothing is transmitted to you in that touch. No human contact crosses the barrier. Even objects around you seem further away, although you know it is not so, and while you are aware that the sun is shining and the birds are singing, you know, even more poignantly, that the colour has drained from the sky and the birds are silent.

How can you describe this experience and convey its meaning to someone else? Saying that you are depressed, or really down, or fed-up, can mean to another person no more than the Monday morning blues, or something you could snap out of if you really tried. But you know that it is not a passing mood or something that will vanish if you try to 'pull yourself together'. The turmoil of your feelings is so great that it is impossible to know where to begin to describe them. So it is better to remain silent.

Yet there is a way of conveying what you are experiencing. If you were an artist or a film-maker, you would be able to create an image which would convey at least something of what you are experiencing. It is for this reason that I always ask my depressed clients, usually at our first meeting, this question. 'IF YOU COULD PAINT A PICTURE OF WHAT YOU ARE FEELING, WHAT SORT OF PICTURE WOULD YOU PAINT?'[2]

Some people answer immediately and describe their image, often in a complex way. Some people are rather shy to answer and fumble for words, sketching their image in very simple terms. But no matter whom I ask, it seems that a person's image of being depressed will be one of the following kinds.

First, there are the images of the person alone in a fog. The fog may be grey, or black, or a tangle of violent colours. The fog may be swirling round the person or still and thick like cotton wool. The person may be trying to find his way out of it, or he may be frozen in fright and hopelessness.

Next, there are the images of empty landscapes, water-less deserts or frozen wastes, or images of boundless oceans. The person sees himself trudging alone towards an empty horizon or caught in a violent storm, or sitting helplessly immobile on a burning rock or a melting icefloe.

Then, there are the images of the person, alone in a space, wrapped tightly in something or pressed down by some heavy weight. The wrapping may be a shroud, or a thick black cloth, or some encasing garment. The weight may be a crushingly heavy box, or a stone lodged over one's heart, or a bird like a heavy black owl which perches on one's shoulders.

The most elaborate images are those where the person finds himself trapped. He may be travelling along an endless black tunnel, or clinging to the sides of a bottomless pit, or grovelling in the crater of a burnt-out volcano, or locked in a cold dungeon, or sealed in a metal sphere or a black balloon. Cages come in many shapes and forms. A person may see himself alone in a diving bell deep in the waters of the cold North Sea, or abandoned high on a ferris wheel in an empty fairground, or crouched in a small cage which is suspended by a fraying rope over a bottomless abyss.

All the images are terrible. Some contain a modicum of hope. Perhaps one could find one's way through a swirling grey fog, or lift a weight from one's shoulders. Help might come from outside – a friendly Eskimo might chance along or someone arrive with the key of the ferris wheel. Perhaps one could gain the strength to help oneself – to clamber out of the pit or unwrap the heavy cloth. But, however the image is expressed, all the images have one thing in common. The person is enduring a terrible isolation. You are alone in a prison.

Chapter 2

INSIDE THE PRISON

'When I wake up in the morning,' said Rose, 'I'm too scared to get out of bed. I've lived in that house for twenty years and I've slept in that bed for just as long, and I'm too scared to get out of it and walk across the room and open my bedroom door. So I lie there and I think the most terrible, terrible thoughts and I get so frightened, I want to get up and rush around doing something so I'll be thinking of something else, but I'm too scared to get out of bed. So I just stay there getting more and more frightened.'

John gets up and goes to work. He feels safe in his small office, but when his boss comes in, first to criticise his work and then to tell him he has to attend a meeting at the factory the next day, John breaks out in a sweat and feels sick. At lunch-time he goes home, gets into bed and pulls the blankets over his head. His wife finds him there, but neither her sympathy nor her abuse can make him move. 'You're just selfish,' she cries as she goes out, slamming the door.

'Selfish' is right. Inside the prison of depression you are very selfish. But then, aren't we all selfish when we are fighting for our lives? Feeling the terror of imminent death, we strive to save ourselves. To the outside observer the depressed person does not seem to be in danger of dying, but inside the prison of depression you feel a fear as great as that of death. If you told people how frightened you are they would think you are mad. Perhaps you are mad. The thought of this makes you more frightened. The fear is so great that death might be welcome as peace, a cessation of the fear. But what if after death there is something worse than here? Or death may bring peace, but dying is so painful. There must be a reason for feeling so frightened. Perhaps you are dying – that pain in your chest – is it a heart-attack – or cancer?

But words like 'death', 'madness', 'heart attack', 'cancer' do not convey the totality of fear that you feel when the totality of your very existence is threatened. If you are a Christian you can call it damnation.

That awful and sickening endless sinking, sinking
    through the slow, corruptive levels of disintegrative
    knowledge
when the self has fallen from the hands of God
and sinks, seething and sinking, corrupt
and sinking still, in depth after depth of disintegrative
    consciousness
sinking in the endless undoing, the awful katabolism
    into the abyss.[1]

If you tell your friends that you are damned, they will hasten to tell you that you are not, that the idea of damnation is silly, that God is not like that, that you are a good person, really. If you tell your friends that you are frightened because you cannot do your job properly, you are not a good mother, that the world is a terrible place and everything is going to get worse, they will say don't be silly, your boss really appreciates you, you're a wonderful mother, don't look on the black side, it'll never happen, worse things happen at sea. They do not know what it is like in the small hours of the morning.

There are worse things than having behaved foolishly
    in public.
There are worse things than these miniature betrayals,
    committed or endured or suspected; there are worse
      things
than not being able to sleep for thinking about them.
It is 5 am. All the worse things come stalking in
and stand icily about the bed looking worse and worse
    and worse.[2]

The fear permeates your life, undermining your confidence, until the smallest decision, 'What tie shall I wear?',

'What shall I have for lunch?', becomes an impossibly difficult task. Sometimes the fear comes raw and brutal as fear; sometimes it comes in the special guise of guilt.

You have become an expert in guilt. Every action or every omission of an action you can interpret as a cause for guilt. You have failed yourself and failed other people. You have not lived up to your expectations of yourself. You have not ensured the total happiness of the people around you. You review the stupidities and failures of your life and punish yourself for crimes known and unknown, while all the time you beg yourself for peace.

> My own heart let me more have pity on: let
> Me live to my sad self hereafter kind,
> Charitable; not live this tormented mind
> With this tormenting mind tormenting yet[3]

You feel guilty about being depressed and you know you deserve the punishment of depression – and worse.

Depression is like a dark mist lurking in the corners of the room, always there, always ready to come surging forward and rising up to envelop you. It is blackness, it is emptiness, it is meaninglessness and total inner despair. Others may think you are fortunate, but you know it is all an empty fraud, and that one day the hollow balloon will burst, you will be found out and your crime exposed. What crime? You don't know; you only know you are guilty; and you can hear them coming down the corridor to get you. The penalty, of course, is Death and you might as well be your own executioner.[4]

You long for death to bring you peace and you fear death for it may bring you something worse than life. Death may bring peace, but it will take away the hope that one day the terrible grief you bear will be recompensed, that your heart will be lightened. You tell no one of this grief, since a sensible person would say, 'You should be over that by now', or 'What a stupid thing to grieve over.'

The grief might be one from childhood when a parent died or deserted the family – or deserted you. How can you describe what that meant or still means? How small and weak you were, how vast and dark and terrifying was the world. No one could understand or comfort you. 'Children soon get over it,' you heard people say. You stopped crying, but you didn't get over it. And sometimes, even now, when you remember that terrible day, you wonder, 'Was it my fault?'

The loss might be more recent, when the person you depended on, or a child you should have protected, died, or when a loved and hated parent left this life without a word of reconciliation. How can you show how guilty you are at your failure, how angry at being deserted, how desolate at being left alone, abandoned, never to make recompense, never to be reconciled, never to be approved of and receive absolute, unconditional love?

Perhaps the loved one has not died but has gone away and loves another. 'Find someone else,' say your friends, but how can you do that when the defection of the loved one proves that you are unlovable. And how can anyone else know how important the unfaithful one was to you? You can well understand the epitaph to the trooper killed at El Alamein.

> To the world he was a soldier,
> to me he was the world.

How can you go on living when your world has ended and everyone else's world is tawdry and dull?

You can grieve over the loss of more than just people. What about grieving over the loss of childhood, and so fearing to grow up? What about grieving over the loss of youth, of beauty and virility, and so seeing yourself no longer desirable, while dreaded old age approaches? Or do you look back to when your children needed you, or you were the man in charge, the leader in your field, and now no one needs you, no one admires or respects you? You fear becoming dependent on others and having them pity you. Or are you mourning a dream, something that was once bright and splendid but now unrealisable in this hard, cruel and sordid world? There will be no promised land, no happy ending. Such losses are hard to name and even harder to mourn.

Griefs like these bring hopelessness. Things will never change, or if they do they will only get worse. What is the use of hoping or striving? Once you were ambitious; now you are bitterly resigned to your awful fate and cannot fight against it. You are filled with grey and heavy indifference, even towards people who were once important to you. Love has fled, leaving only an awareness of an absence of love. Once you were concerned about other people and yearned to right other people's wrongs. Now other people's tragedies do not impinge on you, or only serve as further proof, if further proof were needed, that the world is in a perilous state.

You do not love, but you are filled with bitterness and jealousy. Bitter that your life has gone awry and jealous that other people, quite undeserving, have such easy lives and do not suffer as you do. You hate yourself for feeling such horrible jealousy, just as you hate yourself for being unable to love. You get so angry. But there is so much in the world to make you justifiably angry – and a bit more so.

Loved ones – my wife Sally and the children – all agree I'm less impatient than I used to be. And that was no minor failing. An intolerant, and intolerable, demand that things happen, people act, just when I wanted them to happen and act. I never really thought that the whole line of traffic in the jam ahead should immediately get on to the verge and let us pass; but I spoke and behaved as if I did think this. Possessed by a noxious demon of furious impatience. The rampant, tumescent self.

Not that I'm now a model of saintly patience; far from that. I doubt if I've even reached the average level. But now, when held up on the road, I get out my rosary and repeat my mantra – 'The Peace of God' – and nearly always manage to keep my mouth shut – instead of taking it out on poor Sally. (Though at bad times the beads get rough treatment and the unspoken mantra sounds more like a curse than a blessing.)[6]

Irritable and miserable, you push people away from you, and then get scared that they will go and leave you all alone. So you pretend that everything is all right. You try and smile and to be ordinary, but the pretence is so wearying and inside you are silently screaming.

'When I walk down the street with my friend,' said Jackie, 'I feel there's a glass wall between us. I feel I'm alone. I want to scream and shout out. I try to break the glass but it's like plastic. It bends but it doesn't break.'

One day, despairing that those around her would ever understand what was happening to her, she wrote the following account and gave it to her doctor. He passed it on to me.

Four years ago next January I gave birth to a little boy, it was one of the most happy times of my life, we were told we'd never have children, so you can imagine I'd never felt so happy and elated, for two or three months I set about being a mother although I'm the eldest girl of seven and thought I knew a lot, little things happened every day to prove me wrong, but I coped with everything and enjoyed it immensely. When Neil was three months old we were posted to Holtby, from then everything in my life seems to have changed (mainly me). We settled down into Holtby, I became very lonely, no friends, no-one to chat with, started taking it out on Ron. Neil was not a sleeper, caused a lot of trouble at nights, I became over the next few months very nervous, depressed, aggressive with Ron, I remember feeling very low at the time, I went to the doctors with it but couldn't talk about it, couldn't talk to Ron about it, couldn't talk to friends, couldn't talk to Mum as she's the kind of person who says 'I've had seven kids I never felt anything like this, so it doesn't exist.' This was from April to September 1978, during this six months I started to feel all sorts was wrong with me, I remember getting an awful lot of pain in my right breast, I was so frightened, I couldn't eat over it, couldn't talk to anyone about it, stopped making love out of fear, couldn't bear him to touch me, became lower and lower. Finally I went to the doctors, he sent me for x-rays, etc., it took me months to be convinced it was muscular, now I often get the pain but it doesn't bother me, it's usually when I've done a lot of cleaning or been carrying the babies around. I remember at the time I stopped reading papers, or watching the news. I felt so badly depressed that if I read in a paper someone had this disease or that disease in my mind over the next few weeks I would have it, I tried to snap out of it, I didn't remember being like this before, but no matter how I tried I just kept getting lower and lower. The doctor after a while sent me to see the psychiatrist who treated me with anti-depressants, but I couldn't talk to him I tried so hard but I couldn't sit there and tell him all my little fears. I wouldn't take the pills he prescribed me 'cause all the time I could hear mum's voice saying this isn't real, you don't get like this, so I became more fearful of trying to tell anyone. I became worse and our marriage was beginning to show strain but still I couldn't snap out of it, I dreaded getting out of bed in a morning to start another day, I'd spend all my time shut away crying my eyes out, I'm sure Neil used to sense all this because he never got any better, just used to play us up more and more. After six months I met people and thought it had helped at first but it didn't so I became more depressed than ever.

I went to see the doctor again and whilst we were chatting he asked to take some blood tests as I'd had little dots come up under my eyes and he said it could be caused by a higher fat level. I was petrified waiting for the results. When they came back he said yes, your fat is too high so he put me on a special diet, I tried to talk to mum about everything I'd felt but she said I was silly and there was no reason for me to be like this because of one baby – what would I have been like feeling like that and having seven, so another door closed and that was the last time I talked to anyone about anything. The doctors told me not to worry about having fat level, with the proper diet I could keep it under control and bring it down even. I settled into the diet, but things didn't get any better. I started to get pains in my chest (I must state only when I thought about them), 'cause I'm not a daft person and know that high fat caused heart attacks, etc., I became so obsessed with this that I became even lower and lower, so low that I didn't know anyone could go that far. At this time my dad seemed to be ill a lot, always dizzy and off colour, etc., he was put on blood pressure pills and I noticed that he got the spots under his eye too, so my mind put two and two together and trouble really started then, I got so petrified to ask how dad was when I phoned home and stopped sleeping, stopped eating even more and just started living in a full time nightmare world, I was so closed in my own frightened world there just didn't seem to be a way out. Ron had a lot of patience with me but he got so mad and frustrated with me because I couldn't talk that things got worse if that's possible. I got pregnant again then, I was really off with it, then in the June I was told I was having twins, this is last year 1980. For a while other things didn't matter although deep down the thoughts never left me but I was so intent on looking after myself so the babies would be okay that I felt different for a couple of months, but as soon as they were born everything started again, only I didn't know how to cope with it this time I was so tired all the time, twin babies and a little boy to look after I kept saying to myself who wouldn't be tired. I kept losing weight again, that seems to have stabled off now. We went home for Xmas. At Boxing Day tea time dad had a stroke, my world fell apart, he was in hospital a week then came home, I was convinced then it'd happen to me I became more nervous, more tense I seemed to shut off completely, dad had had pains in his legs for a good few years, all these pains in my legs started, I used to cry over them but couldn't tell anyone about them, two weeks later he died, my god I was so full of grief it was like I'd lost a part of my body, but from then I've become even more down and depressed and still couldn't talk to anyone, until one day I thought I'd explode, I thought I'd really gone demented, that's when I called Mrs. Bates (Health Visitor) in and got taken into the psychiatric hospital. Now I don't seem to have a life. The pains in my legs went, but there's always some fear to take over the next one, now I don't sleep, I'm

frightened all day of the night to come because I know
that I'll get restless and tensed up, won't be able to
breathe, won't be able to swallow, will start feeling
numb and petrified – all the time I drum into myself
that I've got to snap out of it. There's far more going on
in my head than what's on paper, I just feel all the time
there is a way to unjumble it all please somebody help
me find it. I'm twenty-seven with three lovely children,
a good husband, I can't bear the thought of living
another day like I've lived the last four. I've been
shaking and nervous whilst I've written this but I feel
calmer now please somebody help me get rid of
everything in my mind.

Chapter 3

HOW TO BUILD YOUR PRISON

Depression is not a genetic fault or a mysterious illness which descends on us. It is something which we create for ourselves, and just as we create it, so we can dismantle it our creation. Of course there are physical changes when we are depressed. Every emotion, pleasant or unpleasant, is accompanied by physical changes which become more profound the longer the emotions persist. Anti-depressant drugs have the effect of reversing or limiting some of the physiological changes that occur when a person is depressed. There has been no physiological change discovered which invariably precedes a depression, in the way that a deficiency of vitamin C precedes scurvy or the presence of tuberculi bacilli (along with a number of other factors) invariably precedes the development of tuberculosis.

Some people have found that they become depressed after a bout of flu, and some women find that they get depressed or become more depressed in the week before menstruation. But this is not to say that influenza or pre-menstrual tension causes depression. Not everyone gets depressed after a bout of flu and not all women endure a monthly depression.

Whenever we become aware of some change in our body's functioning we have to interpret it in some way, just as we have to interpret or find a meaning for everything that happens to us. (When we say we cannot understand something or we find something to be meaningless we are still interpreting that thing as being not understandable or as being meaningless.) Suppose we trip over a carpet, fall down a flight of stairs and break a leg. How shall we interpret what has happened?

We can see the physical reasons for the leg breaking – the carpet, the fall, the way we landed. But there are other reasons as well. Some of us would immediately see the cause as in ourselves – we were stupid, we should have looked where we were going and been more careful. Others of us would locate the cause in other people – the person who left the carpet like that, switched the light off, designed that flight of stairs, told you to go down those stairs. Some of us would find a deeper reason – it was God's way of punishing me, teaching me a lesson; the Devil or malign Fate is out to get me; this is the second disaster in a week – there will soon be a third. After that the treatment for our broken leg can be interpreted in so many ways – we can have faith in our wonderful doctors and nurses or know that they are all incompetent, especially if they are foreign. We can feel pleased that we are making use of all the money we have paid towards our health care, or we can worry about how much it is all going to cost, all the extra expense of being off work or needing help in the house. We can choose to enjoy a rest in hospital or to fret over what is happening at home or at work. We can feel sure that the bone will knit properly and the leg soon be as good as new, or else we can know that the doctor really is not telling us the truth and that we shall be maimed for life. (Convinced and practised pessimists can think of far worse eventualities than these!)

Such a simple event, and yet no two of us would, when it happens to us, interpret it in exactly the same way. No two people ever see anything in exactly the same way. We all know this, just as we know how there are some things which we see differently now from the way we once did. Everyone has different opinions, and opinions can change.

But sometimes we fool ourselves into thinking that our opinions represent the Real and Absolute Truth about the world and that anyone who does not agree with us is either mad or bad. Believing this, we make life difficult for ourselves and the people around us. We get angry (and frightened) because life does not always conform to our Truth and other people do not always see the error of their ways and accept our Truth as their Truth. Our lives and the lives of the people around us can become exceedingly unhappy because we have ignored the observation of that wise ancient Greek philosopher, Epictatus, when he said,

It is not things in themselves which trouble us, but the opinions we have about these things.

This book is about our opinions and how we can change them.

Nothing in life is so simple that it has one single cause. Everything that happens emerges out of a whole network of causes, and so to understand why something happens we have to bear in mind a number of different things.

To become depressed you have to have acquired over the years a complex set of interlinked opinions which relate to the particular circumstances of your life. When two people meet together in the process of psychotherapy it can take a long time to unravel these opinions and to choose whether or not to change them.[1] Even where two people hold similar opinions each will express the particular opinion differently. One person might say, 'My marriage is very important to me', while the other says, 'I always think of myself as part of a couple.' There are some people who hold opinions about everything under the sun, and some people who ignore most of what goes on in the world and have few opinions. But there are some things in life that no one can ignore and about which each of us must have an opinion. It is the set of opinions we hold about these aspects of life which determines whether or not we become depressed.

So, if you want to build for yourself the prison of depression this is what you must do.

Hold as if they were Real, Absolute and Immutable Truths the six following opinions.

1. *No matter how good and nice I appear to be, I am really bad, evil, valueless, unacceptable to myself and other people.*
2. *Other people are such that I must fear, hate and envy them.*
3. *Life is terrible and death is worse.*
4. *Only bad things happened to me in the past and only bad things will happen to me in the future.*

5. *It is wrong to get angry.*
6. *I must never forgive anyone, least of all myself.*

Now let us see what it means to our life when we hold such opinions.

1 No matter how good and nice I appear to be, I am really bad, evil, valueless, unacceptable to myself and other people

'I've never thought much of myself,' said Jackie.

Helen said, 'I am not worth loving.'[2]

Joan said, 'If someone doesn't like me it must be my fault.'[3]

Mary said, 'If someone gets angry with me it must be my fault.'[4]

John said, 'If I am on my own I cease to exist.'[5]

Peter said, 'If I could construct a model of me, inside it would be something in the form of a bucket which was full of broken glass which was being rattled about rather violently, and bits fly off and this is rather dangerous.'[6]

Siegfried said that a child comes into the world 'a complete savage . . . I think that at an early age I saw this badness (in myself), unpleasantness, nastier features, and by accident or by luck I disliked them. Difficult to change one's mind after fifty or sixty years, isn't it?'[7]

Carol put her opinion of herself in a poem.

What is this self, this me?
Why do I want to change me?
Why can't I accept me?
I just don't like me, why?
Others seem to accept themselves
Why can't I? Am I so different?
Questions, questions, where are the answers?
Why do I swing so fiercely from a too high mood
Down to the miserable depths?
Why can't I be the happy medium?
When in a high mood I'm told
'That's better, more like your old self.'
Horrors. I Don't Want to Be My Old Self.

Little do they know what lay behind the 'Old Self'.
Misery, bewilderment, anxiety, unrest,
Disappointment, all hidden behind a mask,
Which is still put on even now
To face the outside world.[8]

The feeling that you are essentially bad can be expressed in many different ways. It can be felt in many different ways. Some people, like Peter, believe that inside them is something so corrupt and evil that they are a danger to other people. Some people, like Siegfried, are not so much frightened that their evil will corrupt or injure other people as proud that they have identified this evil in themselves. Some people would not so much see themselves as evil as, like Helen, simply and devastatingly dislikable. They dislike themselves and so expect other people to dislike them. Like Mary, they always take the blame for other people's anger. Some people see themselves not so much evil or dislikable as simply inadequate, unable to cope, to do things properly. Sometimes the sense of inadequacy becomes so overwhelming that the person, like John, feels as if he does not exist and has to have people around all the time to confirm that he does exist.

What is a common experience for many of us is that we think of ourselves as basically good people, but then something terrible happens that makes us feel there must be something wrong or evil inside us. Accidents or illnesses may lead us to believe that God is punishing us for sins of which we were unaware; betrayed or cruelly used by someone we thought loved us, we come to think of ourselves as soiled or unlovable or disgusting and horrible. As time goes by we may allow our friends and our common sense to convince us that, despite what has happened, we are good and lovable. But if you are convinced that you are bad and evil, then you resist all evidence to the contrary. Anyone who tells you that you are good and lovable is either too stupid to see what you are really like or is lying and wanting to deceive you, either because he pities you (which you hate) or because he wants to use or to hurt you. When professional people like doctors or nurses or psychotherapists say that they like you, you know they don't mean it. They're just paid to say that.

Knowing that you are bad you must constantly struggle to be good, to present an acceptable face to the world. Like Carol, you need 'a mask . . . to face the outside world'. You can never be yourself, since if people knew what you are really like they would reject you. You might have been wearing a mask or playing a role for so long that, even if you wanted to, you could not be yourself because you do not know who you are or what you are really like and you dare not take the risk of finding out. To know how to behave you have to rely on other people's opinions, and so you live under the tyranny of *'they'* 'What will *they* think?' is the thought that accompanies every action and determines every decision.

When I talk to some depressed women I get the impression that there must be a book of rules of housekeeping which was handed down to Moses at the same time as the Ten Commandments, and while it is possible to break all the Ten Commandments and still be forgiven by God, infringements of the Heavenly Housekeeping Book are Absolutely Unforgivable either in this world or the next. The Heavenly Housekeeping Book contains a large number of rules and regulations, all aspects of the one Universal Law – YOUR HOME MUST BE PERFECTLY CLEAN AND TIDY AT ALL TIMES.

Thus your life must be spent in keeping this rule and in getting your family to keep it as well. God sends his inspectors in the form of your mother (alive or dead) and the woman down the street whose house is always spotless, who has children who put their things away, who gets her spring cleaning done weeks before you and who can easily cope with a full-time job and a family. Even if these inspectors cannot see everything, God knows if it is over two weeks since you tidied the linen cupboard or turned out the spare room.[9]

I often laugh at this kind of keeping up of appearances, but I do know what it means to have the rules of the Heavenly Housekeeping Book branded into your flesh. I know the terrible despair you can feel when keeping the house clean is just beyond your strength, or, when your life is going badly awry, you obsessively clean and tidy your house since this is the only part of your life that you can control and keep in order. Over the years I became able to live with a degree of untidiness and dirt, but I still do extra housework when I am expecting visitors and if I am going away for a while I always leave the place clean and tidy for the burglars.

Men may laugh at women for this kind of keeping up of appearances, but men have an equally silly obsession. Many men experience their badness as being small, weak and inferior, just not masculine at all. To deny this badness they must constantly be involved in competing with other men in every situation which might be remotely construed as being a competition. Like most women I find this constant creation of competitions quite amazing. Getting into the *Guinness Book of Records* is an ambition many people prize, and I suppose being known as holding the 1976 record for eating baked beans one by one with a cocktail stick or for flipping beer mats[10] is better than living your life unknown and unadmired. I find less sympathy in me for the man who wishes to prove his masculinity by having his finger on the button of the greatest collection of nuclear weapons in the world.

Rather than reveal their weakness, their badness, by, as they see it, losing a competition or even compromising on some group decision, some men are prepared to sabotage the institution they work for, or to neglect and reject their wives and families, or to undermine their own health and strength. Not all such men are aiming at great riches and power. All some might want is to compete well enough so as not to be wiped out by the men they see as strong. Such men are scared of everyone they see as being in a position of power, and so they have to work extremely hard to avoid criticism and rebuke. They cannot risk appearing lazy, or less than keen, or insufficiently prepared. Like the obsessively house-proud woman, they fear being found out.

Playing a role, you have to be very careful of your appearance. If you experience the badness within you as filth then you have to become extremely clean. You have to devote a great deal of time and effort in keeping your body clean. If you experience the badness within you as some dangerous force to be kept under control then you will expend a lot of effort in keeping your hair neat and your clothes regular and tidy as a uniform. You might devote much time to painting on a face with which to face the world or buy extravagant, eye-catching clothes to distract the observer from the sham within, or you dress shabbily because you do not want to attract attention and you do not deserve anything better. Some people try to appear good by denying themselves all but the bare necessities of life while others try to obliterate their sense of weakness and inferiority by the acquisition of many objects.

If you experience yourself as bad then you can come to feel that you have no right to exist, to walk upon this planet and to breathe the same air as other people. So you either have to disappear or do something to justify your existence. What can you do? You can look after other people. You can be needed. If you feel that your spouse and children would reject you if they discovered how bad you really are then you can shower (and control) them with such unselfish, loving devotion that only people much wickeder than you would dare to reject you. If you feel that as a child you were deprived of loving care you can try to make up this deficiency by caring for others (victims like you) in the way you would wish to be cared for. Thus you can devote yourself to your family and give them more care and attention than they could ever need or want. Or you can show your family up for the selfish, self-indulgent people that they are by devoting yourself to Good Works. Fortunately our world never lacks the necessity for Good Works, so if you put your mind to it you can find something which allows you to support your prejudices, to annoy your enemies, to ennoble your appearance and to punish yourself. And it is at punishing yourself that you excel. You cannot merely take simple pride and pleasure in keeping your home nice, in doing your job well, in enjoying games and sport and friendly banter, in dressing in a way that suits you, in owning some things that you like, or in helping other people. Everything you do is aimed at hiding the badness within you and at punishing yourself for being bad.

It is the idea of *punishment* that gives us the clue about where the sense of badness comes from. The Bible may teach that each newborn babe carries the burden of Original Sin, but a young child does not know whether it is good or bad anymore than it knows whether it is a boy or a girl. It learns these things from the adults around it. If you have parents, aunts and uncles, grandparents, older siblings who generally define you as good ('Who's the most gorgeous baby in the world?', 'This is daddy's darling little girl', 'Isn't he the cleverest boy you've ever seen?', 'That was a silly thing to do, dear. You won't do it again, will you?'), then there is a fair chance you will believe them, just as you believe what they tell you about how old you are and what your name is. If you have parents, aunts and uncles, grandparents, older siblings who generally define you as bad ('What a pity it's another girl', 'Mummy doesn't love a bad boy', 'You're stupid', 'You're a disgusting, wicked girl') then there is a fair chance you will believe them, especially if your childhood contains more punishments, disappointments and loneliness than rewards, security and love.

Some parents believe that a child's upbringing should prepare him for adult life in a harsh world and so a child should not be 'spoilt' by being indulged and petted. Some parents love their children but are so beset by their own worries and needs that the child never feels the warmth of his parents' love. Some parents do not love their children. Most parents mean well but make mistakes. Whatever the reason, every child, sooner or later, finds himself suffering and he has to explain to himself why this has happened. Is it his fault or his parents'? But if it is his parents' fault then that means that those people on whom his security depends are not looking after him properly. If that thought is too terrifying the child will decide to blame himself for his suffering. The American cartoonist Jules Feiffer showed this process of reasoning in a cartoon of a little girl talking to herself. She said, 'I used to believe I was a good girl until I lost my doll and found it wasn't lost. My big sister stole it. And my mother told me she was taking me to the zoo, only it wasn't the zoo, it was school, and my father told me he was taking me to the circus, only it wasn't the circus, it was the dentist. So that's how I found out I wasn't good. Because if I was good, why would all these people want to punish me?'[11]

So, to preserve your parents as good you have sacrificed your own essential goodness, and this first act of sacrifice has begot a million others. Even today you dare not contemplate the possibility that your parents were less than perfect and that they did things to you which harmed you. Even just to think such a wicked thing about your parents shows what a wicked person you are. You try to forget the pain of childhood, sometimes by blotting out your childhood so completely that your remembered life starts when you are sixteen or seventeen. But some things are hard to forget, like being beaten by your father or your schoolteacher. You cannot forget the pain of that but you can do something about the pain of knowing that your suffering was being inflicted by the person who ought to be looking after you. You can protect yourself from the memory of this second terrible pain by deciding that it was right that you should have been beaten. Not only did you deserve the punishment because you were wicked but also the person beating you was doing you good by punishing you. This just shows how good the person was to take the time and trouble to beat you and when you grow up you would be just like him. 'When I was a boy I was whipped by my father and it never did me any harm.' Anna Freud called this process 'identification with the aggressor'. It is one of the means by which the human race perpetuates its cruelty.

Enjoying the smug satisfaction of being the aggressor instead of the victim is one of the advantages of regarding yourself as essentially bad. There are plenty of others, and if you think about yourself honestly enough you will know what particular advantage you get out of seeing yourself as bad rather than good.

When I asked Jackie what advantage she got out of thinking so little of herself she was surprised at my question and said she could not think of any possible advantage. I outlined some of the advantages that people do find. If you see yourself as weak and always in need of protection then you do not have to take responsibility for yourself. You can blame others when things go wrong in your life. If you are unwise enough to see yourself as having ability you are then under the obligation of trying to put your ability to use, of striving towards something and so running the risk of failing. You can avoid all this danger by seeing yourself as having no ability. If you want to keep a little personal pride you can say to yourself that you could have been the greatest but you are the sort of person who attracts bad luck or other people's envy and spite.

I USED TO BELIEVE I WAS A GOOD GIRL.

UNTIL I LOST MY DOLL AND FOUND OUT IT WASN'T LOST, MY BIG SISTER STOLE IT.

AND MY MOTHER TOLD ME SHE WAS TAKING ME TO THE ZOO, ONLY IT WASN'T THE ZOO, IT WAS SCHOOL.

AND MY FATHER TOLD ME HE WAS TAKING ME TO THE CIRCUS, ONLY IT WASN'T THE CIRCUS, IT WAS THE DENTIST..

SO THATS HOW I FOUND OUT I WASN'T GOOD.

BECAUSE IF I WAS GOOD WHY WOULD ALL THESE GOOD PEOPLE WANT TO PUNISH ME?

None of these advantages struck Jackie as being applicable to her. So we went on talking about other things, which led to Jackie telling me how, although she loved her husband and children dearly, running a home left her feeling unsatisfied. She knew there was something wrong with her for feeling like this and she felt very guilty when people pointed out how lucky she was to have such a good husband and lovely children. Other women were satisfied with their lives. Why wasn't she? She had grown up expecting to get married and have a family. 'It was always expected that my sister and I would leave school as soon as we were old enough and get a job – any job – until we got married,' she said. It was her parents who had expected her to leave school. There had never been any chance that she could stay on at school. I made some remarks along the lines that a woman of her undoubted (in my mind) ability would find housework and three young children exhausting and time-consuming but unsatisfying and that it was a pity her mother had prevented her from staying on at school and perhaps going on to art college.

'Oh I wouldn't have had the ability to do that,' said Jackie sounding as if I had just suggested that she take over as pilot of the Space Shuttle.

'Yes you have,' I said.

'No I haven't – and I can't blame my mother for not letting me stay on at school. It makes me feel too guilty if I think that about her. I'd rather think that I haven't got any ability.'

'There,' I said in triumph, 'that's the advantage in thinking so little of yourself.'

Living is very often a matter of making the best of a bad job, and so if you are taught early in life to see yourself as bad, evil, valueless, unacceptable to yourself and other people then there might be sense in finding some advantages in this. But if these advantages become very important to you you may never inspect your opinion of yourself to discover that it is merely an opinion and not an immutable Truth and that you are free to change it. The advantages of seeing yourself as essentially bad may blind you to the fact that the opinions we hold about ourselves form the basis of our assessment of everything else in our lives, and if we make the opinion 'I am a bad person' the foundation of our world then the cost of our world will prove to be excessively dear.

2 Other people are such that I must fear, hate and envy them

Everything that is fine, beautiful and worthwhile has something to do with the experience of love. When we are entranced by the waves dashing against the rocks or the delicate tracery of black branches against a pale evening sky we experience the love which binds us to our splendid cosmos. When we are enraptured by music, or a painting, or a poem, or a story, or thrilled by the brilliance of the people in a play or a sport, we experience the love which binds us to our fellows. When we create something which we know is good, be it a symphony or a batch of scones, we experience the love which is the joy of creation. When we snuggle into our parent's arms, or hold our beloved in ecstatic union, or cradle our baby on our lap, or share a sympathetic joke with a friend, we partake of an experience which is at the one ordinary yet mysterious. It is ordinary because loving relationships between people are common and to be expected. It is mysterious because without love we shrivel up and slowly die. For human beings to survive they need air, water, food, shelter and the opportunity to love and be loved.

Yet how can you love and be loved when you are certain that at your core you are bad, evil, valueless, unacceptable to yourself and to others? You may be able to love others, but when they return your love you know that you do not deserve it and that sooner or later your loved one will find you out and then reject you. Sometimes, even, the strain of waiting to be rejected is too great and so you reject your loved ones or behave badly so as to force them to reject you. Better the pain of rejection than the anxiety of waiting.

So love to you means not happiness but desolation, fear and guilt. No wonder you fear the people who are the source of this pain, just as you fear the people who, you are certain, dislike you, who criticise and belittle you, who seek to do you down in every competition. Your fear of people extends beyond individuals to whole groups of people. Middle-aged women (just like your mother) may terrify you or middle-aged men (just like your father). As a man you may fear all women whom you see as powerful and destructive beings, or as a woman you may fear all men whom you see as insensitive and cruel. You may fear all people in authority and be reduced to speechless terror by a policeman or a doctor's receptionist. You may fear all Catholics or all Muslims, or everyone with a skin darker than yours, or the rich who make you feel inferior or the poor who are scheming to rob you of all you own. Your fear of other people may be so great that you hesitate to venture beyond your own front door. You prefer not to invite strangers into your home and prefer, as you often say, to keep yourself to yourself. Even if you would like to go out more, to do different things, when you fear other people and see yourself so inadequate and valueless you lack the confidence to mix with other people. It would be easier to jump off a precipice than to walk into a room full of people.

Of course it is very difficult to like people who do not like us and even more difficult to love people who do not love us. We can, if we choose, remain indifferent to the people who dislike us, but if we fear them we soon find that the experience of fear is so painful that we can come to hate the people whom we see as the cause of this pain. We can, if we wish, deny that we are afraid and instead claim some virtue in hating our enemies. By then we have forgotten that, as George Bernard Shaw said, 'Hatred is the coward's revenge for being intimidated.'[12]

You can be sure that people dislike you because you are such a bad person that no one could possibly like you, but you may be uncertain as to whether other people are basically good or basically bad. Neither alternative gives you much comfort. If other people are good through and through then they will despise you when they find you out. Their mere presence makes you feel inferior. If other people are like you, basically bad but pretending to be good, then you have every reason to fear them since their words and actions have meanings which are unknown to you but which may harm you. Some people, you observe, are self-confident and appear to approve of themselves. Like Siegfried, you can despise the people who have not recognised their own essential badness and you can feel most resentful that other people are happy while you are not. In fact, you find that you envy other people just as much as you hate and fear them. In your heart of hearts you know that although some people might appear to have big problems, anyone who does not have your problems really has no problems at all. You look at your relatives, your neighbours and colleagues and you see them coping with their lives and enjoying themselves. You may hate yourself for being so wildly jealous but you stay jealous just the same.

Fearing, hating and envying others robs you of what little self-confidence you might otherwise have, but lacking self-confidence makes you dependent on people in whom you have little trust. No matter how much your loved ones try to impress on you that they are everlastingly devoted to you, you suspect that they are secretly planning to leave you, and even before this happens the disaster which you know is inevitable will overtake them and leave you alone in a dangerous world. So you insist that your parents must never ever leave you; or you demand that your husband must come straight home from work and spend all his free time with you; or you refuse promotion because that would mean spending nights away from home, fearing that on your return you would find your family gone. Such lack of trust you know is preventing your growing up or is destroying your marriage but you feel powerless to do anything about it. However, you may not have entered into your marriage with any great hopes and if the truth were told it would be that to some extent you despise your spouse. When you were young you dreamed of someone wonderful (and still do) but because you thought so little of yourself you married someone who was not as good as you wanted but as good as you deserve. You cannot help but see your marriage as a disappointment.

When we hate ourselves and fear and despise other people it is impossible to behave towards others in any frank, easy, kind and loving way. It is impossible then to achieve a happy life by following the Golden Rule, 'Do unto others as you would have them do unto you.' If you fear, hate and envy other people your life becomes yet another proof of the dictum which my father was very fond of quoting, '*You only get back what you give away*.' If you give away love and kindness you get love and kindness back (though the returning love and kindness does not always come from the source and in the form that you particularly desire). If you give away fear, hate, envy, resentment, coldness and distrust, even though you may try to hide these under the guise of love and kindness, such bad feelings will be returned to you, not only by mere acquaintances but by those whom you love and on whom you depend.

You fear others but you may not appreciate how much others fear you. A person may pride himself on the high standards he sets for himself and other people but, as Goethe said, 'he is a man who is impossible to please, because he is never pleased with himself.' You view your own imperfections and demand perfection of yourself, and fail to achieve it. You demand perfection of your family and when they, mere fallible human beings, fail to achieve it you get very angry, just as you get so angry with the world in general which falls so short of your expectations. Your family have learned to be frightened of your anger. They know that the smallest thing – a missing button, an unmade bed, a loud noise – can provoke in you a rage quite out of proportion to the provocation. They know that the simplest action, an unguarded remark, can bring your response of punishing silence which can last for days, weeks or even years. They know that your good humour cannot be relied upon since your mood can change with frightening, unpredictable suddenness. No matter how much they love you their fear makes them retreat from you, while the one rule which governs all aspects of family life becomes, 'Don't upset your father!'

We fear other people because we see them as wishing to harm us. Sometimes the other person's intentions are quite clear – someone coming at us with a knife or a gun or an upraised fist can quite rightly be interpreted as someone to fear. But when anger and aggression are not so clear we can make mistakes. A friend may sound rather abrupt on the phone and we can think, 'She doesn't like me,' when in fact our friend is ill or tired or distracted by worries that have nothing to do with us. We need to understand the other person to be able to judge accurately what that person's wishes, needs, worries, angers, loves and fears are at any particular time. But if you fear other people understanding others is not easy. If we want to understand another person we need to be able to get close to that person. We can never come to understand a person whom we have always feared, and when we have always feared everyone we can never develop that special form of imagination we call empathy which allows us to understand how another person experiences himself and his world. In fact our understanding of others can be so limited that we do not realise how little we understand and we may even pride ourselves on being good judges of character. Our understanding of other people develops from birth onwards[13] just as other skills develop, partly through physical maturation and partly through having had the right experiences at the right time. Unfortunately, if we do not have the right experiences our ability to understand other people may be more like a child's than an adult's.

Initially we do not understand that other people have perceptions, feelings, needs and desires. They are simply figures in our landscape. As the people around us start to make demands on us, expecting us to behave in certain ways, rewarding us when we do and punishing us when we do not (this period usually starts with toilet training), we begin to see other people in terms of our own self-interest. (Grandmother can be relied on to be rewarding no matter what you do, but woe betide you if you do not obey your father.) As we get older and go to school we begin to see people in terms of the roles they fill – mother, teacher, policeman, school friend. We can carry this mode of thinking into adult life and judge other people according to the categories in which we place them. ('All Scotsman are mean', 'Of course he's unreliable – he's Irish', 'Fat people are always jolly', 'Once a thief, always a thief', 'All of Jack's family are like that', 'Any woman who doesn't want to be a wife and mother is unnatural', 'All men are rapists at heart', 'I don't know what the youth of today are coming to. In my day we respected our parents.')

The immature understanding of other people is where we see other people only in relation to ourselves. In fact we can look at the entire cosmos only in relation to ourselves. The sun shines solely for the purpose of warming us while the malicious wind blows only to chill us. We cannot enjoy a landscape for the beauty in itself, but we see it only as a backdrop to a drama in which we are the central character. Surroundings which do not lend themselves to our personal drama hold no interest, while people whose existence does not enhance our own we ignore or find boring. We do not object if nature is cruel and other people dangerous so long as people and nature do not ignore us. We do not like to think that the world has any concerns where we are not the focus of interest.

But of course it does. Nature takes no account of the existence of the whole human race, much less of one person, and we, as an individual, can be of importance to only a minute portion of the millions of human beings on earth. To understand how other people think and feel we have to be able to see the world they inhabit through their own eyes and not through our own. We have to be able to see ourselves in ways which add nothing to our vanity. We have to be able to accept that other people have opinions, attitudes and feelings which are appropriate for the world they live in but which are different from our own. To understand other people we have to be able to take many different points of view and to accept that our own view of the world is not the Absolute, Real and Eternal Truth.

Where other people are concerned we are often ignorant of the fact that we are ignorant. We can be aware that we do not know anything about nuclear physics or the game of chess, but we can be unaware that the thoughts and feelings of the person who shares our bed or who gave birth to us are a complete mystery to us. In therapy one of the processes is the gradual discovery by the client of how little he really knows of his nearest and dearest. One method of aiding this process is the writing of 'scripts'. I used this with one woman whose fear of other people kept her depressed and lonely in her own home, unable to venture out her door unaccompanied. Her husband would bring her to see me when he could and at other times she would telephone me. Her conversation was full of complaints about her husband – how insensitive he was, how demanding, irritable with her and the children, unable to appreciate how she suffered, how he would leave her alone in the evening to go out drinking, how under his mother's thumb he was and so on. I did not doubt that he was no angel, but from the incidental information she gave me about his childhood, his family and his job I guessed that he was under considerable strain. Attempts by me to get her to view a particular situation as he might view it led either to her changing the subject to something of greater interest to her or accusing me of siding with him against her. Since she enjoyed writing and had already provided me with a long autobiography I suggested that she write a script which was an account of her husband's life. This account was to be in the form of an autobiography where her husband told his own story and described his own attitudes and feelings. She was most enthusiastic about this project, but the next time I saw her she had to report that she had not written the script. When she tried to write it she came to realise that while she knew about the main events in her husband's life she knew nothing of his attitudes and feelings. She did not know how he felt about his mother's illness or being sacked from his first job or even how he felt about her. She was so taken up with her own concerns she had not spared the time to understand him, and now when she attempted to do so she discovered that she did not know how to begin.

Understanding others is a skill we have to acquire if we are to live comfortably with other people. If we do not learn this skill we are always making mistakes in our dealings with other people. We find ourselves always saying or doing something which upsets the other person and we do not know why. We act with the best of intentions, and lo and behold, the person gets angry, or refuses to talk to us. ('I just asked Jimmy what he wanted for breakfast and he slammed out of the house and never spoke to me', 'My wife's always on at me to finish painting the kitchen cupboards. I'll get round to it when I've got time, but she will go on and on', 'I never shop at large stores. The assistants there are so snooty.') If we are not afraid of other people such mistakes do not bother us, but if you are afraid, especially when you are sure that the other person is angry with you, then you worry about these experiences even for years after. You try to get along with other people by being pleasant and doing things for them, but so often you find, as Tacitus observed a long time ago, 'More faults are often committed while we are trying to oblige than while we are giving offence.' You want to show your love, but when you try to do this the loved one does not respond in the way you want, and so you withdraw, hurt.

The disadvantages of fearing, hating and envying other people are so immense and widespread that it would hardly seem likely that there are any advantages in doing so. But there are advantages, ones that you may be reluctant to relinquish.

Fear is an unpleasant emotion but hate can, in its way, be quite pleasant. As Byron said,[14]

> Now Hatred is by far the longest pleasure;
> Men love in haste, but they detest at leisure.

Hating others can make us feel more secure in our own virtue. More than that, our hatred can become the measure by which we define ourselves. We can define the very meaning of our existence as residing in our being anti-Communist or anti-Catholic or anti-Muslim or anti-white or anti-men or anti-The Permissive Society. If we gave up our hatred of this other group we would feel quite bereft. Hating others fills in a great deal of our time and provides us with plenty of things to complain about. If you know that you are quite incompetent, you can enjoy the pleasures of complaining without feeling any necessity to put to rights the matters about which you complain. (One good reason for not attempting to right the world's wrongs is that if you do try to do so you are in danger of discovering that the world does not conform to the picture that you have of it – that human problems are quite complicated and that other people have different points of view.)

Another advantage of fearing, hating and envying other people is that you can see other people as the source of all your misery. You are as you are because of your childhood or your family or society and there is nothing that you can do about it. Thus you are able to avoid the responsibility for your own failures or, at least, avoid the responsibility for changing the situation in which you find yourself. You would do something about it but *They* are against you.

Hatred is simple. Love, real love, is much more complicated. The problem about love is that it is inextricably linked with freedom. Love is spontaneous. We cannot love on demand. We cannot order someone to love us. Psychoanalysts may say that we love someone because he or she reminds us of our mother, and behaviourists may say that we love someone because we have been conditioned to regard that kind of person as a positive reinforcement, and there is some truth in what psychoanalysts and behaviourists say, but we all know that the mystery and wonder of love lies in the fact that it cannot be commanded and it can only be freely given. I cannot love you just because I feel I ought to or because you want me to. The fondness we feel for people who give us things, in the hope, perhaps, that we shall love them, we call 'cupboard love' and know it is not the real thing. We do not love someone just because that person gives us presents and does things for our benefit.

We may like to think that all children love their parents and that all parents love their children, but we know it is not so. Some mothers love their child from the moment it stirs in the womb while others feel no more than a mild benign interest in the child for its entire life. Some fathers would lay down their lives for their children while others can desert the family home without a backward glance. Some children can never in their whole lives think of their parents without feeling a warming of their hearts while others cling to their parents only as a means of satisfying a need and discard their parents as soon as a more satisfying source becomes available. The passion we can feel for someone who meets our deepest needs and who promises the fulfilment of our secret fantasies we often call love, romantic love, but such a passion has more to do with possession than with love. If we do not come to love the object of our passion then when the object ceases to meet our needs and demands, as he or she must as time goes by, we are left with a stranger who at best bores us and at worst repels us. This is the point where marriages come apart or turn into the cold routine of acquaintances who have to share a house.

But love is a risky business. It means getting to know another person. It means loving a person as that person *is* and *not as we want that person to be*. Just because we love someone does not mean that that person will love us or, even loving us, behave in the ways that we desire. Some people think that they can control their loved ones by threatening to turn their love on and off like a tap. ('Daddy doesn't love you when you do that', 'I don't see how you can expect me to love you when you prefer to spend your evenings in the pub rather than at home with me',) but such behaviour rarely inspires everlasting love, rather the feeling of being used and manipulated. Some people believe that if they show their love the loved ones will take advantage of their 'softness' or in some way become 'spoilt'. Such people expect that their loved ones will interpret their sternness as proof of love, but usually the loved ones experience only a lack of love. One of the recurring tragedies in families is that children can grow up thinking that their parents do not love them when in fact the parents do.

Real love cannot be used as a weapon to control others. It can only be freely given, and, as a gift, it can be rejected. Loving is a very risky business. We risk rejection, and if we are not rejected we have to risk opening our innermost self to another person. That is risky enough if you feel quite good about yourself but, if you fear and distrust your innermost

..., letting someone close to you can be too dangerous to
.. Better to keep up a wall of fear, even though you, in some
sense, know that while the opposite of fear is courage, the
opposite of fear is also love.[15]

3 Life is terrible and death is worse

> My apprehensions come in crowds;
>   I dread the rustling of the grass;
> The very shadows of the clouds
>   Have power to shake me as they pass;
> I question things and do not find
>   One that will answer to my mind,
> And all the world appears unkind.[16]

Feeling as you do about yourself and other people, you cannot
help but find that life is terrible. The thought of death does
not comfort you since, though sometimes you dream of peaceful oblivion, you wonder, like Hamlet,

> For in that sleep of death what dreams may come.

Far outweighing your fear of death can be your fear of dying
and the pain and suffering that can entail. You become aware
of every ache and pain and any unusual sensation in your
body, and each of these you can become convinced is a symptom of a fatal disease – a failing heart or the dreaded cancer.
You recall the members of your family who have died and the
diseases they died from, and feel sure that you have inherited
the fatal complaint. You may keep these worries to yourself
or you may hasten to your doctor. When he assures you that
you are perfectly well and good for many decades yet, you feel
a fool, regard his prognosis of a long life as a curse and not a
blessing, and suspect that he is not telling you the truth.

Some people say they never think of death. This may be
because they live such busy, pleasant lives they do not give
much time to meditating on their future, or it may be that
death terrifies them so much that they dare not think of it.
But, if we do think what our own death means to us, each of us
can say what we believe it will be – not the particular circumstances of our death (though we do fantasise about these) but

what will happen to us at death. There are only two possibilities. Either death is the end of my identity or it is a doorway to another life. Some people say they can imagine both alternatives applying to them, but when they are asked which alternative they would bet on, they have no doubt on which one they would place their money. We all know whether we see our identity vanishing with our death or our identity in some form passing to another life, since it is this choice which has determined what we see as the purpose of our life. If we see death as the end of our identity then we have the task of making this our only life in some way satisfactory; if we see our death as a doorway to another life then we have the task of living this life according to the rules of entry to the next life. We can define 'satisfactory' life or 'rules of entry' in many different ways, but whatever definitions we choose we know when we are not meeting the standards we have set. Feeling that life is terrible and death is worse means that if you see death as the end you see your life as a failure and death as no recompense, and if you see death as a doorway to another life you know that you have not lived up to the standards required. You see yourself as dying to be forgotten or cursed by those you leave behind you, or being consigned to hell or limbo or to an even worse life on earth than your present one, or left a lonely, wandering ghost. You know you are damned without hope.

When I first began talking with people who were depressed to examine how they saw themselves and their world we would talk about immediate realities – relationships, work, and the person's tumult of feelings. As I got better at understanding what I was being told the sooner we began talking about death, not just the losses the person was suffering ('My mother died when I was a child. I know it's silly but I still feel it was my fault', 'My son died four years ago. People tell me I should be over it by now and I feel guilty because I'm not', 'My father died last year. I never got on well with him. I didn't know he was dying. The family kept it from me because they didn't want me to be upset'), but how the person felt about his own death. This would often lead on to a discussion of the person's religious beliefs. And here was a great problem.

British people are not great church-goers when

compared with people in some other countries, but whenever surveys are taken of religious beliefs a large percentage of British people say that they believe in God and an afterlife.[17] Similar surveys in the USA give even higher percentages of believers.[18] Such percentages would seem to suggest that religious beliefs are normal and important, but to a great many psychiatrists and psychologists the possession of a religious belief is, at best, evidence that the person is naive or stupid and, at worst, neurotic or even psychotic.[19] Whenever I ask a group of clinical psychologists whether they believe in an afterlife most of them say they do not, and when I advise them that in therapy with a depressed person it is a good idea to discover what that person's religious beliefs are, many of my colleagues look at me strangely and think that I have ceased to be a rational person, having discovered religion in my old age. I have been shocked to find that some of my colleagues whom I have always regarded as the most open-minded of people have shown themselves to be so against religion that they refuse to take seriously the religious beliefs of other people. They do not realise that if a psychologist believes (and does not say) that the purpose of therapy is to help the client live a happy and successful life and if the client believes, or hopes (but does not say), that therapy will help him be a better person and to make his peace with God, then the therapeutic enterprise must fail, since the therapist and client are travelling on different paths and not hand-in-hand. The therapist needs to understand that when you are in the business of saving your soul, happiness is irrelevant. However, that psychology is a science and science is opposed to religion is the justification of such attitudes by psychologists. Moreover, Freud stated authoritatively that the possession of religious beliefs was evidence of a neurosis and that religion was a universal neurosis. Jung opposed Freud in this, but it was Freud's views, not Jung's, along with the scientific attitudes to religion which influenced British psychiatry. As a result, the basic textbook, *Clinical Psychiatry* by Slater and Roth carries only one reference to religious belief,

Jung is probably right in holding that some neurotic subjects seeking help are really groping for *some system of religious belief* which will provide them with a source of strength and render their lives meaningful. These probably include the individual whose problems were in former times dealt with by the priest, the confessor or the head of the family; the hesitant, the guilt-ridden, the excessively timid, those lacking clear convictions with which to face life.[20]

So it is that if you tell a psychiatrist that the worst part of your misery is that you are shut out from God and that you dread life and death because you know you are damned, he will nod sympathetically and note that you are exhibiting one of the symptoms of a depressive illness. Your statement carries the same significance as the red spots in measles.

But such an experience is more than a symptom of an illness, and you feel angry and hurt when it is dismissed as such. Once in a letter to Gerald Priestland, the then Religious Affairs Correspondent for the BBC, I made a flippant comment about choosing one's religious beliefs. He shot back at me, 'The experience of damnation can be as compelling as the experience of salvation. You must figure that out for yourself, but unless you understand it your work among depressives is in vain.'[21] Alas, it is not just the atheistic psychologists and psychiatrists who fail to understand this experience but also many ministers of religion and committed Christians. If you are unfortunate enough to take your problems to such a person you find that their platitudes about the certainty of God's forgiveness do nothing but cast you further into the darkness. Better to remain silent.

No one can live his life using only rational beliefs. Even the most scientifically minded person must hold, if not religious beliefs, beliefs which cannot be proved but only taken on trust. Believing that life ends in death is just as metaphysical a belief as believing that death is a doorway to another life, since neither can be proved in the way that Brand X washing powder can be shown to wash better than Brand Y. Philosophers have had a lot to say about the differences between rational and metaphysical beliefs, more than I wish to mention here. The difference I want to stress is that where our metaphysical beliefs are concerned, proof is irrelevant. If you believe that life ends in death, no account of the joys of salvation and eternal life will change your belief. If you believe that Jesus was the Son of God who died and was resurrected, no argument backed by the best of historical studies will prove to you that Jesus, if He existed at all, was only a man. Of course, sometimes people do change their religious beliefs quite dramatically, being either converted to a religion or losing their faith altogether, but such changes usually occur not so much through reasoned argument as through the profound emotions created by a significant crisis point in the person's life where such a change in belief brings some sort of solution to his problems.

Over the past few years I have spent a great deal of time talking to people about their metaphysical beliefs. Some of these people were my clients who were living lives of great misery; some were friends, acquaintances or colleagues who, despite many problems, not only cope with their lives but enjoy them. The group of people altogether included atheists, committed Christians, vaguely Christian humanists, Jews, some people who believed in a form of reincarnation with or without a mixture of Hinduism and Buddhism, and some people whose beliefs were more mystical and magical than religious. The variety of possible beliefs amazed me. But, whatever the beliefs, they fell into one of two categories. Either they gave the person who held them courage and optimism or else they rendered the person who held them fearful and pessimistic. The first category were the beliefs of the people who coped with their lives; the second were the beliefs held by my clients.[22] People who cope with their lives hold metaphysical beliefs which liberate or at least do not impede them. People who do not cope have beliefs which serve to trap them in a life of misery, like this woman who, in the debate about shelters for battered wives, wrote to the *Observer*,

> Why has nobody yet mentioned the part religion plays
> in the endurance by women of physical violence from
> their husbands?
>   Although the fact that I had no money and no place to
> take my young children were contributory reasons for

my remaining with my uncontrollably violent husband,
the main reason was that, having been brought up in a
religious home, I believed that my marriage vows were
binding and that 'for better for worse' really meant
what it said.

Indeed, the greater the misery, the more I believed
God was putting me on trial.

It took me 10 years – during which I sought in vain
for help from my parson, my doctor, a lawyer and the
police (all of them, incidentally, men) – before I
managed to shake off the religious teachings of my
upbringing sufficiently to seek a divorce.[23]

Before I began asking people about their religious beliefs
I had assumed that when we were children we might believe
in God whom we saw as an old man with a long beard who
kept a benevolent eye on the world, but as we got older we
might realise that this was just a myth, like Santa Claus,
since no benevolent God would ever allow such horrors as our
world contains. I was quite shaken by what my clients told
me. Some of them, like Elizabeth,[24] had been told that gentle
Jesus looked after little children, but painful events soon
showed them that this was not so. Elizabeth prayed that
Jesus would make her well when she was sent home from
school for being ill. She knew her mother would be angry.
Jesus did not answer her prayer and she was punished by her
mother. Later she asked her teacher, 'What if one sparrow He
missed, or one child?' She was told that the child or the
sparrow must have met with His disapproval. Elizabeth may
have given up believing in Jesus, but not before she took
these events as further proof of her essential badness. Some
people, I have discovered, do not give up their belief in God
when they suffer grievous blows. They simply give up their
belief in a benevolent God. Their faith in God is unshaken,
but God for them is an evil God. Siegfried told me that if God
exists, 'He's a shit . . . He couldn't intentionally and with the
ability to do something about it, run the world like this,
surely. How can He tolerate man being intolerable to man?
What end can possibly be served by Auschwitz, the IRA, this
wretched business we read about this morning? I could do

better than this.'[25] Tony said, 'I have a great fear of the Christian God – He must be a bastard, what a bloody sick joke creating this world. There must be some gods up there, sitting around, and He's a baby God among the bigger immortals, and the baby's been given the world to play with, stirring things around in the world, seeing what havoc can be caused. If there is a God, then this God is some sort of holy maniac, an evil maniac. Evil because He allows enough food to keep the dream going. It's the biggest con trick ever played – the dream that you're getting somewhere.'[26] You can hardly feel safe, at home and at peace in a world created and managed by an evil God.

When the wife of C.S. Lewis died of cancer he kept a diary through the period of intense grief and later anonymously published some of his thoughts. He had discovered that

> You never really know how much you really believe
> anything until its truth or falsehood becomes a matter
> of life and death for you . . . not that I am (I think) in
> much danger of ceasing to believe in God. The real
> danger is in coming to believe such dreadful things
> about Him. The conclusion I dread is not 'So there's no
> God at all', but 'So this is what God's really like.
> Deceive yourself no longer'.

Friends tried to console him with the assurance that his wife was in God's hands. However, he could only wonder,

> But if so, she was in God's hands all the time, and I have
> seen what they did to her here. Do they suddenly
> become gentler to us the moment we are out of the
> body? And if so, why? If God's goodness is inconsistent
> with hurting us, then either God is not good or there is
> no God, for in the only life we know He hurts us beyond
> our worst fears and beyond all we can imagine. If it is
> consistent with hurting us, then He may hurt us after
> death as unendurably as before it.[27]

Trying not to see your God as evil and malevolent causes you great conflict and pain, and, like Gerard Manley Hopkins, the Jesuit priest whose experience of depression

brought forth the most poignant of poems, you might argue
with God and plead,

> Thou are indeed just, Lord, if I contend
> With Thee; but, see, so what I plead is just.
> Why do sinners' ways prosper? and why must
> Disappointment all I endeavour end?
> Wert thou my enemy, O thou my friend,
> How wouldst thou worse, I wonder, than thou dost
> Defeat, thwart me?
> . . . .
> birds build – but not I build; but strain,
> Time's eunuch, and not breed one work that wakes.
> Mine, O thou lord of life, send my roots rain.[28]

We can go through life untroubled by the pain and misery of our fellows, but once we allow the knowledge of this
suffering to penetrate the cocoon of our well-being (while I
was writing this, five days before Christmas, the military
took over in Poland, sixteen people were drowned as a ship
and a lifeboat were wrecked off the Cornish coast,[29] and in the
space of one day 40,000 children were, and are, dying of
starvation[30]), we have to face the problem of evil. When the
suffering is personal, our loss and pain, the question of why
this has happened to me and mine demands an answer. (The
night before last my friend Margaret Templeton, whom I met
when we did a phone-in on depression for BBC Radio Sheffield in 1978 and who since then has organised self-help
groups for depressed people in Sheffield, phoned to tell me
that her youngest son, aged ten, had been knocked down by a
car and killed. 'I didn't know he was outside,' she said. 'A
child came to the door and said he'd had an accident. I tried to
hurry' (she wears a spinal corset) 'I had to crawl up the bank
to reach him. They'd thrown a blanket over him. I lay down
on the road beside him. Someone said he was just unconscious. I didn't know he was dead. The car had gone right over
him. I tried to wipe the gravel off his face. He was always such
a happy boy – my baby. I feel I've lost part of me.' A good
Christian woman. Why?)

How can we account for evil? If we do not believe in God
we have to account for evil in terms of the unpredictable ways

of nature (floods, fires, earthquakes, blizzards, typhoons, the deadly virus, the burgeoning cancer cells, the blood clot) and the cruelty and stupidity of human beings. People who cope with life and who do not believe in God accept with some degree of equanimity the randomness of nature, regard scientific knowledge as largely beneficial and exciting, and see the cruelty and stupidity of people not so much as evidence of their inherent badness as of their poor education. Faith in man's capacity to learn from his mistakes gives hope of improvement.[31] But if you fear the randomness of nature, regard scientific knowledge as dangerous and frightening,[32] and believe that most, if not all, people are inherently evil and through wilfulness or stupidity refuse to learn from their mistakes, then you have no hope that life on this earth will improve.

If we do believe in God we have to ask why God allows evil to exist. If you believe that God inflicts suffering to punish the guilty and to show them the error of their ways, when you suffer a grievous blow you can interpret this as evidence of your essential badness. You can interpret the misery you feel, your state of depression, as the punishment you deserve for being so evil. If you believe in the justice of this punishment you will resist having your depression taken from you in case worse punishment will follow. If you were not such a bad person your mother would not have died, or your child would not have been born handicapped, or your husband's heart wear out before its time. Even as you accept this as proof of your badness you have to ask, 'Why should the innocent suffer? Why should they be made to pay for the sins of the guilty?' And not all people appear to suffer. Indeed, evil, as ever, seems to flourish like the green bay tree.

The ways of God are indeed mysterious. If He is all-powerful He hardly seems to be all-good; and if He is all-good, He cannot be all-powerful. At the very least He is inefficient. If you try to discuss these problems with members of your clergy you are likely to be told that you have to take God on trust. Now this is something you find impossible to do. You know quite well that you cannot trust other people. You are always being disappointed in other people. They are always letting you down, even your nearest and dearest whose behaviour you can usually predict. How can you trust God who is likely to come up with anything?

Trusting means accepting uncertainty, and that is one thing you are not prepared to accept. One way to be certain about God is to decide that He is harsh and cruel, if not malevolent, and that He is more likely to inflict suffering rather than to create happiness, and when He does create happiness He always follows it by pain. Another way of being certain is to see God as entirely good but not omnipotent. He is in battle with the source of evil, the Devil.

Quite a few people believe in the Devil as a potent force in the world.[33] Belief in the Devil certainly makes the world appear as a dark and dangerous place, especially when you see the Devil as more powerful than God. Sometimes God and the Devil are seen as personages locked in combat; sometimes God and the Devil appear as the Force of Good and the Force of Evil. Felicity[34] described to me how 'I can remember as a child trying to think "How did the world begin in the first place and if it was made in seven days, and this is a God sitting up there, well, where did that God come from? Where did the space come from?" You could go mad thinking about that.' She came to an answer when she got older. 'It's some kind of good and evil forces which are at war with one

"Oh, we have no end of trouble over people's preconceived ideas about the life hereafter."

another, and I can only think that the evil forces are winning because certainly the world is not improving, is it?'

Whether we believe in God or not, we all find it difficult to conceive of the complete and absolute end of our identity at death. We speak of death as going to sleep, but in our sleep we are aware of time passing, and we experience ourselves in dreams. Dreams are still a puzzle and for some of us a source of fear. As small children we found it hard to distinguish dreams from waking, and even as adults we can appreciate the quandary of Chuang Tsu who dreamed he was a butterfly and on waking wondered if he was a butterfly dreaming that he was a man.[35] We can argue that we know what is a dream because it is something from which we can awake, but when your dreams are nightmares you dread to sleep lest you never wake but stay trapped in your dream. The blessing of some sedative drugs is that they abolish dreaming, and their curse is that ceasing to take the drug brings the dreams back with greater intensity. Death as sleep can be something to dread. There is another kind of blanking out which death may resemble. This is the experience of the general anaesthetic used in surgery. As the anaesthetist murmurs soothing words a black tide rises and you know no more until you hear a nurse's rousing voice and feel some strange discomfort. There are no dreams, no sense of time passing. If you had not awakened you would not know you had not awakened. If our identity perishes at death this must be what death is like. For many people the thought of disappearing like this is quite intolerable. Their identity must continue in some form.

It is easy to conceive of my identity, that which I call I, continuing to exist after my death. The problem is to decide what this post-death existence will be. Will it be the same for all of us? If we feel that one of the greatest imperfections of this world is the way virtue is not always rewarded and vice not always punished, we may look to the afterlife for the justice denied in this world. We can believe that the good (including the sinners who repent) go to heaven and the unrepentant bad go to hell, or that the good are reincarnated to a better life and the bad to a worse. Such beliefs may satisfy our need for justice, but they create an ever-present anxiety that we may fail to qualify for heaven or a better life. If we see ourselves as basically good with a few, not-too-terrible faults and if we set ourselves standards of goodness which are not too difficult to meet, then our anxiety is not very great. But if you see yourself as basically bad with none or only a few minor virtues and if you set yourself standards of perfection which are impossible to meet, then your anxiety is great. Heaven or a better life may not be for you.

As great a sense of hopelessness and failure can pervade the lives of those who do not believe in a life after death. If you see yourself as essentially bad and if you set yourself standards of perfection, then you can never be the person you think you ought to be or achieve the things you feel you ought to achieve. You can never be the perfect child of perfect parents, the perfect housewife and mother, the perfect and brilliantly successful man, husband, son, lover, father. You have been cheated of your birthright, badly used, wasted your talents and opportunities, disappointed those who love you, behaved badly, selfishly, foolishly. You may believe that your luck has run out[36] or that you are the helpless victim of a terrible Fate. You will leave behind no work that you will be remembered by; your virtues will not be extolled by your relatives and friends; you leave no children behind you to revere you, or if you do have children they are no credit to you. When you die you will be forgotten. It will be as if you never existed.

Whether we believe that our identity ends in death or that we go to another form of existence we all like to believe that we shall leave some trace of ourselves behind on earth, through our works or in the loving memories of our children and friends. Some people's passionate ambitions are not simply to obtain an enormous share of the world's goods but to leave some permanent mark upon the world. Some people enter politics not only to make their country, in their terms, a better place but to enter the history books as well. Some people want to have children not just for the delight of having children but to secure the immortality of one generation succeeding another. Some people are kind to their fellow men not just because they love them but because they want to be remembered and praised. For such people the failure of their enterprise is not just the failure to become rich, or to receive acclaim as an artist, or to be elected to high office, or to beget children, or to win friends and influence people, it is the failure to achieve a kind of eternal life, and it is felt as keenly as the failure to enter the Kingdom of Heaven.

When we imagine our own death we summon up a scene where we are both the central participant and an observer. We are there seeing ourselves die. I rather fancy the death-bed scene favoured by the Hollywood movies of the forties, where I die beautifully and gracefully, without pain or discomfort, murmuring a few memorable last words, surrounded by my loved ones who, while regretting my leaving, are not too painfully distressed since I have reached a Great Age and had a Good Life. I do not fancy one of those deaths which are recorded in the funeral notice as 'after a long illness bravely borne' and I hope that no one is so dependent on me that my death will leave that person bereft. Not everyone has such faith in a Hollywood ending. If you have written a scenario for yourself which includes much pain and suffering, or circumstances which produce a terrible death scene, then this scene can take on a strange reality and haunt all your waking and sleeping moments.

When we imagine our death we consider not just the circumstances of our death but the kind of funeral that we want. I have discovered that people who do not believe in life after death can feel most passionate about their funeral, and the simple question, 'Do you want to be buried or cremated?' can produce a fierce argument.[37] Our preference can be based on positive reasons stemming from how we see ourselves in relation to life in general. We may want to be buried so we can become part of the life cycle or we may want to be cremated because we see burial as using up the scarce land resources of this small island. Or our preference can be based on fear and mistrust. If we cannot trust other people's judgment we may fear that we shall be placed in our coffin not dead but unconscious and awake to find ourselves being – well, which is preferable, being buried alive or burnt alive? For many people this is not an idle question.

John was referred to me because, since the death of his closest friend from cancer, he had been depressed and extremely panicky. I wrote of him,

John had a recurring nightmare about Paul's cremation. 'It starts where the coffin is just coming in. Then it sort of builds up from there. The noise gets louder and louder. The shouting is in the background, then it seems to build up and – it's really unbearable. It's like the shouting in the panic attack, but I can make out the words in this one because Paul's mother kept on saying, "Bury him, bury him". The voice gets louder and louder and then suddenly I'm awake.' . . . I asked John to imagine what would happen in the dream if he had not woken at that point. Reluctantly he thought about this. 'I think I would see the burning – all I can imagine is that he is still alive, you see.' I asked him to imagine that he was the person in the coffin. He said that he would be fighting to get out but would not be able to do this because it would be too late . . . John was against cremation, 'because there's nothing there. Nothing to show respect to. You can go back to a grave. You can carry on the love side, the respect. Whereas with the cremation it's final. There's not anything left.'[38]

Rose was terrified of being buried since it made her feel 'as though I was going to be suffocated. I dread being shut up.'[39] Mary accepted burial but expected that her grave would be neglected. She said, 'I'm frightened of being on my own when I wake up in heaven . . . When I'm depressed I often wish I was dead myself, though I don't know what good it would do. I feel everybody would be better off without me.' She pictured her husband and parents 'carrying on without me . . . I can imagine my grave being overrun with weeds and people not remembering – I can't imagine Robert at a funeral, not even mine. I can imagine him laughing and cheerful. He hates people crying all over the place. . . . I imagine them carrying on as usual – I suppose they would. It's as if I'd never existed at all. As if I'm completely forgotten.' To me it seemed unlikely that her family would forget her, but she had a good reason for wanting this. If her family remembered her, mourned her, and kept her grave tidy, this would mean that she, through her death, had upset them, and, as she said, 'I don't want to hurt anyone's feelings – I'm always frightened of upsetting anybody and anything. Even if I don't like them I shouldn't want to hurt them.' Rather than upset other people she would be a lonely ghost.[40]

It is the fantasies that you have about death that determine whether you will commit suicide when you are depressed. You think about death a great deal. It both terrifies and charms you. It may look attractive as the end to your misery, but if you cannot bear to cause your loved ones suffering or if you fear an afterlife which is more terrible than your present life, suicide is no solution. But if you welcome death as an end without waking, a complete ceasing to be, or if you are indifferent to the feelings of those you leave behind, or see your death as a triumphant vindication of your life, or as a means of a kind of rebirth, a second chance, or as a way of making the world a better place, then suicide can hold a promise which you may find hard to resist.

Jacky Gillott wrote about her years of depression in an article for *Cosmopolitan*. She said,

Depression is suffered by people who see no reason to like themselves at all. Depression *is* a state of self-hate. It is the horror of feeling oneself inescapably bound within the body of someone you fear, loathe and despise. Depression is a state of mind that inevitably invites paranoia; if you find yourself loathsome, you expect the rest of the world to find you loathsome too. What's more, you feel you have no business infecting other people's existence with your unpleasant presence . . . Because I have this loony belief that I am somehow contagious, and that those who might catch whatever it is hate me anyway, I become hysterically frightened of other people. I ignore the phone and hide if someone knocks at the door. If I have to go to the bank or the shops I will either walk miles the long way round to avoid people I know, or travel to another town where I can be fairly sure of going unrecognised . . . Many depressives commit suicide, I'm sure, as the last act of unselfishness . .˙. I'm convinced that many of the neat, quiet, unexpected suicides are committed by

depressives who quite simply wish not be a nuisance
any longer . . . I find it quite easy when I'm at my lowest
to present a logical case for my removal. It would, for
instance, be infinitely kinder to my family. Hours are
spent working out which would be the least
inconvenient moment to lay my head in the gas oven.
There never is a convenient moment, of course, because
I've learnt over the years to crowd my schedule with
certain unavoidable commitments . . . I always make
sure I'm permanently in debt because I would feel it
rather disgraceful to go leaving other people to pay my
bills.[41]

Unfortunately for those of us left behind, in 1980 Jacky paid
her debts and found a convenient time to take a lethal dose of
tablets.

Taking an overdose of drugs is a popular way of commit-
ting or attempting suicide since it seems to offer a fulfilment
of that desire for peace and the cessation of struggle which
every depressed person feels at some time or other. Val
expressed this in a poem which she wrote when she was very
depressed.

Desired Haven?
Battered by waves of desolation,
Tossed in a sea of despair,
Sucked in spiralling whirlpools,
Clutched by an icy hand.

I struggle to ride out the storm.
Progressively weaker I thrash about, but,
As the seventh wave gathers fear paralyses me.
I become helpless and am swamped.

I plunge deeper and deeper into a green oblivion.
All is silent and still now.
Inert I languish in the sudden tranquillity.
Alas, this is but transitory.

I am pitched back into the turbulence,
And continue the struggle for survival.
I am heaved from crest to crest,
Between wallowing in the gaping troughs.

The effects of exposure take their toll.
The clammy coldness slowly destroys me,
Until a salvage job seems worthless.
Now I look for an end to the tempest.
I long to sink deeper and deeper,
I yearn for the cool, calming caress of gentle ebb
  and flow,
To surrender to the peace it offers.

That is the desire. The actuality is different. Whether a person quietly takes an overdose or dramatically plunges from the top of a cliff, it is a violent act of self-murder. Suicide is an act of violence against that part of ourselves that wants to go on living. If every part of us, body and soul, wants to die, or if we are totally convinced that death is inevitable, then we die without having to inflict any violence upon ourselves. Many old people give up and die. An Australian aborigine who has been expelled from his tribe, no matter how strong and healthy he is, will die within days of being expelled, as will an Azande who knows himself to be the recipient of bad magic. Research on the life expectancy of women with breast cancer shows that the women who are determined to go on living do very well while those who give up hope are less likely to survive. If you have to do violence to yourself in order to die, then somewhere in you is hope and the desire to go on living. A large part of you wants to go on living. You should stick with that part of yourself.

Of course it is easy for me to say that because I think that life is worth living. You don't. Whether you see death as the end or as a doorway to another life, whether you believe in God, or the Devil, or the Forces of Good and Evil, or whether you have no religious beliefs at all, your particular beliefs about the nature of death and the purpose of life inspire in you fear rather than hope. They ensure your suffering – and yet they have their advantages.

Every belief, like everything else in our world, has its advantages as well as its disadvantages. The God of vengeance will deal with your enemies just as He deals with you, while the belief in sin certainly adds a piquancy to life. Some activities which might otherwise be quite dull can be found to be exciting because they are sinful and forbidden. There is some satisfaction to be gained in believing in a universal system which is just and perfect, even if the application of that justice means that you are punished, and the vision of perfection illuminates your faults. Your beliefs may make you fearful, but because you know them to be Real, Absolute, and Eternal Truths your beliefs give you *certainty*. You prefer to be certain of the future, even if the future is tragic. And a tragic figure has a particular distinction which a contented mediocrity lacks. As much as we fear our death, it is the knowledge of our death that gives the point and purpose to our life, and we want our life to have to have some significance to ourselves, even if not to other people.

Of course we must be aware of death in order to survive. We learn to be careful crossing the road, to eat the right foods, not to walk down dark alleyways, to wrap up warmly in cold weather and not to smoke too much. A careful respect for death can help ensure a long life not just for yourself but for those around you. Respect rather than fear, for, as Epictatus said,

> *Why, do you not know then, that the origin of all evils, and of baseness and cowardice, is not death, but rather the fear of death.*[42]

Our death lies in the future, so if you fear death it is the future that you fear.

4 Only bad things happened to me in the past and only bad things will happen to me in the future

'I just feel that my past is getting larger, my future's getting smaller and I haven't got time for the present,' said Bob, one of the heroes of the BBC TV series 'Whatever Happened to the Likely Lads?' (Bob and Terry, once likely lads, are now approaching thirty, and look back to their childhood and adolescence as their golden age. The theme song of the series ends with the words 'The only thing to look forward to is the past.') Bob's words, uttered in his usual rueful, anxious way, made us all laugh, the kind of laugh that comes when we are presented with something which we know is, sadly, only too true about ourselves.

If time were a house, then our present should be a large, airy, sunlit room where we can move freely in it and from it, whenever we wish, into the past, a small, cosy, cheerful room, or into our future, a wide open doorway on to a welcoming vista. But if *your* time were a house, your past would be a huge, dark, menacing room, containing your present, an insignificant treadmill where you have to run fast to stay in one place and your future a dark tunnel ending in a blank wall. There was a time when you thought that if you turned your back on the past and ran as fast as you could the future would open up, rosy with promise. However, once inside the prison of depression you know that running on a treadmill makes no progress, that there is nowhere to progress to, and all you are left with is a past which is filled with fear, anger, jealousy, regret, grief and loss.

The famous French psychiatrist, Henri Ey, considered that the most important feature of depression was the way in which the person's perception of time changed, not just the slowing down of time so that twenty-four hours pass like a week, but the relative importance of past and future, so that the past and not the future engages the depressed person's attention. It is not the kind of interest in the past which many people develop as they approach old age, when they spend a lot of time thinking about past events and telling their stories to every willing and unwilling listener available. Usually the story is told in the framework of 'things were better then than they are now', even when the events recalled involved suffering and hardship, since the person is in the business of showing that he had not been conquered and defeated, but that he had mastered life and enjoyed it, and, since the contemporary world is inferior to that of his youth, nothing is to be gained by living forever. In such a way do elderly people become reconciled to their lives and so reconciled to their deaths. They recall their past to redefine it as good.

But your living in the past is quite different. When you do recall something that was good and happy, you do this not with pleasure but with painful regret. Something, or somebody, has been lost, never to return. When you see this loss as having occurred not by chance but by carelessness or malice, your memories are filled with bitterness, anger and resentment. You have suffered many losses, rebuffs, unsettling changes, some of which would be categorised by sociologists as the 'life events' which depressed people, so research shows, collect in greater numbers than non-depressed people[43] (you always knew you were unlucky!) and some of which were the small betrayals, deceits, disloyalties, treacheries, cruelties, dishonesties, denunciations, threats, belittlings, rejections, criticisms, reproaches, indignities, jealousies, animosities, ingratitudes, meannesses, enmities and ostracisms that take place in every community which is not guided by love and forgiveness.

None of us grew to adulthood without having suffered some 'life events' and some measure of inhumanity. How do we come to terms with the unhappiness of our past so that it does not dominate our present? What most people do is that they talk things over with someone. A good friend listens, commiserates, and helps us get things in proportion. But what if there is no one in your life who is interested enough in you to listen? Or no one you would dare to talk to, since the people you know would get angry with you, or belittle you, or punish you in some way? Or if you believe that family matters must never be discussed outside the family, and there is no one in the family you can discuss such matters with because you do not want to hurt anyone in your family? How often a client has told me a story of what I would call everyday family unhappiness and ended with the words, 'This is the first time I've ever told anybody about this.' No wonder the past remains the burdensome present.

It is not just that you have never been able to reassess, redefine, master and lay to rest the past events which still trouble you, but you have been unable to redefine yourself in relation to these events. Long ago you decided that you were a bad person, and subsequent painful events served only to confirm this. In fact, you only remember bad things about yourself, and, if by any chance someone reminds you of an occasion when you did very well at something, you can instantly prove your badness by saying, 'I should have done better.' Now it is a curious matter that what we call 'I' or 'myself' is composed almost entirely of memories, so that to have a sense of identity means being constantly aware of the past. If you ask me what sort of a person I am, much of what I would answer would refer to the past. If I answered you in terms of the present (right now I am in bed on a cold winter morning, writing this, drinking coffee, coughing, and aware of a vague pain rumbling around inside my pelvis) you would feel that I had told you very little about myself, but if I answered you in terms of the past (I was born in Australia fifty-one years ago, came to England thirteen years ago, have a son of twenty-four, work as a clinical psychologist in the National Health Service, live in an old cottage in a small village, enjoy my work, the company of my friends, reading, writing and travel), you would feel that I had told you a good deal about myself. My past, it seems, tells more about me than my present. This is curious, as Alan Watts, in his excellent book, *The Way of Zen*, explains,

> We learn, very thoroughly . . . to identify ourselves with
> a . . . conventional view of 'myself'. For the conventional
> 'self' or 'person' is composed mainly of a history
> consisting of selected memories, and beginning from the
> moment of parturition. According to convention, I am
> not simply what I am doing now. I am also what I have
> done, and my conventionally edited version of my past
> is made to seem almost the more real 'me' than what I
> am at this moment. For what I *am* seems so fleeting and
> intangible, but what I *was* is fixed and final. It is the
> firm basis for predictions of what I will be in the future,
> and so it comes about that I am more closely identified
> with what no longer exists than with what actually is![44]

Thus it is that we use our past to predict our future, and if that part of our past which we call 'I' is defined as 'bad' it must follow that the predicted future matches it in badness. Of course, when you were younger you dreamt of a future which would recompense you for the pain of your childhood. All children have such dreams, but soon there crept upon you

> The conviction that life
> Is coming up with some colossal romantic musical
> For which the casting director has, yet again,
> Overlooked you.[45]

You might abandon, but still mourn, your romantic dreams, while you acquired what you call a more realistic appraisal of the workings of the cosmos –

> Life, you know, is set up by this great random
>   computer,
> But it has been poorly programmed.
> Someone has fed in more bad news than good,
> And the messages tick out mad irrelevancies
>   and ironies.[46]

But such a cynical attitude cannot keep at bay your deep, all-pervading pessimism. You know that Robert Lowell was right when he said that always,

> if we see a light at the end of the tunnel
> it's the light of an oncoming train.[47]

However, although you are convinced that the future holds nothing good for you, until the isolation of your prison brings you to a complete halt, you are forever rushing, rushing, rushing to get things done. You never pay attention to what you are actually doing since you are busy thinking about what you must do next, and after that, what next, and so on and so on. If hell is ceaseless activity, then this is it. Only by running on the spot can you avoid falling into the bottomless abyss under your feet. And some fool tells you to take it easy! How can you stop when you must work so hard to overcome your badness, to placate and please others, to earn the right to exist, to grasp at a life which might any moment be wrenched away from you, to get hold of something which might fill the horrible void within yourself.

Philip Toynbee who, in the last years of his life, set out to discover the *purposes* rather than the *causes* of his depression wrote,

> I suspect that each of us suffers from some *besetting* sin, which we must diagnose with great care and much hard thought. Often that dominant sin is not what seems the most obvious one; or rather it lies half-concealed behind some of its more ostentatious forms. In my own case it might seem that lust (in the days of lust in action!) and

gluttony (drunkenness) have been my major sins; but
now I believe that what lies behind these, and most of
my other faults, is a sort of wilful metabolic frenzy; the
constant urge to hurry as quickly as possible out of the
present moment and into the next one. Get this woman
now; *at once*! Drink these drinks *immediately* in order to
take instant possession of the whole evening ahead.

He described how he rushed at everything, eating, dressing,
gardening, repairing his house, just to get the job over and
done with.

How calmly and thoroughly S works at her windows,
scraping off every bit of old paint and crumbling putty!
How I rush at my walls, wielding the brush like a
weapon!

He realised that

With the old and obvious error about possession goes a
slightly subtler error about accomplishment. 'I want *to
have read* this book; and therefore contain it . . .' 'I want
to have made this garden; I want *to have written* this
book . . .' In fact it is desire for possession in another
form; another notch on the stick for another Indian
killed . . . A greedy grabbing for the future.

No matter what you acquire or get done, nothing assuages
your sense of guilt.

The reason why guilt is so useless [wrote Philip
Toynbee] is that it keeps our heads buried, and
suffocating, in our own past.[48]

So you live in the horrendous past and the hopeless,
fearful future and never in the present. And yet the curious
thing is that the past and the future have no reality, except as
ideas in our mind. All we ever experience is the present. In
the present we can remember (think about) the past and
imagine (think about) the future, and our thoughts are *in the
present*. Of course, we can be so absorbed in our thoughts that
we are oblivious to everything else in our present, and our
thoughts may make our present quite unbearable, but, as

Alan Watts said, 'There is never anything but the present, and if one cannot live there, one cannot live anywhere.'[49]

However, there are advantages in seeing your past and your future in the worst possible light. We can always try to avoid responsibility for our actions in the present by blaming the past – our parents, our schooling, our social conditions. 'I can't help being like this' is a wonderful excuse for behaving badly. How easy it is to change a cause into an excuse, to claim that a disadvantaged past necessarily means a disadvantaged present and future, and that no effort toward change needs to be made. Even if we do not want to excuse our bad behaviour in this way, we can absorb ourselves in our past so as to avoid the challenges of our present and future. We can be so terrified of adulthood that we resolve to remain a child forever, or we can be so absorbed with the mother of our childhood that we ignore the needs of the old woman she has become, or we can be so lost in the nostalgia for our children's early years that we can ignore the problems with which our adult children are trying to deal. It is so much better to concentrate on the problems of the past, because we are always experts on those. It is the problems of the present that keep on being new and different and demanding flexibility and creativity for their solution. Better to stick to what you know.

When it comes to the future, it is always better to predict disaster than success, since you have a better chance of being right, for the simple reason that it is always easier to destroy than to build. You can always make sure of failure, and then you may not be happy but you will be certain.

As a child I was very slow in learning to ride a bike, and I was an adult before I could walk down a flight of stairs without feeling nervous. I had no physical disabilities, but a mother who followed my infant steps with cries of, 'You'll fall, you'll fall!' To oblige her I did. Then she would say, 'I told you you would fall.' Fortunately I had a father who was encouraging and optimistic, so my inhibition in learning was not too great. But I was often reminded of my mother when I talked with Carol.

Carol often told me anecdotes of family life in which she had expected the worst and was not disappointed. On a visit to a neighbour, 'I was just waiting for Peter to smash that Chinese lamp. I was thinking all the time, he will do it, he will do it. Anyway, he knocked over some plastic ornaments – but I knew he would.'

When I asked how she knew these things would happen she said, 'Premonitions. More often than not when I've thought of something it's happened.'

'Does that worry you?'

'No. I think it's an advantage in one way. I think there must be something in it. I get a sort of feeling. You can't always say directly what's going to happen. It's an inspiration that suddenly comes over me that there might be some trouble. It doesn't worry me. In fact, I think it's an advantage.'

'It allows you to start worrying sooner.'

'Possibly. When the car didn't pass its test I wasn't a bit surprised. I could not get out of my mind about the accident my cousin had. Whether somebody's given me a bang on the head and giving me all these premonitions! I wish they'd give me nice premonitions – so that things would still be all right – so I didn't have to guard myself.'[50]

Being constantly on guard against the future is exhausting, but it does have the advantage of directing your attention away from the present. Since the past and the future are ideas in our minds we can insist that the past and the future are exactly as we see them. The trouble with the present is that it has the habit of suggesting that my ideas may not be entirely right. How can I maintain my belief that everybody hates me if I recognise here and now the love you have for me; how can I maintain my belief that the Catholics are in league with the devil if I recognise the concern of the nun who nurses me in hospital; how can I maintain that everything turns out badly for me if I recognise that the trouble I predicted for today has not eventuated. And if I discover that my ideas are not entirely correct, how shall I know how to behave? Instead of following the rules of behaviour which my ideas demand, I would have to behave spontaneously. Now some of us quite like behaving spontaneously. But you do not. For you, spontaneity means not joy but anger, and anger, you know, is dangerous and evil.

5 It is wrong to get angry

In the journal of the last two years of his life Philip Toynbee
spoke very briefly but very poïgnantly of his childhood. He
wrote,

> All that period of my youngest childhood is filled and
> suffused with love of my mother. She seemed a wise,
> strong and tender giantess, holding my hand on a walk
> or swinging me high above her head; a tall figure in
> doorways or towering beside my bed. During those
> years, and probably for many years afterwards, the
> thought that she might be wrong in anything she did or
> said was as far outside the reach of my mind as the idea
> that she was capable of dying. (It wasn't until I saw her
> dead body, nearly fifty years later, that I realised what
> a small woman she had been.)
>
> So my mother was also a storybook queen except that
> she was so palpably present to Tony and me,
> warm-fleshed, always sweet scented and often singing.
> Although she reproached us when we behaved badly,
> and sometimes punished us, *that* mother was never
> angry. To have lost her temper would have been a
> breach of the impeccable serenity which belonged to her
> as closely as her beautiful hair and face. . . . Tony was
> much more shy and withdrawn than I was. He was
> terrified of being made to look a fool in public, while I
> was a natural clown, and always happy to attract
> attention. I was also the more quick-tempered of the
> two, and my mother used the same device to tease Tony
> out of his sullen self-consciousness and me from my
> noisy tantrums. She would raise her first fingers to her
> temples, point them down at us like horns, purse up her
> mouth as if in awe of us and waggle her fingers at our
> angry faces. We understood that this forbade us to sulk
> or rage any longer: her gesture was almost an order to
> us to laugh at ourselves.
>
> Although Tony and I often quarrelled I know now, as
> I have always known, that we were closely bound to
> each other under all the apparent ferocity of our rows
> and arguments . . . Yet our quarrelling was the usual

cause of my mother's displeasure, and in most cases she
was shrewd in deciding who was the more to be blamed.
So we were usually in disgrace separately, and in a
disgrace which divided us further. This may be why I
remember so clearly an afternoon when we had been
equal accomplices in some nursery crime. My mother
had spoken to us with that air of amazed disgust which
was the worst punishment we ever received; and even
my father had been called to our bedroom to add his
uneasy quota of disapproval. [His father was] a
shadowy figure [but sometimes the two brothers] were
allowed to come into our parents' bedroom in the
morning; and when I saw them sitting side by side in
that great bed I was deeply assured of their strong and
unbreakable union. Or rather I was never aware of my
need for such assurance. We used to climb into the foot
of the bed, pulling the eiderdown over our legs; and
when the whole family of four were together I imagined
the bed to be a boat which would sail down the river and
over the sea.

　Certainly this concept of the close family was deeply
planted in my mind, and my father was just as
necessary a part of it as either my mother or my
brother. I never admitted to myself that I loved him less
than the other two, for I know from as early as I can
remember that such inequality in love is a terrible and
dangerous thing.

At that time Philip knew other terrible things, like the Ger-
mans (he was born in 1916), and nightmares, like the recurring dream

　of a high wind blowing down the river as we crossed the
Albert Bridge for our afternoon walk in Battersea Park.
I was clawing at the smooth surface of the bridge as the
wind blew me back and back towards an edge which no
longer had any protective paling. But my mother
always saved me before I fell into the wrinkled water.
[Then] a very clear memory of my grandmother
skipping across the hall at Yatscombe, holding a piece
of paper above her head and singing, 'A new-born baby!

A new-born brother for Tony and Philip!' I suppose we
must have been warned of this, but all I remember was
a feeling of mildly uncomprehending surprise. There
was certainly no conscious shock of jealousy and not the
least apprehension of what this birth would mean to us
. . . What I remember best is coming into a bedroom and
seeing the new baby at my mother's breast; but even at
this moment of confrontation I can remember no very
strong emotion. I said that the baby looked weak, and
asked my mother whether it was going to die. Today the
'true' meaning of my question seems too obvious to
mention,[51] yet I know that I felt quite a genuine concern
for the wrinkled fragility of that tiny, spluttering
creature. And I would guess that this concern was at
least as real as any fratricidal impulse in my
unconscious mind.

But how did it come about that within a year of that
birth I was boarding at a private school half a mile from
our St John's Wood house? I wasn't even a weekly
boarder, although my mother must have paid
occasional visits to the school in term-time.

Children usually accept whatever happens to them
without question, and I doubt if it even seemed odd to
me that I was boarding at a school where Tony was a
dayboy, and where the parents of all the other boarders
seemed to be living in Africa or India.

Many years afterwards, when this state of affairs,
and many others that followed it, *had* begun to seem
strange to me, my mother explained that I had become
so intolerable soon after the birth of my brother
Lawrence that it was impossible to keep me at home.
Indeed she had always dreaded the holidays, when the
exiled monster would again start to raise hell in a house
which had been a bower of peace in his absence.

What I do remember is that I was often in trouble
now, and that the notion of my exceptional naughtiness
was one which I learned to accept as a fact in life. I told
the dirtiest stories in the dormitory. I was often beaten
by the tough but charming Mr Campbell, whom all
wished to please. I got myself lost whenever we went on

school outings to Hampstead Heath.

Most home memories of those years have been obliterated; but I remember that my mother, who had never seemed capable of ill-temper in Chelsea, was often fiercely angry with me in St John's Wood. And still it never crossed my mind that she might be wrong, or even mistaken, in anything she said or did. (How curious it seems to me now that we were brought up to believe that all the adults we knew were good, and that both our parents were impeccable.)

Some time in my ninth year, and second year at Arnold House, the headmistress was taking a group of parents round the garden when they came upon Toynbee Minor peeing into a flowerpot. This had been of course, the culmination of my offences, the last straw on that broad back which made her decide that her school could tolerate me no better than my mother could.

This first expulsion from school must have greatly strengthened my conviction of sin, for my mother's accusations had now been endorsed by a quite separate authority.

After this, with a minimum delay, I was sent off to board at the Dragon School in Oxford, an institution which prided itself on being able to lick even the most misshapen boys into place.[52]

But whatever reshaping this school did of Philip Tonybee, it did not change his belief that he was essentially evil nor did it teach him how to control his quick and violent temper.

What Philip Toynbee described here is the process by which a small child comes to believe that he or she is bad, evil, and unacceptable. His early childhood was presided over by a strong, good and loving mother who protected him from all sorts of unknown terrors. She had already made clear to him her disapproval of anger, but this did not become a major problem for him until the birth of his younger brother. He could remember nothing of the year between the birth and his expulsion from the family home, but a great deal must have happened. He wrote,

A family friend saw very clearly that my mother transferred much of her overt love from Tony and me to the third-born son. The same friend also saw that while Tony seemed almost unaffected by this – perhaps he had already worked off his quota of jealousy on me – I was soon disturbed by obvious though confused resentments. And so, the much-told story continues, I was made captive to these emotions, and remained their captive for forty years.[53]

What were these emotions aroused in the small boy? No more than what any small child would feel in a situation where he feels insecure and unloved. Fear and, because he wants to go on living, anger. He protests. He wants the object that caused these dangerous changes to be removed. He wants to feel secure and loved. But the object stays. He is frustrated and, being a human being, like all other human beings, when he is frustrated he feels angry. But his mother will not accept his anger. He is punished for being angry, and so he feels more frightened and more unloved. But if he decides that it is his mother who is wrong (why did she not put her arms around him and assure him that he was safe and loved?), he will be in even greater peril. So he must decide that his mother is good as she has always been, that he is the wicked one, and the evidence of his wickedness is his anger.

The birth of younger siblings often forces a child into a situation from which the only escape is to define both self and anger as bad. Jackie who, when she first met me, would not utter one word of criticism about her mother and who lived in fear of her mother's disapproval was explaining to me that she was the third child in a family of eight and mentioned, in passing, how when she was small she would go to bed at night and then begin to worry whether her tiny brothers and sisters were still breathing. She would get out of bed and go and investigate. As soon as her parents heard her moving about they would come upstairs and slap her hard and order her back to bed. Jackie had not connected this with the terrible terrors that had come upon her after the birth of her own babies. What mother has not crept to the side of her sleeping baby to check that the baby was still breathing? But what if she has already had it beaten into her that this is a wicked thing to do?

For many children it is not the birth of siblings that convince the child that he is evil. It can be any situation where the child's desires come into conflict with those of the adults around him. Often the clash comes over toilet-training, where the adult's disgust with the natural products of the child's body is taken by the child as disgust with the child himself. Parents who themselves have been taught, and never questioned, that anger is wrong, find any sign of temper in their child quite intolerable. Rather than teaching the child how to cope with frustration and how to use his anger constructively, they demand that the child inhibit a response which for human beings is as natural as breathing. Sometimes the child decides that anger is wrong, not because he is forbidden to express his own anger, but because the anger of the adults around him, amongst themselves, is so violent and uncontrolled that he lives in terror. Children who grow up in households where everybody is angry all the time, or in households where nobody gets angry with anybody ever, grow up believing that anger is wrong. Consequently they cannot manage to live with anger, their own or anyone else's.

So, for whatever the reason, you have grown up believing that it is wrong to get angry. How do you manage to live with this belief?

What a great many people do is to deny that they ever get angry. No matter how difficult or provoking other people may be, no matter how much your desires are thwarted, you never get angry. You are always calm and smiling. Except, of course, when you have those dreadful migraines that usually come on after you have visited your mother, or when your ulcer plays up, usually on the morning of the monthly conference at work, or when you are stuck in a traffic jam and you start trembling so much you can hardly drive once the traffic starts moving. But you do not like to complain about these things at home or at work, because you do not want to upset your family and you would not want anyone at work to suspect that you do not do your job perfectly all the time. You know how quick some people are to criticise, and if there is one thing that really upsets you, it is criticism.

When Chalky Giles came to see me to find out why he could no longer cope with his job of deputy-headmaster of a local school, I told him about the six beliefs one must have if one wants to be depressed. He laughed ruefully and agreed that he had them all. (His image of his prison was being trapped in a dyke, the deep ditch which lines most of the roads and lanes in Lincolnshire.) At the end of our first talk I set him some homework, to write a character sketch of himself as it would be written by a sympathetic friend. This, he protested, was a very difficult task, for while he would have no difficulty in listing his faults and in berating himself, to say anything good about himself and to talk about himself with sympathy was quite impossible. I insisted. So the next week he presented me with the following account.

I have known Chalky for the last ten years when he married Rachel and came to live in Huxby. To me he seemed perfectly happy and quite a witty and effervescent person. He could always be relied on to make some cheerful, humorous comment. He appeared confident when chairman of the tennis club and could organise his committee and was liked and respected by all who met him. However, over the last few years I have seen him in a depressed state when he is like another person, as if he has a split personality. Gone is his humour and ability to joke, to be replaced by moaning about the mess he is in and the gloomy outlook that lies ahead. On the surface of it all I can't see what he has to get depressed about for he appears to have all the material needs for a comfortable life, and has a good wife and a beautiful daughter. He is fit and healthy physically when not depressed and always seems to be bursting with energy. I know now that 'he sails close to the wind' most of the time. If only he would believe in himself and realize that he can do his job well. He tries to please everybody all the time and sets himself too high standards. He is not content with what he has achieved and worries far too much about the future and what people might say or do to upset him. He never really enthuses about anything but tries to appear

happy, contented and on top of things. He never tries to
offend people or show annoyance but always wants to be
the peacemaker.

He is very concerned and helpful when anyone else
needs a helping hand, but he doesn't seem to like to help
himself when he is depressed. He is quite capable at his
work and is well liked and successful with nearly all the
pupils, both past and present, from the village.

He is a fool to himself because he could so easily
destroy his job security and family by letting himself
get so low and depressed. It always seems to happen in
the early part of the year when the weather is bad and
he tends to stagnate when coming home from work.

Chalky had run into difficulties when he had been prom-
oted from class teacher to deputy head. Now if you take as
your rules for living trying 'to please everybody all the time'
and trying never 'to offend people or show annoyance' but
always wanting 'to be the peacemaker', then you must never
take a position of authority and decision making. In a position of authority, whatever it is, you cannot avoid offending
some people and you cannot avoid being criticised. Rather
than offend others and be criticised by others some people
refuse to accept any role which might confer some authority
('I always go along with what my husband wants', 'Do what
you think best, dear. Don't ask me to decide'), but this solution will run counter to the need to justify one's existence by
achieving or by doing everything perfectly. You can then find
yourself in the difficult position of trying to win by letting all
the other contestants come first. (My solution to this problem
has been to realise how much we all enjoy complaining about
and criticising other people, especially people in authority
over us, and so that when people complain about and criticise
me I can rejoice that I am making them happy!)

One of the problems of never wanting to offend people is
that you find yourself doing things which you do not want to
do. Mary said, 'It's just that I get put upon. People will say,
"Oh, Mary will do it." In the bank I keep changing my job to
get the hang of the work, and it's surprising how many things
follow me around from job to job . . . I don't like to say no . . . I

get given a lot of things other people don't want. People give me clothes that's too small for them. I don't want them but I can't say no. I feel awful if they find out I don't wear them.'[54] Being put upon in this way makes you feel resentful, but, if you dare not speak out and protect yourself against the encroachments of others or even complain to someone else, then the resentment destroys whatever enjoyment or satisfaction that might have accrued from doing something for somebody else.

One of the ways through which people manage to deal with the frustrations and irritations of living or working together is through humour. Every group of people that get along well together has its own special jokes and teases, most of which are developed as commentaries on the curious and often irritating characteristics of the individuals in the group. The ability to joke and be joked about, to tease and be teased, is something we usually learn as small children in our families. The person who grows up in a family where there are no jokes, where everything is taken absolutely seriously, usually has great difficulty in being able to tell whether another person is being serious or joking. Since the most outrageous and aggressive things are said in joke and since all jokes carry a kernel of truth, if you cannot tell whether another person is joking or not you will often be hurt, confused and offended by the people around you. Of course, if you can recognise a joke but believe that to joke about a person means that you do not like or admire that person, then all jokes about you will be taken as insults.

Mary had married a very witty and humorous young man who used his humour to cope with all sorts of difficult situations. But Mary took everything he said very seriously and so was often confused about whether or not she had angered him. One day I asked her what she thought would happen if she upset people. She said, 'They won't love – get cross with me. I'm terrified people will get angry with me – Sometimes I worry about things I've said that don't upset people but I think they might do. They don't appear to be upset, but I wonder when I've said something I don't really mean, and I think I've upset them even if they don't appear to be upset, and I'm always worried in case they are – and I get upset so easily. I think everybody's like me. Nobody has to shout at me to make me really upset. I take things the wrong way. I suppose everybody is just like me.'[55]

Everybody is not like Mary. There are some people who cannot possibly deny that they get angry, since their anger is a violent, raging torrent that rises in them and bursts forth, crashing against and damaging everything and everybody that gets in the way. And even when the raging torrent is still, the person lives in fear that it will burst forth again, a force which cannot be subdued or controlled. Some people in the grip of such anger inflict real damage and injury on their possessions, their loved ones, or even a passing stranger. Others use only the weapon of their tongue, but their murderous fantasies show them what they are capable of, given the opportunity, and they see the opportunity all around them. Sometimes the murderous fantasy becomes so powerful and engrossing that the person finds it hard to distinguish thought from action and comes to believe (as young children do) that wishing someone dead actually causes the death of that person. Sometimes the person may not fall into this fallacy but still believe that the guilt should be as great for the thought as the action. (As if thinking about scrubbing the kitchen floor is the same as doing it, or thinking about sending money to Oxfam is as virtuous as actually giving money to Oxfam.)

Jean and I met only a few times since she and her family were moving north to an isolated farm. I suggested that we continued contact by letter, which we did. In one letter she told me about a friend whose wife had multiple sclerosis, and she went on,

> Something enormous like that presents such an emotional challenge. It's the mundane, small darknesses that I seem to have more difficulty with. It seems that every time I forget that life is cruel and foul something happens to remind me fairly forcefully. Last Sunday morning I had one of my infantile outbursts of insecurity concerning my surroundings. We went to church and listened to a sermon on security and inner peace, came home and had another go at one another.

We pretty well decided that we weren't fit company for one another and I asked Jack to remove himself plus all livestock from the house for the afternoon so I could be left to my black thoughts. So he took himself off and shut the two dogs and the kitten outside. About an hour later I went out to get some more wood for the fire and there was blood all over the doorstep and all over the collie's legs. I immediately thought that she had got caught up in barbed wire, but on looking round saw the kitten lying dead on the gravel. Why she had killed him we haven't a clue, but it was a fairly sharp reminder that we are not living in a fairytale cottage in the country. I long to be able to look at the countryside and find total poetic peace. There is so much beauty, and so much cruelty: finding beauty and peace in the horror of it all I think is the problem. I read a review of a new collection of Sylvia Plath's poetry; and was struck by the 'blackness' with which she became so involved. I do find myself in touch with the blackness. Coming to terms with the sheer violence of life causes problems. The realisation that beauty is so impermanent, that each organism is destined to decay. Everything returns to the earth. I find that the question arises as to whether there is much justification in the struggle to survive? I can see that suicide, to the depressed mind, offers comfort as the obvious solution. It fits the pattern. Sometimes I see violence in almost everything I look at. I fear that poker, the axe, the kitchen knife – I fear their potential – as I realise I fear my own potential. Facing my own potential violence I find very hard. We visited the Art Gallery in Aberdeen on Monday and I could marvel at the violent emotions at work in a lot of the works there. The stairs were made of marble and so cruelly cold and hard. As I carried Emily down them I could feel their threat. I know in myself that what it says on your wallposter is true – that the world is not how it seems but how you are (though I can't remember the precise words[56]). I suppose that in my 'perfect' world there is no cruelty or violence. Or harsh words or guilt or whatever. There seem to be different explanations of these feelings.

'That I fear the violent feelings in myself.'

'That I fear loss of joy and am therefore busy destroying it before it leaves me of its own accord.'

'That I simply can't bear to admit that I'm boring and ordinary so I imagine all sorts of horrors to make me a little bit different. I can therefore be irritated by this lack of stillness in my surroundings because I cannot yet find that stillness within myself. The countryside is supposed to be quiet – but I can be irritated by the grass moving and the smoke coming out of our chimney if I'm not careful. I cannot find the source of all this irritation yet. I can't seem to totally let it go either.'

Some people feel very guilty about their bad temper but use their temper as a defence against a cruel world. Carol said, 'I have to hurt or be hurt. The minute I put my defences down nearly always something happens and I get hurt. I might be looking for it – I don't know. I don't know how to cope with being hurt.'[57] Peter's rages were extreme but they gave a subtle reward. As he told me, 'The person who suffers after a row – I know other people do, don't misunderstand me – the person who suffers extremely is myself. I get shattered. I think about it for months afterwards. I suppose in a sense I punish myself for it. I'm not sure that there aren't times when I promote anger in order to lay the stick on myself. In a sense, one sort of feels that for some reason or other it's appropriate that I should punish myself. I deny myself things on occasion. Self-denial. I think it does me good – it's like "If I don't do this God won't punish me".'[58]

There is one great advantage in regarding anger as wicked and evil. If you see anger as simply part of the drive to survive and to create, the drive which has enabled puny humans to overcome enormous obstacles, then as you develop ways of mastering and using your anger (e.g., don't thump the mechanic whose ineptitude has damaged your car; write a stern letter to the Managing Director, demanding recompense and suggesting ways in which the work of the garage could be improved), all you can claim is the gaining of wisdom. But if you regard anger as a vice, evidence of your essential badness, then all your attempts to control your anger you can regard as evidence of virtue. How delightful is the vanity of practising our virtues! In fact, you can devote so much time to being angry and being guilty about being angry, and feeling virtuous because you are feeling guilty about being angry that there is no time left over to do or even *to be* anything else. 'It's exhausting being angry,' said Julie, 'but if you subtract the anger there's nothing there.'[59]

For some people, in the last analysis, not being angry is more dangerous than being angry. Peter deplored his bad temper, but, as we explored the ways in which he might come to curb or dissolve it, he said, 'I can identify with anger. I can say, "Yes, I'm angry about this", and the reason I am angry about it is so and so – I can and I will on occasions say to myself, "Well, it's not something to be angry about", and it may make me angry, but it's an unrealistic action on my part because it isn't important enough. I tell myself that I can translate virtually any situation into this sort of equation and whatever it is, life is short, it's only me getting angry over something I feel and it doesn't justify anger. And then I get frightened because I think, okay, if that's the way it is, then I'm in danger on a long-term basis, and if I spread it over the whole of my outlook, my attitudes, my behaviour, maybe I shall stop feeling. I don't want to stop feeling. I want to feel pleased about things and cross about things because I feel that, without feeling, motivation goes and I don't think I'll become a vegetable, but I'd become so bland that I'm no longer a person, and I know that's not a good argument but it's where I come to war with myself about feelings. I would like to be serene and wise and able to take everything in my stride and that would be a lovely ego thing, I tell myself, I think with my head. But I don't feel that with my gut. My gut says that I've got to care because if I don't care about this or I don't care about that, then I cease being *me*.'[60]

And it is better to be *me*, even if me is a wicked me, than not to be me at all.

I am often asked if being with depressed people makes me depressed. I always answer no, but in truth there is one thing about being with a depressed person which I always find very worrying and wearying. This problem does not arise with my clients since when we talk together it is in a time and place which have been set aside, free from interruptions and harassments, and where I can relax and give my full attention to the other person. Where the problem does arise is when I am in the company of the members of a self-help depressives group. This might be at a group meeting which I attend after work or after travelling some long distance, or in the psychology department which I administer or in the shopping precinct in my lunch hour. On these occasions I am not always full of sweetness and light. Sometimes I feel tired, distracted, harassed, ill or crabby – sometimes all five together, and consequently not on my best behaviour. A trivial matter, like the windscreen wipers on my car not working when I am driving my depressive friend home, can irritate me, but woe betide me if I let any of this irritation show, for my friend will immediately assume that I think it is all her fault, that it *is* all her fault, that I do not like her, I have never liked her, I shall never like her. What follows is an ominous silence (she will not speak to me because she knows I do not like her, but when I finally realise that I am not being spoken to, I think I must have done something to offend her, but do not know what), or else protracted apologies with each of us trying to take the blame for the incident. To avoid all this I have to remember never to show any anger or irritation when in the company of my depressive friends. Thus I have to dissemble, something I dislike doing, first because I am too lazy a person to be an effective liar, and, second, if I am found out it will only reinforce my friend's belief that other people are not to be trusted. I think to myself, 'If only she would realise that just because a person gets angry in your presence, or even gets angry with you, it doesn't mean that that person does not like you.' Then I realise that this is simply my way of seeing things. It is not hers. She knows quite well that if someone gets angry with her that person does not like her and will not forgive her for what she has done. Why?

Because this is the sixth rule that builds those prison walls so firm and high. You know that when someone gets angry with you that person dislikes you and will never forgive you. You know this is so, because, when someone hurts and angers you, you never forgive.

6 I must never forgive anyone, least of all myself

When we were children we each spent a lot of time working out what we hoped and believed would be the story of our life. We dreamed of growing up to be like the adults we admired and we feared turning into the kind of people we despised. Sometimes we despaired of being able to live up to certain standards (I knew I could never attain the immaculate beauty of the Hollywood heroines of the 1940s, and what a relief it was when I gave up trying to) and sometimes we became angry and frightened as we found ourselves being pushed by our families and teachers into something which did not fit our dream (I dreamed of escaping school and family to lead an exciting life of travel and writing. My heroine was Dorothy Thompson, an American journalist whose wartime travels were recorded in the newspapers I read. But I was told, 'Girls don't do things like that. It would be different if you were a boy. You should become a teacher. That's a good, safe job.') The fate of our childhood dreams always bears out what George Bernard Shaw said, that there are only two tragedies in life. One is not getting what you want, and the other is getting it. If our childhood dream does not eventuate, we mourn it; and if it does eventuate, we discover that it does not bring the complete happiness that we expected. Prince Charmings can make dreadful husbands, and what do you do after you become rich and famous? Life is always different from our dreams.

However, that does not stop us trying to make life conform to our dreams, especially when our dreams are our only defence against a harsh and cruel world. When we were little and made up the story of what we wanted our life to be only part of that story followed from our belief that life was wonderful and that good things were in store for us. Part of our story sprang from our joy, but only a part. The other part, and for some of us, the major part, sprang from our fear, our experience of being cruelly and unfairly treated. When we were small children we were weak, fully in the power of other people, and, when these people used their power to punish, shame and ridicule us, we did what all impotent human beings do when they are threatened with complete destruction and annihilation by their enemies. We vow revenge. We vow never to forgive.

Sometimes the dream we create is based on the theme of 'I'll show them'. We dream of becoming so brilliant and famous that our family and teachers will be able to do nothing but stand amazed and abashed, overawed by the magnificent figure that we have become. Some people do achieve great success in the pursuit of this dream, but rarely do they find that the returning hero gets the welcome home of which he dreamed. Teachers have the habit of dying or forgetting who you were, and relatives are either singularly unimpressed with anything you do or else they appropriate to themselves all the credit. Thus success can seem very flat, stale and unprofitable. If, on the other hand, you have vowed to heap scorn on your enemies by becoming a world-famous figure and you fail to do this, then you find it very difficult to accept what most of us who dream of fame have to accept, that world fame, or universal, total acclaim is a fate reserved for very few people. You can make yourself very miserable by rejecting all your successes on the grounds that they are not good enough. They do not confound your enemies.[61]

Sometimes the dream we create is based on the theme 'They'll be sorry'. Tom Sawyer enjoyed the perfect working out of this dream when he and his friends hid in the church to listen to their own funeral service. How lovely it would be to hear our relatives saying how sorry they are that they hurt us and treated us unjustly, and what good and wonderful people we were! The trouble with relatives is that they never seem to do this, and some of the relatives I have met in the course of my work could not do this, even to save their own lives. But that will not stop you trying. There are many depressed people who are prepared to starve themselves in the hope that their family will kneel round their deathbed and beg forgiveness. There are others who are prepared to let the locked doors of the lunatic asylum clang behind them, just so they can say to their grieving, repentant relatives, 'See what you made me do!' However, relatives who drive you to these extremes are usually the sort of people who never beg forgiveness nor ever admit any responsibility for your distress. Your dream fails, and the reality is that you have entered upon the career of a psychiatric patient, a career which, once begun, is difficult to leave.

Fortunately not all the people who get depressed carry revenge to such extremes. Instead, behind the facade of pleasantness, compliance, graciously agreeing with everybody, never (or rarely) saying anything nasty about anyone, you remember all the injuries done to you and you still feel angry and unforgiving. Some of you find it impossible to voice these feelings because you dare not criticise the people on whom you depend. Some of my clients have given me the impression that they still more or less have the childhood belief that Mother knows everything you think and do. Other clients I have found feel obliged to report to their mothers and spouses what is discussed in the therapy session. One woman I knew went straight from my office to her mother's home, while another woman knew that the minute she arrived home her mother would phone her from the other side of England to check on what I had said and especially to see if I was blaming her for her daughter's predicament. Another woman found it very hard to talk to me about the things her husband did which upset her (not very terrible things really – just the acts of a typical loving, obtuse, unthinking man) because he would question her about our therapy session. I suggested to her that she simply say that she had forgotten. This was not a complete lie, since she was in that stage of depression where it is very difficult to think straight. (A bad memory is a wonderful alibi and should never be relinquished.) The problem about not being able to talk about your resentments is that you are then prevented from going through the stages necessary to achieve forgiveness and reconciliation. By giving expression to our anger in some direct and truthful form (that is, saying how you feel instead of saying nothing and being upset), by talking the matter over with a sympathetic friend, by thinking about our feelings and our relationships freely, not inhibited by rules of 'I mustn't criticise my mother/father/husband/wife', we come to terms with the painful experiences we have suffered. We master them, learn from them and, by forgiving and so forgetting, we cease to be oppressed by events in our past and are better able to cope with events in our present.

But to do all this we have to believe that it is right to forgive. Not everyone sees forgiveness as a virtue.

Some people who get depressed do not always present themselves as pleasant and compliant, not speaking evil of anyone. They may do this outside the home, but inside the home, whenever anyone offends they sulk – not quietly and unobtrusively but in as dominant and noticeable manner as possible. (Actually, there is no point in sulking if nobody takes any notice.) Some of you have perfected the art of Not Speaking. This is where you go about your usual domestic chores but without saying one word to anybody, no matter what anybody says to you. (Heavy sighs which mean 'Here I am yet again sacrificing myself to an ungrateful family' are allowed, as are cries of distress in the kitchen, following some small accident, while the family are settled watching television in the living room. The cries of distress are particularly effective if the accident has been caused by the laziness or negligence of your family.) Some of you prefer Retiring to Your Bedroom in a High Dudgeon. It is necessary to have a well trained family for this. You have to be sure that they will hover around your door, anxious to cater to your every whim. It is no good if they laugh at you, or scamper off to attend to their own affairs and leave you to starve or to perish for want of a cup of tea. The games of Not Speaking and Retiring to Your Bedroom in a High Dudgeon can give a great deal of satisfaction (if revenge was not sweet we would not bother with it), but they do have the problem of how do you start speaking again or leave your bedroom without feeling foolish. If you have succeeded in getting your family to apologise to you in the way you feel is appropriate then you can graciously agree to overlook their errors and to rejoin family life, but so often families not only fail to understand how they have offended you but they also fail to understand how they should mend their ways. It is all very difficult.

But there are even greater difficulties when you decide never to forgive. Jesus summed up this problem when he said,

> Judge not, that ye be not judged. For with what
> judgment ye judge, ye shall be judged: and with what
> measure ye mete, it shall be measured to you again.[62]

That is, the rules or judgments that we apply to other people we expect other people will apply to us. So, if you believe that it is wrong to forgive, you must expect that other people will not forgive you when you harm or upset them in any way. This is one of the reasons why you find other people so frightening. Even when they are nice to you, you cannot be sure that they are not harbouring grudges against you, and when you feel certain you have offended someone you are often too scared to meet that person again. You try to avoid all the places where you might encounter the people you might have offended and so the number of places where you dare to go become smaller and smaller. It never occurs to you that that person might have dismissed the offence entirely or, if forgiveness was required, to have forgiven you. You expect to be judged as you have judged.

This, of course, is the rule you apply to yourself. The one person you must never forgive is yourself. You never let any of your mistakes go by saying to yourself, 'That was bad luck', or 'No point in worrying over it' and forgetting what you did. You go on and on at yourself, never forgiving yourself, no matter how many punishments you inflict on yourself. In your eyes your crime is that you exist, and you will never forgive yourself for that.

If you believe in a God who judges us then you know that God will not forgive you. Jesus had a great deal to say about forgiveness. He told Peter that he should forgive his brother not seven times, but 'seventy times seven'.[63] He preached,

But I say unto you, Love your enemies, bless them that curse you, do good to them that hate you, and pray for them which despitefully use you, and persecute you.[64]

He told the parable of the servant who was forgiven by his master for not repaying a debt of ten thousand talents but who would not forgive another servant a debt of a hundred pence.[65] On learning of this the master withdrew his forgiveness. When Jesus taught the prayer

And forgive us our debts as we forgive our debtors

He explained,

For if you forgive men their trespasses, your heavenly

> Father will also forgive you. But if you forgive not men
> their trespasses, neither will your Father forgive your
> trespasses.[66]

So, if you cannot forgive yourself or other people you know
that you are damned.

Jesus had a lot to say about forgiveness but it is one
aspect of His teaching which has been largely ignored by
most of His followers. Had it been accepted and acted upon
world history would be quite different – no pogroms, no
religious persecutions between different Christian sects, no
wars or acts of vengeance. Northern Ireland would be a haven
of sweetness and light, and nuclear weapons would never
have needed to be invented. All too fantastical. Much better
to justify our aggression by remembering Jesus saying, 'I
come not to send peace but a sword.'[67]

While Jesus was quite clear that we should forgive one
another and so obtain God's forgiveness, He did make some
rather obscure remarks about the unforgivable sin of speaking against the Holy Ghost.[68] Just what this sin is and why it
is unforgivable has caused much debate, and many simple
believers have worried terribly that they have unwittingly
committed it and so are irretrievably damned. The Catholic
Church lists the sins against the Holy Ghost as presumption,
despair, resisting the known truth, envy of another's
spiritual good, obstinacy in sin and final impenitence. These
categories could be narrowly interpreted to fit every crime
and peccadillo, but they can also be interpreted to encompass
what Simon Phipps, the Anglican Bishop of Lincoln,
explained to me was the interpretation he gave to the unforgivable sin against the Holy Ghost. He said,

> I suppose it would mean absolutely basically turning
> your back consciously, deliberately on what you saw as
> what God stood for. There are lots of sins, lots of things
> which you might do which might be called sins,
> categories of ways in which we do damaging things, but
> this sin against the Holy Ghost means not so much that
> you *do* something as you actually decide to *be*
> something which is totally over and against what you
> see God to be. I think the Holy Ghost, the Holy Spirit, is

an attempt to put a name to the actual impinging upon
our experience of God.[69]

What Simon was saying and what religious thinkers of
all faiths have said in their own particular ways is that if,
when we glimpse some profound and awesome aspect of our
existence as an individual and as part of the cosmos, an
aspect which we know without the necessity of proof is true,
and then we deny that truth, we do ourselves great damage.
Such a discovery was not confined to religious thinkers.
Freud rejected the religious account of how we damage ourselves by rejecting what we know is true, but devoted his life's
work to showing how such denials created the splitting of the
psyche which is the essence of neurosis. Psychoanalysis is
concerned with healing the divided psyche and rendering it
whole. Sartre considered the problem from the existentialist
point of view and spoke of 'bad faith' when we pretend we are
something we are not. The trouble with pretending is that if
you start it early enough in life you end up forgetting who you
were before you started to pretend, and so you fear that if you
stop pretending you will disappear. The 'holistic' therapies
which have developed over the past forty years aim at finding
ways of discovering who you are and of making yourself
whole. If, as a small child, you decided to see yourself as bad
so as to preserve the adults you depended on as totally good
(which they were not, and you knew they were not, since they
were fallible human beings and not angels) and to put from
your consciousness the realisation which came to you when
you were under threat that we are part of a formless, ever-
changing, moving, shapeless nothingness and everything-
ness, and if in adult life you have not reviewed all this by
accepting the awesome uncertainty of which you are a part
and by reapportioning responsibility and then generally forgiving and forgetting all round, you have, in fact, decided to
be something which goes against what you know, and deny,
to be the truth, and so you have wilfully done great damage to
yourself, something which we all know is unforgivable, if not
in God's eyes, then in our own. We are each responsible for
ourselves and we should cherish ourselves.

The various religions of the world all have ceremonies of

healing, cleansing, forgiveness and rebirth. The various psychotherapies use non-religious rituals and words, but they, like the religions, help the person become whole again by creating a sense of being forgiven, if not by God, then by one's own conscience. (Some people would argue that the words 'God' and 'conscience' refer to the same thing, that being at peace with yourself means being at peace with God, and vice versa. But this is not important. What is important is for you to know the right words *for you* for your experience.)

So these are the reasons for forgiving. You have lots of reasons why you should not. It can be that you just hate saying sorry and admitting that you have made a mistake. (Rather than risking making a mistake you prefer to avoid all decisions.) Forgiving means letting go of the hurt as well as the cause of the hurt, and, like Carol, you may not be prepared to do this. As she said, 'I think I can forgive but I don't think I could forget. This is my trouble. I never forget. With us when the air gets heated between us we tend to bring all these things back. I've got to have something to fire at Bob when he starts on me. I'm grateful that Bob has put up with me. But gratitude can only go so far. You get to the point where you're just taken for granted. I've realised after thirteen years of marriage I was never a person that could say I was sorry. That was a lot of our trouble. I keep things inside and build up a resentment.'[70]

Of course, if someone hurts you and you forgive that person you just put yourself in a position to be hurt again. When I asked Joan what she did when a shop assistant got angry with her she said, 'I should be hurt and I wouldn't go into that shop again . . . If I know somebody who's nice and then they're angry, I don't want to know them any more.'[71]

There is another danger which Kay described. She and her husband often argued, and when he said and did wounding things she 'would just stop speaking. Because I detested him at the time. It would go on for a day or two and after that I would wish I were speaking. He would say, "You silly thing. Why aren't you speaking? You know you've got to speak in the end." I enjoyed it. But I didn't enjoy it for long. I've gone on for over a week, but after two days I wished we were speaking. It's a wanting to go back to normal, really. After a couple of days I wouldn't feel the same and I wouldn't eat either . . . Since I have been like this he has said, "If only you knew how much you have hurt me." But he'd never shown me. If only he had shown me that I had hurt him in a way I should have been pleased to think that in some way I had hurt him, but I think we would have had a better relationship. But I just wanted to see that I had hurt him. I wanted him to feel like I did. Sometimes I would break down and cry when he had upset me, but I didn't want him to go that far. I just wanted to know that I had hurt him. But he never did . . . Sometimes I wanted to say I was sorry but I just couldn't.'

Kay described how they had quarrelled and to hurt him she had refused to go to his firm's dinner dance, a function she very much wanted to attend.

'I just lay on the settee and I was miserable with myself. I wanted to go, but I couldn't tell him.'

'What did you want him to do when you said you weren't going?'

'I was laid on the settee and I wanted him to come and say, "Please come, please come, darling". And he didn't you see, and it shook me. That was three years ago, and, looking back, that, I think, was the start of this depression. I should have said nothing and should have gone with him. We should have been all right then.'

I asked her, 'What do you think would have happened to you if you had never stood up to Jack?'

'Well, I might have done better. It might have made him feel small. Or I might have just become a servant to him.'[72]

If you experience yourself as weak, or so bad a person that you have no right to stand up for yourself then you do see yourself as being in danger of being wiped out by those people who hurt you and whom you see as much stronger than yourself. So you build a fence around the emptiness, the void you feel inside, by vowing never to forgive. Indeed, you can come to define yourself almost totally in terms of your vows never to forgive but to seek revenge. Right now there are little children in Ireland and in the Middle East who are being told by their elders that the very reason for their existence is to avenge the crimes committed by their enemies. Unfortunately, many of the children will believe this, and, like so many of their elders, will resist the resolution of the conflict between Protestants and Catholics, Arabs and Jews, because such a resolution would take away their purpose in living, the very means by which they define themselves.

Sometimes we call not forgiving 'intolerance' or 'righteous anger' and define it as a virtue because we are intolerant of the evils we see in the world. Tony scorned 'tolerance' because he saw tolerant attitudes as no more than a cover for cant and hypocrisy. His ferocious intolerance caused him and the people around him a great deal of pain. The pain did not end until he 'had what he described as a profound and revelatory experience when he discovered that he could contrast his intolerance not just with pusillanimous tolerance but with the assured detachment which is the essence of Zen Buddhism.'[73]

That forgiveness is a strength and not a weakness is part of the Buddha's teaching in the terms that *dukkha*, suffering, is the result of our trying to impose our desires on the world and to insist that what happened in the past is still with us. To desire revenge is to suffer. If you do not wish to suffer, give up the desire for revenge. We may try to hang on to the past by not forgiving. We can try to keep our dead alive and with us by not forgiving, with reproaches to ourselves ('I should have looked after my mother better'), or to the dead ('Why didn't you say you loved me?') but all we achieve out of trying to make reality repeatable is *dukkha*, suffering.[74]

And you have indeed made one part of your reality repeatable. You try to protect other people by blaming yourself, you feel guilty about your shortcomings and misdemeanours and fear that you will be punished, you get more frightened, and then angry with the people who make you feel guilty and frightened, then you feel guilty about being angry with the people you should protect, so you blame yourself and feel more guilty, more frightened, more angry and so on forever and ever. There seems to be no way out. There *is* no way out, since you forbid yourself the key that will unlock the door. You will know no peace until you discover how to forgive yourself, to forgive other people and to let others forgive you. Only then will you be free of the past, be able to live in the present and to look to the future with hope. But how can you do that when you believe that it is wrong to forgive?

These six opinions, held as Real, Absolute and Immutable Truths can be expressed, interpreted and acted upon in many different ways, and each person who gets depressed has his or her own individual way of doing this. Of course, opinions are not just ideas in our heads. They are feelings, emotions and actions. To understand how these six opinions can combine together to form the peculiar sense of isolation which is the essence of being depressed we need to look at these opinions in terms of one basic essential feeling, a feeling that is so intrinsic to our existence that we do not have a single word for it but a number of words which have all sorts of meanings and connotations. Some of the words which refer to this feeling are —

> Spirit, soul, heart, psyche, quintessence, vital principle, energy, vigour, vim, force, intensity, potency, dynamic energy, verve, fire, drive, vivacity, liveliness, outgoing, radiance, vitality, life force, élan vital, vital spark, joie de vivre, passion.

Now when we think to ourselves, 'What a lovely day it is. I'm really looking forward to what I'm going to do today. Life's turning out really well. What nice friends and colleagues I have. How I love my family! I did that really well. I do enjoy meeting people. We had a good laugh together over old times', and such like, that feeling of life within us goes out towards everybody and everything. 'We experience a sense of the outgoing of the spirit, a sense of the force of life, a sense of freedom and movement which may range from mild placidity through vigour and vitality to immense and marvellous joy, relish and delight. Such an experience is accompanied by some degree of confidence, creativity, optimism, courage, and benevolence.'[75]

But when we think to ourselves, 'What a horrible day it is. I dread what the day will bring. Life is terrible. I haven't a friend in the world. My family are a great disappointment to me. I make a mess of everything. I'm terrified of other people.

I can never forget the dreadful things that have happened to me', and such like, that feeling of life within us does not go out to anybody or anything, but rather it shrivels within us. Then we feel that 'we merely exist, that we are diminished, constricted, isolated, inhibited, helpless, despondent, anguished, barren, desolate, fearful, pessimistic and bitter.'[76] We are enclosed and isolated within ourselves, and we learn the truth that torturers down the ages have always known. Many people can manage to survive the greatest pain, injury and privation, but the one torture that affects even the strongest and bravest of us is solitary confinement. We need, just as we need air, food and water, to be part of the woven pattern that is human life. If we are isolated from it, if we isolate ourselves from it, then we suffer the torture of the damned, and the longer we stay in solitary confinement, the greater the torture becomes.

So it is that if we hold these six opinions and make them the basis of our every action and decision then we impose on ourselves a sentence of solitary confinement.

Now some people go through life believing that they are not so much evil as simply not good enough. They struggle hard to make up their deficiencies, but since they see themselves as unacceptable to other people, other people make them nervous. They find anger hard to deal with, but they value forgiveness so they do not brood too much on their past. They have some hope for the future since they have based their life on a philosophy which allows some optimism. Such people would not call themselves depressed but they may, at times, be aware of a sense of being burdened in a world of muted colours. A stone lies on their heart. This might be the pattern for their entire life, or, if they are lucky, great happiness, a success which they are able to accept, removes the stone forever and they feel light and free in a colourful world. But if disaster comes upon disaster, or if one day they realise that they are no longer young, that the opportunities for the life they dreamed of are lost forever, if the love they need has vanished, then they despair and mourn and do not forgive. The burden on their heart becomes the prison walls of depression. However, for many such people their depression is no more than a walk through a dark valley while they come to

terms with their life. Because they have always allowed the
possibility of forgiveness they have the capacity to accept
change. Because they have always allowed the possibility of
love they do not turn totally against themselves but give
themselves a measure of kindness and allow others to be kind
to them too. Love and forgiveness (aided perhaps by the
cheering effect of anti-depressant drugs) leads them out of
the dark valley.

Susan described her experience of depression as being in
rough and dangerous waters, and trying to gain a foothold on
a rocky incline. The first time she was depressed she could, in
her image, see figures on the top of the incline, reaching their
hands down to help her. She was able to find the strength
within her to scramble to safety. In the words of her psychiatrist, she responded to anti-depressant drugs. But in each
succeeding period of depression the water got deeper and
rougher, the helping figures fewer and further away, and the
less strength she had to secure a firm footing. Even when she
felt herself to be on dry land she was not secure. She was only
one step away from a precipice. On her next admission to
hospital she 'did not respond to medication or ECT'. She saw
no figures offering to help her and she was not able to help
herself. And neither should there be any help for her. She
believed in a forgiving God but a just God. She was wicked
and lazy, and had not helped her family in the way that she
should. So she was being justly punished for her wickedness.
Her depression was her punishment and it was right that she
should accept her punishment and not try to escape it.

So, if you have not taken love and forgiveness into the
dark valley with you, you will not discover the path out of the
valley. Those people who get depressed and stay depressed, or
who go from one period of depression to another, with the
time between each period filled with the sense of the depression lurking in the background are those people who see as
Immutable Truths that they are essentially evil and must
work hard to be good, that other people are dangerous and
must be feared, that the only religious and philosophical
ideas which reveal the Truth are those which lead to fear and
despair, that the past is unreconcilable and the future hopeless, that anger is to be feared and that it is wrong to forgive.

If you are one of these people then you know how for some of your life, before you became depressed, you were strong and active enough to work hard at being good. You had found some limited ways of coping with other people and there were one or two people in your life you could risk loving and trusting. You put from you all awareness of death and when you thought of the disasters that would certainly befall you, you thought, 'Not yet.' You avoided anger as much as you could, and while you cherished your injuries like a miser cherishes his gold, you did not spend too much time counting these for you still had some hope for the future. But then something happened. Perhaps it was the last of a line of disasters which destroyed your hopes, perhaps it was the death or defection of a loved one, or perhaps it was the gradual realisation that you cannot keep up the pretence of being good any longer. The edifice which you have built so carefully crumbles. The bottomless abyss yawns beneath your feet. The black cloud descends, the door clangs shut. You are in the prison of depression.

Chapter 4

WHY NOT LEAVE THE PRISON?

The short answer to this question is 'I'd rather be good than happy.'

However, preferring to be good rather than happy is not something that only people who get depressed do. To some extent we all do. A few weeks ago I said this in a lecture on depression to a group of psychology students and teachers. They all looked surprised since, like most psychologists, they regarded themselves as hedonists, preferring pleasure to pain. To explain I simply said, 'It's Saturday afternoon.' They all laughed and acknowledged I was right. There we were, crammed into a dreary lecture room, applying ourselves to serious matters instead of taking part in all the delightful things that we could do on a Saturday afternoon. We certainly were preferring to be good rather than happy.

There were some people in that room who knew how serious a point I was making. Others, the ones devoted to joyous and successful living, would have argued that they followed the principle of enlightened self-interest, that they were prepared to endure some discomfort in order to gain future pleasure. But those who knew what it was to be depressed knew that they were involved in a continuous battle to be good, and in this the sacrifice of a Saturday afternoon was a small matter.

I first realised the significance of wanting to be good rather than happy back in 1968 when I was learning about a form of psychological testing called the repertory grid and when I was spending much time talking to patients who were quite severely depressed. One of these patients was a woman,

Mrs A, who had had all the usual treatments of drugs and ECT, all without any sign of permanent improvement. I asked her to do a grid where, first of all, she drew up a list of twenty people, including herself, who were in some way important to her. Next she drew up a list of the terms she used in assessing these people. Then she grouped the people she had listed according to each of her assessments. This gave a grid of numbers which was then analysed on a computer to see how her ideas or opinions clustered together. What this showed was that she divided the people in her world into good and bad. Her good people were 'not critical of other people, are affectionate, easy-going, soft, generous, are used by other people but do not complain. The bad people are mean, hard and cruel, aggressive, nasty and hurtful, have no feelings, are fault-finding and self-opinionated and use other people.'[1] Mrs A put herself among the good people. A sensible way of judging people, you might say – except for one thing. All the good people, she said, were poorly; all the bad people were well. 'Poorly' in Yorkshire covers every physical and mental state where one is not well. It certainly covers being depressed. In Mrs A's way of viewing her world, every time the doctors tried to move her from being 'poorly' to being 'well' they were trying to move her from being a good person to being a bad person. No wonder all their treatments failed!

None of us want to be changed from being a good person to being a bad person, and most people accept a degree of unhappiness so as to meet what they see as their responsibilities. Looking after husband, children and a house, or doing a dull job, day after day, year after year, in order to support a family certainly does involve a degree of unhappiness in order to be good. But this is different from seeing your unhappiness – depression – as evidence that you are good, or, at least, that you are trying to be good.

'Oh, no,' you cry, 'I don't want to be unhappy. I don't want to be depressed. I'm not like your Mrs A. I'm not making myself into a good person by being depressed.'

Are you sure?

In the effort to be good we all do peculiar things. (Why have I woken up early to be writing this? Why aren't I relaxing over a novel or having another hour's snooze?) When we start in life believing that we are not good enough we have to do all sorts of things to improve ourselves. The more bad and unacceptable you see yourself as being the more drastic the things you must do to be good. Being depressed is one of these drastic things.

There are many ways in which a person can work out the equation

Being depressed = being good.

If you regard yourself as essentially bad, then you can think that you do not deserve to be happy. Being depressed is what you deserve to be. Not just not deserving happiness, you can see depression as your punishment for not being good enough. You should have tried harder, done better. At the one and the same time you can see your depression as the punishment for your badness and the evidence of your bad-ness, because no matter how much you strive to overcome your depression you fail. You try to pull yourself together, to make an effort, to do the things your doctor and your family tell you you should do. But all this effort does not work. You are still depressed. So you must accept your depression as punishment (good people always accept their just punish-ments – good little children hold out their hands to be smacked and do not run away or hit Mummy back, and good adults always pay their fines) and you must work harder to overcome your depression (good people always try again and do not give up).

It is no wonder that you get confused, trying to do these two opposing things at the same time.

Probably all of us, when we were little, were told by some adult that if we were good we would be looked after but if we were bad we would be abandoned. A common sight in any shopping centre is of a child dawdling behind his mother who, exasperated, turns to him and yells, 'If you don't hurry up I'm going to leave you behind.' The child who knows she does not mean it continues to dawdle, but the child who fears she might obeys and hurries to his mother. Sometimes, when a child loses his mother in the crowd and in fear begins to cry, the mother, returning, instead of comforting him, says, 'You're a naughty boy. If you did as you're told, this wouldn't have happened.' Some children in these situations are wise enough to know that his mother would never leave him and that it was her fault that he lost sight of her (that is, on occasions his mother lies and is careless) but the child who would not dare think such dreadful things about his perfect mother grows up believing that if you are good, really good, there will always be someone there to take care of you. You might devote your life to trying to get your parents to care for you totally, or, if it is borne in upon you that parents cannot protect their adult child totally and make your life smooth and secure, you expect *them*, the government or society or the medical profession or God to protect you and make your life smooth and secure. You want to live in a world organised by immutable laws derived from an infallible source. (A colleague told me recently how an adolescent client was in difficulties over her Social Security benefits but she assured my colleague that she would be all right because, she said, 'They aren't allowed to let you starve.' Really?) However, when you do discover that *they* are incompetent at protecting you, you get very angry. How dare the government be so stupid! How can the medical profession be so ignorant when they ought to know how to cure every illness! How dare God go back on His promises!

What promises? The promise that if you are good you will be safe. Don't ask where the government, society, the medical profession, or even God made this explicit promise. You know that this is the way the world *ought* to be. The idea that we have to be responsible for ourselves and that the ways of the world are neither good nor just is too terrifying for you to contemplate. You cannot tolerate such uncertainty. You do not trust yourself, so how can you take responsibility for yourself? You would rather stick to the belief that if you are good someone, somewhere, somehow will look after you.[2]

But right now it seems that you are not being looked after. Perhaps it is not because of the incompetence of the powers that be. Perhaps it is because you are not good enough. You must try harder.

If being good means being depressed, then you cannot afford to leave your prison.

Chapter 5

WHY I WON'T LEAVE THE PRISON

1 I have high standards

We all want to be good, and most of us are prepared to put up with some unhappiness in order to be good. But there are many different ways of defining 'good', in setting goals and standards for ourselves and in dealing with ourselves when we fail to reach these standards. People who do not get depressed see themselves, although with some faults, as essentially good. Since they do not have to battle to overcome great wickedness they regard themselves as good if they are 'good enough', that is, they do not expect perfection but just a reasonable attempt to do as well as can be managed in the circumstances, and when they fail to achieve this modest goal they chide themselves in the mildest of terms and feel reasonably sure that next time they will do better. But you who get depressed despise such wishy-washy mediocrity. Since you regard yourself as essentially bad with insufficient virtues to redeem yourself you expect – nay, demand – perfection, and when you fail to reach it (as you must, since you regard yourself as inherently flawed) you berate and chastise yourself harshly as you believe you deserve. Even as you suffer you despise those who lack your high standards. You have before you the image of perfection. You know what Melvyn Bragg meant when he wrote, 'Most of us have known a time – however long ago, when the notion of perfection seemed worth the sacrifice of everything else.'[1] But you still feel that perfection is worth the sacrifice of everything else – or at least your happiness – while Melvyn Bragg was saying that this is a youthful belief that most of us outgrow. Most of us come to realise that the world is imperfect and to accept these imperfections as best we can. But not you. You will not forgive the world for not living up to your expectations, for not being perfect the way you want it to be.

Because you are frightened of other people and because you are not sure just how to make the world perfect (that is, to get everyone to do what you want, and to abolish death, old age, suffering and natural disasters like earthquakes and blizzards) you concentrate on making your family perfect. You can reject the world for failing to live up to your standards but unfortunately the world is unimpressed with your rejection. You can, though, make your family very aware that you will reject them if they do not live up to your standards. You can make your love conditional on their good behaviour, and if they accept this, you have them in your power. So you demand that they be perfect parents and children and spouses, that they keep their bedroom perfectly tidy, be in at your stated hour, get their hair cut a decent length, cook food as it should be cooked, never have friends of whom you do not approve, keep to your routine and so on. They do try – at least, sometimes – but they fail, because children cannot help but be their age, and parents get tired of adolescent demands, and wives get tired of mothering their husbands, and husbands get confused by conflicting demands. Sometimes you feel confused yourself about the demands you hear yourself making. You find yourself wanting to do something in an easy fashion, or to stop, or to rest, or not to be so demanding of others, but there is a voice within you that drives you on. You obey because if you do not you will be overwhelmed by guilt. Jackie described to me how she and her husband Ron decided that on Saturday mornings she would lie in while he minded the children, but every Saturday morning she would get out of bed soon after him and follow him around, telling him where he was not doing things properly. 'I can't stay in bed,' said Jackie, 'when I was a child it was a rule that the girls had to get up and do the housework. I feel guilty if I stay in bed. I know Ron knows how to look after the children but I can't let things be.'

Not letting things be, constantly carping over faults, impatiently wanting things to be done, being resentful and unforgiving when your standards are not maintained, all adds up to what Jung called 'the well-known bad moods and irritability of the over-virtuous'.[2] Since your family soon come to fear your bad moods, irritability and constant criticism, it is no wonder that you sometimes feel that they do not love you.

As much as you rail at your family, you criticise yourself even more. It is as if you are two people, your wicked self and a harsh, punitive critic whose standards can never be met.

What is this self inside us, this silent observer,
Severe and speechless critic, who can terrorise us
And urge us on to futile activity,
And in the end, judge us still more severely
For the errors into which his own reproaches drove us.[3]

Carol's mother had taught her that 'The easy way is never the best way'[4] and now the critic in her head was scornful if she looked for ways of making her housework easier. Chalky said, 'If I don't feel tired at the end of the day I don't feel I've worked hard enough.' Who sets these crazy standards? Is a floor more virtuously clean because it was scrubbed by hand not by a machine? Does a child's knowledge increase proportionately to his teacher's increasing exhaustion? But there is no arguing with these kinds of rules. I might joke about them and you might smile in sheepish acceptance of my jokes, but, if underneath you still hope that there is a book of immutable laws from an infallible source, and that this source or power will protect you if you keep these laws, then there is nothing I can say or do that will help you take life easier. Your mother or father might be many years dead, but if you still scurry to obey the parental voice when it speaks in your head, giving orders applicable in another time and place but not here and now, and if you still hope that your obedience will secure your parents' protection and love, then you have sentenced yourself to a lifetime's hard labour, and much good it will do you. Sometimes the parents you obey are not your earthly parents but the ideal parents in your head. When Tracy was nine years old her mother left the family. Tracy was very upset by her mother's desertion, even though she had not been, in Tracy's eyes, much of a mother. 'I'd go into her bedroom when Dad was at work,' Tracy told me, 'and she'd be in bed and I'd see a man's head coming up from under the covers. And I never had any clean knickers.' Tracy vowed that she should never forgive her mother, and she constructed a picture of an ideal mother, someone who never deserted her family, who looked after her children and her home perfectly. By the time she was nineteen Tracy had a house, a husband and a baby. She rarely left the house because she had to keep it perfectly clean all the time; she had to keep the baby clean, dry, neat and tidy in good clothes and healthy and properly fed. Her husband would have to ask permission before he touched anything in the kitchen, and usually he complied, but sometimes he would grow so exasperated with her he would hit her. 'I ask for it,' she told me, 'I say dreadful things to him. I get so panicky. I get this tight feeling in my chest and I think I'm going to explode. I can't stand going to my friend's house – she lets it get so mucky. I don't think she's a fit mother. I'm worrying now what my house is like while I'm here talking to you. I don't want people to think that I'm like my mother.'

However, no matter how much we try to be good and to obey our parents, or our ideal parents, and our conscience, no amount of good behaviour will make our life secure and save us from our death. We are all fallible mortals. We all die. But for you death is the Great Imperfection.

You come to believe that you can attain perfect security if you can have complete control over yourself and your relationships with other people. You set high standards in your relationships. You want your loved ones to be completely truthful and open with you and always loyal and trustworthy. You want to be sure that the love and care you bestow on them is not wasted but responded to in what you consider the proper manner. (i.e., 'If you really loved me you wouldn't upset me by coming home late/tramping mud across my clean floor/expect me to go visiting with you, etc., etc..') You expect your loved ones to be perfectly self-controlled, but this is no more than what you expect of yourself. You set yourself the standard of perfect, composed self-control, and when rage or misery or even joy pours through some small chink in your armour you berate yourself and fear that you are going to pieces, going out of your mind. Even when the self-control appears, at least outwardly, to be perfect, inside you are angry and frightened, since, as Alan Watts said, 'Any system approaching perfect self-control is also approaching perfect self-frustration . . . I cannot throw a ball as long as I am holding on to it so as to maintain perfect control of its movement. . . . This desire for perfect control, of the environment and of oneself, is based on a profound mistrust of the controller.'[5] Because you see yourself as bad, you cannot trust yourself to *be*. Because you cannot trust yourself to be, you cannot trust yourself *to become*, to allow yourself *to grow* as a plant grows. Rather you have *to make* yourself, like you make a box. A box can be made just as you want it, perfectly symmetrical, whereas a plant grows by unfolding itself in its own asymmetries. In regarding yourself as a manufactured box rather than a growing plant you see yourself as an object, not as a living being.

In making yourself do all the things that your high standards demand, you turn everything you do into joyless work rather than pleasurable activities. You expect that other people have the same high standards as you (or even higher) and so you can be constantly trying to reach these standards and constantly feeling exhausted, and frustrated and angry at your failure. You encourage others to depend on you (after all, you know better than they do how to be the perfect mother, father, son, daughter, student, boss, counsellor and comforter), and when the burden of these dependencies begins to weigh you down you start to be angry and resentful, and then guilty, because being angry and resentful does not meet your high standard of being the Perfect Comforter and Friend, the one who is responsible for the well-being and happiness of all those around you. Not for one minute will you allow yourself justified anger with the people who lean on you rather than be responsible for themselves. After all, they do not have to be responsible for themselves while you are there looking after them and knowing what is best for them. Left to themselves they could make mistakes and that would never do.

Some people who get depressed have set themselves the rule Never Complain. No matter what happens they Say Nothing. Not for them the pleasure and relief of complaining. But then those people who get depressed and who do complain do not find that complaining produces any pleasure and relief. It can never be a relief, since no matter how much you complain the feeling of anger and frustration never goes away. You cannot find complaining in any way pleasurable, since you are trying to keep your anger in check. Moreover, when you do complain, the people you complain to either take no notice or else they give you stupid advice like, 'You work too hard. You ought to take things easier', or 'You do too much for your family. You really ought to let them look after themselves. You ought to go out more. When did you last have a holiday?', or 'You worry over things that are never going to happen. What's the point? Take each day as it comes, I always say.' How could you possibly take such advice? You must keep up the high standard of your work. Who will look after your family if you don't? And you know quite well that the only way to stop terrible disasters from overwhelming you suddenly is to identify all the possibilities and to worry about them. Not being able to maintain your high standards is something that you can always worry about.

You have to maintain your high standards because you cannot bear the thought of being mediocre and ordinary. You want to be the Most Perfect, Wonderful, Intelligent, Beautiful, Successful, Admired and Loved Person the World Has Ever Seen (don't we all!) and if that does not work out you are not going to be mediocre and ordinary like the rest of us. You would rather be the Worst, Most Despised, Confused, Evil, Failure and Outcast the World Has Ever Seen. You hate yourself, but, like those people who discover that notoriety can bring the same rewards as fame, you come to take a secret pride in your very badness. There is, you are sure, nobody in the world like you. You might find your essential badness, as you see it, quite unacceptable, but there are aspects of yourself which you deplore but which, viewed from another angle, fill you with pride.

Some of you suffer painful loneliness but take a pride in keeping yourself to yourself. At school you felt an outcast, but secretly you despised the other children who were rough, common, or snooty, or stupid. You grew up regarding everyone outside the family as foreigners. Now neighbours rarely cross your threshold and you rarely cross theirs, and you can be certain that this is the correct way to behave. People should know their place. You are as formal in your dealings with a bus conductor as you would be with the Queen. You do not join sporting and social clubs because you have better things to do with your time. You cannot spend time just chatting to people when there are all those important things that you have to do. (Concentrating on the virtue of not wasting time banishes the recollection of the breath-taking, paralysing fear you feel when you have to join a group of people.)

Your fear of other people and your pride in being independent may be so strong that you want to remain alone all your life. If this is unbearable you may risk a close relationship with one other person, but you can come to see this relationship threatened by your inability to share a joyous sexual union. To deal with this you may pretend to enjoy sex, and you achieve a good performance, but the pretence is wearying and makes you feel that what should be the most important relationship is nothing but a hollow sham. Since sex can be a metaphor for all kinds of power struggles among men and women there is no single explanation why things go wrong in bed, but there is one idea still around, despite Freud and the sexual revolution, that lays its chill hand on a loving couple. It is the belief that sex is disgusting. A virtuous woman does not like sex but endures it for the sake of the family. A virtuous man worships his wife, a virtuous woman. He has sex with bad women. There are still many men who can see women only as sex objects or as sexless good women. Such a man cannot relate to his wife as a good, sexual person but can only alternate between seeing her as bad and sexual, and good and asexual. (Seeing women as either a sex object (that is, stupid, of little value, discardable without guilt) or wholly good (that is, submissive, unaggressive, non-competitive) is an excellent way of dealing with your fear that women are more powerful than you.) Knowing that her husband has never actually *met* her, much less accepted her, the wife feels very lonely. If a woman believes that a virtuous woman does not like sex, she is torn between trying to please her husband (if she does not he will reject her) or maintaining her virtue (if she takes part in sexual activities, or worse, enjoys them, her mother will reject her), and always there is the fear that if suddenly she loses control and acts spontaneously and joyously her husband (and her mother in her head) will turn on her and berate and reject her for being dirty and evil. (Here I have used the words 'wife' and 'husband', but the terms for all sexual partners are applicable.) If you have been brought up to believe that sexual desire is evidence of the evil inside you, and that you must strive to hide and to control this evil, then no matter what pain and despair you feel in your loving relationships, you will take a certain pride in your virtue. You take great pride in your self-control.

Requiring such self-control of yourself, believing that you know best at least in all matters concerning yourself, and wanting to do everything perfectly, you find it very difficult to admit that you have made a mistake. In the face of all evidence to the contrary you go on and on, making the same mistake, keeping yourself in an unfulfilling job or a barren marriage, rather than let the world see that you are capable of failure like everyone else. Sometimes you will not even admit to yourself that you have made a mistake. You berate yourself for not doing things well enough, but you never question your basic assumptions about how you should live your life. However, while it is possible to lie successfully to other people, lying to oneself is never a good idea. Deceiving oneself is as life-enhancing as feeding oneself chocolate-coated cyanide pills.

Easy for me to say that. You know that if you look too closely at yourself and your life, if you discard your childhood dreams of perfection, then the despair you feel now will be as nothing compared to the despair that would overwhelm you. I make it sound all too easy. Buck up your ideas and everything will be all right. I know it is not like that, as Jean reminded me when she wrote to me recently. She said,

> I have managed to re-acquire all my depression and bitterness . . . and am having an indulgent time . . . My

overriding feeling is that it isn't really fair to write to you like this. I want to write letters of blue skies and birdsong. I think I get close to the pain sometimes. I can remember it as a child, the tightness in my chest when I was alone and I didn't know what to do with myself. Always waiting for stage directions. God, I hope I'm not doing the same to Emily. I wonder if living in an isolated situation intensifies the feeling, as I can always remember taking long, solitary, painful walks. I wonder what mother was doing at the time – probably wondering what her mother had been doing when she was spending solitary hours. Anyway, I know the pain is there, and that I want someone to make it better and tell me what to do to stop it coming back again – and guess what – I'm going to have to start all over again. I know vaguely where the path is. Is it common to step back onto the shore having once plunged into the raging torrent? Actually, I suspect I only dipped my toe in to test the water, knowing my inability to commit myself to anything beyond self-torture. I have had glimpses of the raft that carries one in the choppy water though – there always is that confounded chink of light that in the end has to make you laugh uproariously at the whole farce.

I apologise for this letter, as I don't suppose it does anything for you to read it – but it has made me feel better to write it. Harry Williams wrote something rather good about feeling even more angry than ever after receiving Holy Communion – I can't remember the exact context, as I have lent the book to my sister, but I know the anger well. There is a perfection – of thought and emotion that the human mind is capable of, and the human heart of accepting – I wonder if some of the rage has to do with getting small glimpses of such from a million miles away.

And indeed it has – to glimpse perfection, to reach out for it and to be frustrated, again and again. You reject the imperfect and reach out for the perfect. Yet as Father Harry Williams[6] knows well, we cannot reach the perfect until we

accept the imperfect and see them fuse together in a perfection more wonderful than we could ever construct in our
narrow imaginations.

That, of course, sounds like mystical nonsense. You
know quite well that you must reject the bad and concentrate
on the good. You want to be entirely good, entirely right. The
trouble is it is so hard to get hold of what is good and right,
and if you relax your grip for just a moment what you have
grasped will be swept away. If only you could get hold of the
good and the right in all their entirety.

> If we could get the hang of it entirely
>   It would take too long;
> All we know is the splash of words in passing
>   And falling twigs of song,
> And when we try to eavesdrop on the great
>   Presences it is rarely
> That by a stroke of luck we can appropriate
>   Even a phrase entirely.
>
> If we could find our happiness entirely
>   In somebody else's arms
> We should not fear the spears of the spring nor the city's
>   Yammering fire alarms
> But, as it is, the spears each year go through
>   Our flesh and almost hourly
> Bell or siren banishes the blue
>   Eyes of Love entirely.
>
> And if the world were black or white entirely
>   And all the charts were plain
> Instead of a mad weir of tigerish waters,
>   A prism of delight and pain,
> We might be surer where we wished to go
>   Or again we might be merely
> Bored but in brute reality there is no
>   Road that is right entirely.[7]

You are prepared to be bored, in fact you usually are,
rather than see the brute reality that no road, no course of
action is entirely right. You want to see the laws of right and
wrong, prescriptions of how people ought to live their lives, as

immutable laws of the universe, and not as conventions which people create to guide them through their lives. You prefer to see them as immutable laws, fixtures of the universe, since that way you gain certainty. You prefer to know where you are, even if it is in a prison. If you see our rules about right and wrong behaviour as something that people create, then you cannot rejoice that you are free to change the rules. You do not consider the pleasure of creating something better; you fear the uncertainty that any change brings, and you are quite sure that any change can only be for the worse. You cannot accept with your heart, though you may know with your head, that good and bad, right and wrong, are inextricably intertwined. You reject the wise words of Lao Tsu,

> Under heaven all can see beauty as beauty only
>   because there is ugliness.
> All can know good as good only because there is evil.
> Therefore having and not having arise together.
> Difficult and easy complement each other.
> Long and short contrast each other;
> High and low rest upon each other;
> Front and back follow each other.[8]

Without dark we would not know the light. Without death we would not know we were alive. Without imperfection we would not know perfection.

Imperfection is all around you and inside you. Perfection is somewhere else. This is so clear to you that if I say to you, 'I'd like you to consider how you see yourself and your ideal self', you know exactly what I mean. 'Self' is that bad, useless thing you see yourself as being. 'Ideal self' is the person you aspire to be. If I asked you to tell me about the values you use to judge yourself and other people, and then I asked you to rate your 'self' and 'ideal self' on these values you would put a very great distance between 'self' and 'ideal self'. If I computed the relationships among your ratings and set the results out in a graph, it would look something like this.

Not everyone produces a graph like this. Some people, I have found, look at me strangely when I talk about 'ideal

```
                                    • does things
                                      right
                                                • IDEAL SELF


              • cares about others          • happy
          • sensitive
    ─────────────────────────────────┼──────────────────────

                      • depressed
    • SELF
                  • gets angry
```

self'. It has never occurred to them that they could be, much less should be different from what they are. Some people can see the point of considering an ideal self, but when asked to describe their ideal self, give no more than a slight gloss to their present self. They would like, perhaps, to be a bit more confident, achieve a modest success, in short, to gain the goals which they have set themselves and which they see themselves as eventually achieving.

Only the people who get depressed put between self and ideal self an unbridgeable chasm. And in the chasm is great despair – and pride.

2 I am a sensitive person

Many of the people who get depressed describe themselves as being sensitive. I often hear this word being used when my client is telling me how much she or he cares for other people. As I listen to accounts of how much my client does for other people, how much other people's problems become my client's concerns I am impressed, yet again, with how good my depressed clients are. They would reject the idea that they are good, but they would agree that being sensitive to others is a virtue. Being sensitive means caring about others, and this is what we all should do.

You would agree that we all should be sensitive. So many people are not. They are completely hard and uncaring. Not you. You feel sometimes that your awareness of another person's suffering is especially keen. You do not just know how the other person feels, you feel it yourself, right inside you. It is not just the suffering of the people around you that distresses you, but the suffering of every person in the world. You feel other people's suffering so much that you get to the point where you cannot bear to read the newspapers or to watch television. The sight of such suffering can make you feel very depressed.

Being a sensitive person also makes you very vulnerable to the rudeness and bad temper of other people. Some people, hard, uncaring people, are never upset if someone is rude or angry with them. They can just shrug it off. But you can't. You get hurt, and the hurt stays, and as often as not this makes you feel very depressed.

In short, being a sensitive person means that you are a caring, loving person, which means that you are being good. Also, being a sensitive person means that you get upset which means that you get depressed. Therefore, to be good you must get depressed. Being depressed is evidence that you are being good.

Some people who get depressed have linked their notion of themselves as a sensitive person with their notion of themselves as a creative person. They value their artistic ability and see it as coming from the same source as their sensitivity to everything around them. Beauty excites them joyously; the suffering of others pierces them like a sword; while criticism and anger all but destroy them. Their depressions may be terrible, but they resist any therapy which might abolish the depression since any method which could eradicate their depression would threaten to destroy their creativity, the source of their being, their reason for existing. This kind of reasoning can be seen in the writings of Virginia Woolf and Sylvia Plath, both of whom preferred to die rather than to put their creativity at risk.

Still, both these women did achieve a great deal, and, as much as criticism hurt them, they were prepared to risk it and to present their work to the world. Unfortunately, some people who get depressed argue to themselves that, 'My sensitivity shows that I could be a great artist but my sensitivity makes me too depressed to create.' Thus one can have a sense of being special without having to prove it. It is much better to think of oneself as someone who would have been a great artist if only I was not such a caring person/I had had a chance/the world had not been against me, etc., etc., than to have tried and – worse than to have failed – to discover that one was merely ordinary.

Whether or not you regard yourself as a creative person, you do regard yourself as a sensitive person, easily upset by other people, even though you do not always show it. One of the things that does upset you is the way other people do not understand you. Now all of us like to be understood, at least by one or two people in our lives, and the people who get depressed do seem to have inherited and collected relatives who show a remarkable inability to understand other people. You have no one you can really talk to.[9] This makes you feel desperately lonely, but for some of you the longing to be *understood* outweighs the simple need to talk to some sympathetic, uncritical friend. If you experience this huge need to be understood, you get impatient with relatives and friends who offer you sympathy and a willing ear but who clearly do not understand you. They say they love you, but you know quite well that if they truly loved you they would understand you, and so their incomprehension upsets you even more.

If this is how you see not being understood then you have never considered the possibility that we can love someone without understanding that person. Not only is it possible, it is extremely common. Children cannot understand their parents fully, yet they love them. Parents do not always understand their children, yet they love them. Romantic love can only flourish in an atmosphere of mutual incomprehension. (In the middle years of our marriage, my husband would say, jokingly, that as a wife I had only two faults – namely, I could not iron his shirts as well as his mother did, and I understood him. His joke reflected a mutual disenchantment.)

But wanting to be understood can mean wanting to possess that person. We can want the other person to be so absorbed in the business of understanding us that he or she has no time for other people. A child deprived of his mother's loving attention (he might have got plenty of her angry attention) can grow up desperately wanting this lack to be made up, and so comes to express this need as a longing that his mother understand him. Since his mother is now an ordinary, middle-aged or elderly woman who could become a nuclear physicist more easily than she could develop this superhuman understanding, he is bound to suffer terrible disappointment.

We can also desperately want people to understand us because we see that as a way of avoiding being hurt. Since cruelty is always a failure of the imagination, if someone really understands how we feel, if they feel our hurts as their own, then they will do all in their power not to hurt us. You don't like upsetting other people. You wish other people wouldn't upset you.

But understanding other people is quite a complicated business. Sometimes we feel that we understand another person because we see that person as being very like us in character or in what has happened to that person. We identify with that person and feel sympathy for him. Sometimes we are correct in seeing a similarity. The person sees it too and is pleased to accept our sympathy. But sometimes we are wrong. There is no similarity, and so the way we express our sympathy is not appreciated by the recipient. Haven't we all, at some time in our lives, squirmed with embarrassment when someone has gushed, 'I know exactly how you feel'!

For, in truth, no one can ever know *exactly* how we feel. Each person's experience is different from everyone else's, since each person is different from everyone else. Each person sees his own world in his own terms, his own values, attitudes and opinions. If we want to understand another person we have to set about the task of discovering what these values, attitudes and opinions are, and in doing so we ignore our own needs and feelings. The other person occupies the stage while we are the audience, involved in the action of the play, as an audience is, but not taking part in it or influencing the action. We can seek this kind of understanding with equanimity when we have no personal connection with the person we are trying to understand. Therapists can do this with their clients who come to them as strangers, provided, of course, that the therapist does not have a theory to prove or a passionate desire to prove himself to be the world's greatest therapist who cures all his clients. (Avoid all therapists who need, for their own sake, to make you better, but be warned. They come in many guises.)

But if we set out to understand, really understand, someone who matters to us, then we are in danger of being hurt. We may discover that the person is really very different from what we thought he was. Or, worse, we may discover that the person does not value us in the terms in which we wish to be valued. Discovering this, we may feel rejected. And being rejected is something some of us are not prepared to risk.

3 I will not risk being rejected

Anyone who is rejected by someone he loves and needs discovers why our language contains metaphors like 'heart-broken', 'sick at heart', 'heavy hearted'. Rejection pierces the heart like an arrow. You actually feel a sharp, violent pain in your chest, just where your heart is. Your breath does not reach your lungs, but stays caught in your throat. You sweat and feel faint. If only someone would come and pull the arrow from your heart and make you whole again. Sometimes this does happen, and you feel your heart mend. But when this does not happen and time goes by, the sharp pain of a broken heart turns into a dull, heavy ache. The sharp pain can return at any time – when you awaken from a sleep or see something that reminds you – so sharp that tears come to your eyes, and with it the terror of a world from which all security has fled. (When we lose someone we love we often say, 'The bottom has fallen out of my world.') The months go by, and the dull ache in your chest becomes a heavy weight pressing on your heart. The years go by, and you become so used to this weight that you forget what it is to be free and light-hearted.

People who get depressed have suffered a great deal of rejection in their lives. Some of this rejection has been the kind a child experiences when he is brought up by parents who, though meaning well, are so wrapped up in their own concerns that they do not take the time to understand how the child feels. If these rejection experiences start early enough and are frequent enough, the child can be so sick at heart that he does not know what it is to be light-hearted. To know that we are sad we must at one time have been happy, and so, if a child feels from birth unloved and rejected, he grows up sad but not knowing he is sad. He cannot name his wretchedness but acts upon it, usually in ways which conflict with the demands of society. People like this cannot name their state as being sad, rejected and depressed (until they come in contact with psychiatrists and learn to mimic their language) since they do not know what it is to be happy, accepted and free. People who get depressed and who know that they are know what it is to be happy and accepted, even though they may never have allowed themselves to be free. As a child you experienced your parents' love and so were aware when it was withdrawn. So painful were these experiences that you had to do something to reduce the pain quickly – to remove the arrow yourself. You exchanged the sharp pain of rejection for the slow misery of guilt. Your good parents had not rejected you. You were a bad child who deserved punishment. Your badness meriting punishment was a continuing state, so you went on feeling guilty. Expecting more pain, you did what you could to prevent it by trying to be the good child your parents wanted and by resolving never to risk being rejected. You desperately wanted people to love you, but you became very wary of giving your love to others. You reasoned that the less you loved another person the less it would hurt when the inevitable rejection came. You loved, but never completely, never enough to forgive the person for being what he or she was or to let that person go. You might come to hate your parents or your spouse, but you hang on to them in the desperate hope that one day they will say the right word, make the right gesture, and your bleeding, broken heart will be healed and you will be a loved and happy child again. You have not realised that to heal the wounds of rejection there must be mutual love and forgiveness.

The problem with growing up fearing and expecting rejection is that you cannot enter into any adult relationship in the expectation of happiness. With friends and acquaintances you cannot help but be reserved, suspicious and easily offended. You may decide never to marry, or, if you do, you choose someone you see as being safe, and you place very great restrictions on your love. You hope you have guarded against rejection, but in this world people rarely value us to the degree and in the terms which we desire, so in every relationship something is sure to happen which we can interpret as rejection.

When I first came to England I went to work in a clinic where there was a good deal of research going on into the physiological changes that occur in depression, and in particular in the changes in people who become depressed at regular intervals. The doctors were sure that the regularity of mood change must be caused by some metabolic change, but in case some 'psychological factors' played some part in these changes I was asked to do some testing of these patients. Not many patients did get depressed at regular intervals, so there were not many patients for me to see. However, when I started work there was one such patient. The case notes showed that she became depressed every August. Unfortunately, over the years, the periods of her depression had become longer and longer and her response to pills and ECT slower and slower, so she no longer came to the clinic but was on a ward in the large psychiatric hospital. I went to see her. The ward was bleak and dingy, affording little privacy to the women there. Maud was a quiet, gentle woman in her late fifties. My tests showed nothing extraordinary about her. She was very intelligent, very depressed, and, so I gathered from what she said about herself, very lonely. I was a complete novice in the business of therapy. All I could do was to give her some companionship and to listen. After she had known me for quite some while she told me something which she had never told any of the doctors because, she said, she did not wish to be disloyal to her husband. Years ago she had, one evening, been putting her daughter, her only child, to bed when the little girl, prattling on, told her mother something which made her suspect that her husband was unfaithful to her. This all but wrecked her marriage. They stayed together, but the estrangement from her husband and later her daughter whom she saw as siding with her husband continued. It was in August that she discovered that her husband had rejected her. It was in August, another August, that her beloved grandfather died, and in another August that her mother died. (Deaths, we know, can be felt as rejections.) August was the cruellest month of her year. It seemed to me that it was unnecessary to look for physiological reasons for her annual depression. I shall always be grateful to Maud, because she removed the pain I was experiencing (I was helpless in my sorrow for her) since she eventually ceased to be depressed, left hospital and re-established a loving relationship with her husband and daughter. Moreover, she did raise many questions in my mind about why people get depressed and what should be done about it, and so she launched me on what seems to be turning into a lifetime's work. In the course of this I have learnt a great deal.

One of the things I have learnt is to have a greater appreciation of how much people need people. It is not just that no man is an island. No man or woman can *be* an island. We do not exist just within the boundary of our skin. Our body may have the skin as its terminus, but we, ourselves, exist as part of an indivisible network of human relationships. We may set up boundaries and barriers – black and white, men and women, Jew and Arab, Catholic and Protestant, communist and capitalist, nobles and peasants, rich and poor – and we may insist that those outside our barriers have nothing to do with us, but our very act of exclusion simply serves to underline the fact that one group only exists in relation to the other. I define myself by the existence of the Other, the Foreigner. I know I am a woman only because there are men; I know I am white only because there are blacks; I know I am I because you are you.

We try to make the divisions between ourselves and other people real, and we may act as if these barriers are real (and so we do not speak to our neighbours because they are Pakistani, or we send our children to private schools so they will not mix with rough working-class children, or we would not contemplate worshipping God in any church other than our own denomination), but we must be careful not to exclude everybody. We must include some people in a group with us for, as each of us knows quite well, if we stay on our own for long enough we become odd. I like my own company and I really enjoy taking time off work to get on with some writing in solitude, but I am home only for a day or two when I find that I am holding imaginary conversations out loud. I begin to wonder whether this will become a permanent habit and I shall be like those solitary people I have seen (and heard) on the streets of London and New York who speak aloud only to themselves and never to others. My solitary conversations cease once I am in company again, but in awareness of our need for others I always respond when some person, usually elderly, in a shop or on a bus, starts a conversation with me about the weather or the cost of food. We can starve for lack of conversation just as we can starve for the lack of food.

We need other people to define our existence. Let me try to explain what I mean. It is always difficult to talk about experiencing our existence since it is hard to find the right words. When I talk to people about this they start by looking at me uncomprehendingly and, one by one, they nod and agree. I hope this happens with you now.

When I talk about this in a workshop I get the people there to do some 'laddering'. (I shall explain about laddering in the therapy part of this book.) In this way each person discovers what is the central concept or idea on which he has built his whole life. This central concept always has to do with how we experience our existence and our annihilation. It is often hard to find words to express this profound feeling, but each person knows exactly what it is. A person may never have thought about it consciously, but has always acted upon it and will continue to act upon it as the absolute, real, essence of his existence. It can be expressed in many different ways, but, from my studies, it does seem that there are two forms by which existence and annihilation are experienced, and each of us uses one of these two forms.

For some people existence is experienced only in relationship to other people, and annihilation is seen as complete isolation. Such people always see themselves as existing as part of a family, part of a group, being loved and loving, needed and needing. They are the ones who would have to escape from a desert island, since isolation has for them the terror that they would look into a mirror and see no one there. Happiness is being part of a group.

Such people probably comprise half the world's population. The other people are those who see submergence in a group, not as bliss, but as chaos. What these people need for existence is clarity, a sense of being a well defined individual. Yet they need other people, just as much as the first group, since to gain clarity, to be an individual, one needs standards to measure oneself by, and other people provide these. Those of us who seek clarity and fear chaos need the approval of other people.

Thus none of us can escape needing other people so that we can exist and not fear annihilation. But you who get depressed have decided to express your need for other people in ways which make it very hard for you to live.

Take the first form of existence – wanting to be part of a group and fearing isolation. If you see yourself as basically a good person and therefore with something to offer other people, you have no fear of joining groups, of being part of a family, having friends, being accepted. If disaster wrenches you away from your family, as much as you suffer loss, you know that you are able to find new friends and to help other people. But if you see yourself as basically a bad person, then the threat of expulsion from your group is expected and feared. Since you do not value yourself, you cannot see people as wanting you to join them, either as a friend or a helper. If disaster wrenched you away from your family you could not see yourself surviving, and so no matter how much you come to hate your family you cannot let them go. They are your reference points of existence, and you fear that if you lose them you will disappear.

In the second form of existence – clarity of the individual versus chaos – the person who sees himself as basically good can pursue the goals of clarity and the development of self without fearing that he is basically flawed, that the dark chaos is part of his being. Seeing yourself as basically good reduces the need for other people's approval. If you see yourself as basically good, you can set up a select group of people whose approval you desire and you can be indifferent to the opinion of the multitude. But if you see yourself as basically bad then you need everybody's approval. When the approval does not come, or when you try to meet so many differing standards, you despair of finding clarity, and annihilating chaos threatens to overwhelm you.

So all of us need others for acceptance and approval. Rejection is always a threat, but if we allow this threat to dominate our lives we can never be free to be ourselves. We can find our individuality being submerged in a group, or, in seeking the approval of all others, we become afraid to act. And this is what you have done. Having decided never to risk rejection, you hesitate to make any move which might upset other people. It might be so long since you expressed any personal preference that you have forgotten what your personal preferences are. (I could ask you, 'What do you do when you give yourself a treat?' and you would look at me uncomprehendingly.) Or in your endeavours to win universal approval you have discovered to your cost the truth of that old saying, 'Try to please all and you shall please none.' Of course, all this desire to please and to avoid rejection does not mean that you always behave peaceably and meekly with your nearest and dearest. Sometimes you behave very badly, so as to test the limits of your family's acceptance of you and to show by hurting and being hurt that you matter to them.

But as much as you provoke your family with temper tantrums or by saying bitter and cruel things, you keep to your family's rules about what are the limits of what is allowed to be said or done. No one leaves home. All families have rules, usually unspoken, about how arguments are to be conducted. In some families shouting and abuse, verbal and physical, are allowed, while in others fights are conducted silently with tight lips and closing doors. In some families one person may be the overt target for attack while it is forbidden to attack openly another person who, yet, is the focus of all family fights. In some families it is forbidden to let the neighbours know that there is a row going on, while in others certain family members are allowed to slam out of the house and go to the pub or to put on a token show of leaving home and never coming back. But playing out the pattern of the family row serves only to reaffirm the unity of the family.

You often wonder why your family puts up with you, and you feel guilty and try to repress your anger and resentment. But at the same time you are striving to be so very good since you are trying to make people love you because you are so good. Surely, you think, if I am very, very good then my family will love me. After all I do for them, they must love me.

But do they? Does anyone love us just because we are good? Can we make anyone love us? Will being the perfect daughter stop your mother preferring your brother to you? Will being the perfect wife stop your husband from noticing other women? Will being the perfect husband stop your wife preferring the children to you? Alas, the answer to all these questions is no. The curious thing about love is that it can only be freely given. We can force people to obey our orders. We can coerce them into behaving respectfully towards us. We can even coerce them into behaving as if they love us (the greetings card industry flourishes on this), but that warmth of the heart which we call love does not spring into being at command, either the command of those who wish to be loved or those who feel they ought to love. No amount of good behaviour or feeling that one ought to love will create love or bring it back when it has fled. You have to learn to leave the table when love is no longer being served.

But that is a very difficult thing to do when you see yourself as needing the love and approval of others to survive and as fearing rejection as you fear death. You dare not upset other people, since by their possible criticism and rejection of you they have the power of life and death over you. You are helpless.

But are you? Are you *really* helpless? Or do other people have only the power that we give them? Any form of government will collapse if the majority of the people cease to acquiesce to it. The pomp and ceremony of government are no more than the Emperor's new clothes which exist only in the eyes of the beholder. It is just the same in individual relations. We can see other people as being powerful and important, and feel frightened of them, or we can dismiss them like Alice in the Court of the King and Queen of Hearts with, 'You're nothing but a pack of cards!' We can invest other people with the power to harm us by their criticism and rejection, or we can say, like street-wise children, 'Sticks and stones'll break my bones but names'll never hurt me.' We make ourselves sensitive to the words and actions of others.

We can choose whether we shall be hurt, or whether we shall ignore them, or whether we shall see them as ridiculous and so be amused.

However, there is one great advantage about seeing yourself as helpless and in the power of others. You don't have to be responsible for yourself. Other people make all the decisions, and when things turn out badly you can blame other people. And things always turn out badly. You know this. That's why you always expect the worst.

4 I prefer to expect the worst rather than to risk disappointment

One of the first words I learned when I was a small child was 'pessimist'. At home something would happen or be about to happen and I would hear my father make a favourable or joking comment, and then my mother would say, no, it wasn't anything to be pleased about, I always knew it would turn out badly, you're too soft, you ought to know better than to trust these people, remember when so and so happened, that was bad enough but this is going to be worse, you shouldn't be so stupid as to think that this was going to turn out all right because it won't ever be better. My mother was fond of that saying, 'It's an ill wind that blows nobody any good', but as far as she was concerned the only winds that blew were ill winds. My father would counter her arguments with, 'Why do you always look on the black side? Why are you such a pessimist?'

My mother never deigned to answer this question. I did not know why, but I did know what a deadening effect her relentless pessimism had on my small world. So I tried to counter it by holding steadily to the hope that things would turn out well and that I would have a happy life, just like my father promised that I would. Thus I acquired what my clients call my foolish optimism.

Now I know why my mother was always pessimistic. If you are an optimist you live a life full of uncertainty, always at risk of being struck down by the pain of disappointment. As a pessimist you may not ever feel cheerful, but life is certain. Everything, you know, will turn out badly. There is the bonus that occasionally you might be surprised by something actually turning out well, but this is rare and something to be suspicious about since, as you well know,

> The Victorian moralists understood these things.
> If you were greedy, they said,
> And wished it to rain chocolates,
> It would rain hard centres, and knock you down.[10]

Bearing this in mind you try never to incur the crime of hubris, of getting above yourself, proclaiming your virtues and thus incurring the wrath of the gods. You might not fear being struck down by one of Zeus's thunderbolts, but you do fear that if you come top of your class, win the race, collect the prize, you will be dangerously exposed to the malicious criticism and rejection by others. You fear success for you know that if something good happens then something worse must follow. You may see the hand of God in the inevitable disaster, but in case God is slow in evening up the score or simply because you cannot stand the tension of waiting for the inevitable disaster, you rush in and create your own disaster. The ideal disaster combines a confirmation of your pessimism with self-punishment. Thus the tension of waiting for a disaster and the tension of guilt may in one action be relieved by being turned into the pain of a broken leg or the inconvenience of being without the car for a month. You may not be happy but you do feel more in control of your life.

Even when you do not do anything as drastic as crashing your car or falling down a flight of stairs, you can render the outcome of most events certain by your pessimism for the simple reason that it is easier to destroy than to build. It is easier to lose the race than to win, to refuse to enter rather than compete, to undermine confidence rather than to encourage it, to stress the dangers without seeking the courage to face them, to carp, criticise and reject rather than to risk building something positive yourself. You also have the feeling that if you concentrate on small, manageable disasters you can avoid the fearful chaos which you see as threatening to overwhelm your world. As a client said to me once in a burst of candour, 'There is a great, heart-thumping fear out there, but I can deal with that by creating my phobias.' Phobias are manageable, domesticated fears, defences against worse terrors and therefore not easily relinquished. By concentrating on what you know would happen if you ignored your phobia – say you actually left the house to go shopping, you *know* that you would faint and everyone would stare at you and that would be *terrible* – you can avoid bigger problems and even bigger calamities over which you would have no control.

Optimists are so often proved wrong. No matter what success, there is always a fly in the ointment. Something always goes wrong. What satisfaction you can feel when you have your convictions confirmed! And what security there is in suffering!

5 My problems are greater than anyone else's

or

Anyone who hasn't got my problem has no problem at all

People who get depressed are often amazed to discover that there are other people in the world who feel as they do. Sometimes it is a relief to find that you are not alone in experiencing what you suspect may be a peculiar madness. But even after you are told just how common depression is in the entire human race, you still have a sneaking suspicion that no one has ever felt as bad as you do. You look at the people around you who show no sign of depression and you feel that, although these people have the occasional practical problem, they do not suffer as you do. In feeling this way you are, in fact, operating under that universal law that 'Anyone who hasn't got my problem has no problem at all'. People in rich nations look at those of the Third World and say how lucky Third World people are, not having to endure the tensions of the modern world. Men look at women and say what an easy life women have, just caring for a home and children or doing women's work which is always easier than men's. Women look at men and say aren't they just like kids, playing games and avoiding all the real responsibilities that women have. I have met homosexuals who have told me that heterosexuals never experience uncertainty, jealousy and rejection. There are stammerers who believe that fluent people never have problems in communication. Then there have been all those clients who have sat opposite me when, I was sure, I was showing signs of illness (sometimes I cough a lot) and tiredness (it shows when I don't get my eight hours' sleep) and who have told me how they know that a wise and competent person like me could not possibly have any problems. They also tell me that the opposite of being depressed is being perfectly happy. Anyone who is not depressed is perfectly happy all the time.

Usually my depressed client does not say this to me directly but by implication during a discussion, say, about his brothers and sisters. He asks me why it is that he is the only one in his family to suffer like this. Everyone else is perfectly happy. He goes on talking and mentions, in passing, his oldest sister who gave up a good job to stay at home to look after their ageing parents and who now rarely leaves the house, and a younger brother who ran away from home and has never been heard of since. Matters like these my client does not see as reflecting a degree of unhappiness. He is sure that he alone suffers, since he alone in his family is the bad one, born bad, and his evidence for this is the fact that his brothers and sisters are happy, as they must be since they were born good and were brought up by such excellent parents. So we go on talking over the weeks, and then one day he tells me, in great amazement, how his favourite sister, who he *knew* was happily married, had phoned him, greatly distressed, to say that her husband had left her, how she had wasted the best years of her life, how she had never wanted to marry, how she had wanted to go to university but their parents had prevented her, saying that education was wasted on a girl. He is appalled by these revelations, not just in his concern for his sister but by the realisation of how little he knew of his closest and dearest sister. Sometimes this is the point where he suddenly sees that the role he has written for himself in the drama of his life as the patiently suffering scapegoat, noble in his tragedy, his self-sacrifice allowing his family to live their lives in peace does not fit reality. Sometimes this is the point where my client stops and considers. Sometimes it is not.

I could tell this story over and over, in many different versions, and show how, when we are entranced by our own suffering, we become oblivious to the suffering around us. This happens to all of us when the pain of toothache or cancer dominates our thinking. All of us, too, missed a great deal of what was going on in our families, especially when we were in our teens, since we were so wrapped up in our own concerns, and thus in adult life we can come to discover all sorts of things about our parents and siblings that we never knew. Of course, my burdens are heavier than anyone else's, since mine are the only burdens I have to bear. But if we want to convince ourselves that nobody suffers the way we do, if we want to measure our significance in the world by the degree of our suffering, then we have to ignore the suffering of others. We dismiss suffering humanity by saying it is not our concern – by switching off the television and by refusing to read the newspapers – and we dismiss the suffering of those close to us by denying that they are suffering, by saying that they are perfectly happy, have nothing to complain of, don't realise just how lucky they are and so on. Of course there are many people, not just those who get depressed, who adopt such attitudes to other people's suffering. They wish to be simply totally selfish and so they make themselves quite unaware of other people's suffering, while you who get depressed would say that you can't bear to read the newspapers or to watch television because they upset you too much, while you care deeply about your relatives. And so you do. But caring does not always include knowing about and understanding. Caring about can become a way of increasing your own suffering rather than a way of opening out your understanding of another person. Of course, if you are one of those people who believe that 'worrying about' is the same as 'loving', then even as you show concern for others you increase your burden of suffering. It may not have occurred to you that if you habitually say to your family 'I worry about you' instead of saying 'I love you', your family will stop telling you things so as not to worry you and thus you go on, unaware of the kind and the full extent of the burdens each member of your family carries.

Even as your family tries to relieve you of burdens by

trying not to worry you, you hang on to them and grow very skilful in turning every new event into another burden. ('Tom got me a new vacuum cleaner. I'd hate to tell him it's too heavy and makes my back ache', 'Joan's baby's lovely but it upsets me to see how tired she looks', 'Dad wants to buy me a new car but I said no. I'd feel terrible if anything happened to it.')

You can collect burdens too because you do not like to upset people by saying no. You also collect burdens because you are the only one that does things properly. Once the burdens are collected you do not relinquish them. There is a certain nobility in having more burdens than other people. You can take pride in your burdens and reassurance in the suffering they bring.

6 I would think there was something wrong if I wasn't suffering[11]

Suppose you were alone on a spaceship which was fast running out of fuel and you had to decide on which of the two available planets you would land. Both planets had adequate food and shelter which you would need since you were likely to be there a long time, but the inhabitants of each were very different. On Planet Alpha the inhabitants would simply not notice you. They would go about their business and ignore you. They would never speak to you or acknowledge your presence. On Planet Beta the inhabitants would certainly notice you, but only with hostility. They might not kill you outright, but they would harass you, plot against you, and appear friendly only to do you harm. Your life would be one long engagement with an enemy.

Which planet would you choose?

If I put this choice to Captain Kirk or Dr Who the answer would have to be Planet Beta. Planet Alpha would yield no stories, no adventures. Without opposition, nothing happens in our lives. Some of the people I have put this problem to have said that after a lifetime of harassment and opposition they would quite enjoy some peace and quiet, and so would choose Planet Alpha, but even they admit that such a life could be very lonely. One would need to have considerable inner strengths to survive such isolation. So, many people choose Planet Beta, even though it means being the object of other people's malice. At least you are noticed. Your life has some significance for yourself and other people.

Not many of us, as yet, have found ourselves on space-ships, but many of us do find ourselves in environments where we are ignored. Think of all those elderly people without families, living in a busy city where no one stops to pass the time of day, much less to care whether they live or die. Some resilient old people make strenuous efforts to establish and maintain contacts with the postman or the woman next door and to create relationships with a budgie or a radio, but some old people take the option of believing, not that no one notices them, but that everyone does. They see themselves as the object of a vast conspiracy. They are being watched by their neighbours, or by bugging devices in the television. The governments of Russia and the USA are trying to poison them. In secret headquarters all over the world plans are being drawn up for their destruction. Doctors call such people paranoid and deluded, but the good thing about delusions is that they make the person who has them seem more important, at least in his own eyes. And the good thing about paranoia is that you are never alone. Someone, somewhere, is thinking of you.

Many of us, too, were faced with the choice of Planet Alpha and Planet Beta when we were children. Many children grow up in homes where they are more or less adequately sheltered, fed and clothed, but otherwise they are largely ignored by their parents. So each child has to find some way of gaining the parents' attention. Some children discover that if they fall ill or have an accident their mother is suddenly at their side, giving love and comfort. Thus the child is soon set fair for a lifetime of illnesses and accidents. (If you are like this and have defined your depression as an illness then you will have to find other ways of seeking love and comfort rather than through illness before you will be able to give up your depression.) Some children discover that if they are naughty their mother takes notice of them. True, being noticed means being punished, but at least it does mean that you are important to your mother. Many children

soon learn that the only way for them to be noticed in school and in society is for them to break the rules. Then, at least, the headmaster, the police, the judge, and, if you are lucky, the newspapers, take notice of you. Your life has some significance. (The moral of this for parents who want their children to turn out well, is to reward good behaviour more than you punish bad behaviour.)

Most of us grow up in homes where sometimes we were ignored, sometimes we were noticed and loved and sometimes noticed and punished. For some children the belief 'I suffer; therefore my life is significant' is established in complex ways. The child who decided to see himself as bad so as to see his parents as good has to follow the first act of self-sacrifice by many, many more, and such sacrifice is always accompanied by suffering. Thus suffering becomes a way of life. You may not consciously think 'I suffer; therefore I am', but you do get very nervous every time you are threatened with happiness. (One woman told me, 'I don't think I ought to be comfortable.' She did not risk saying 'happy'. Another woman, when I asked her how she had enjoyed a particularly nice party, replied, 'I didn't enjoy it as much as I ought to have enjoyed it.' See the devotion to suffering revealed in those answers.) You may not feel that if you stop suffering you will disappear, but you do feel that you can only justify your existence by your suffering, and so after a lifetime's practice you become an expert in suffering.

When the light-bulb jokes were doing the rounds, one went, 'How many Jewish mothers does it take to change a light bulb?' and the answer was 'None. I'll just sit here in the dark.' I am sure there are plenty of Jewish mothers who change their own light-bulbs – it is all those depressed people who sit there in the dark. I have been so impressed with the way depressed people can turn any event into an opportunity for self-sacrifice, self-blame and suffering that I once considered writing a book called '1001 Ways to Be a Martyr', but gave up the idea when I realised that a thousand and one was too small a number to cover the inventiveness of the committed martyr. Another project much discussed in our psychology department was the Suffering Olympics, to find who was the Greatest Sufferer in the World. (There were, and are, some expert sufferers among the psychologists as well as among the clients.) We had to abandon this idea since we could not work out a way of giving a prize to the Greatest

Sufferer since one of the necessary attributes of the Committed Sufferer is that you Never Win.

It is all very well to joke about these matters, but we live in a culture which has suffering and sacrifice as the central theme of its main religion. The symbol of Christianity is the Cross and Christ's bleeding, broken figure. He sacrificed Himself so that we can have eternal life. Not just by baptism but also by martyrdom can we wash away our sins and enter into the Kingdom of Heaven. The Church does not encourage martyrs the way it once did, but the idea that we should consider other people before ourselves is central to the teaching of the different Christian churches. Judaism makes much of atonement through suffering, especially the suffering of the innocent, while Islam teaches that the martyr in the Holy War has secured his entry to heaven. Through suffering and self-sacrifice we reach salvation.

Since the human baby takes so long to grow to self-sufficient maturity it is necessary for the survival of our species that we have some rules about caring for other people and putting their needs before our own. If we are to live in any kind of harmony we need to have rules about sharing and considering other people's needs. But when it comes to putting our rules into practice we run into all sorts of difficulties. When I have the flu, should I stay home and expect other people to do my work, or go to work and spread my germs around? Should I put my parents' needs before those of my children? Is it permitted to lie or to kill in order to save the lives of other people? Is my first duty to society or to my family? And so on. Endless moral dilemmas.

These moral dilemmas have been argued by theologians and philosophers for hundreds of years without any satisfactory resolution being reached. The sad thing about our lives is that such dilemmas do not wait until we are grown up and educated to present themselves. We meet them when we are children, in situations fraught with fear, anger and uncertainty, and from which there is no escape. Jackie wrote the following story from her childhood.

The Noddy Clock
It was a sunny day. My brothers, sisters and I had been

playing out, so it was decided that an early bath was in order. Normally we didn't run for a bath but today was different. The box of paints and left over wall paper was too tempting for us to mess about. We were told to hurry up and get bathed. My mum and dad were in the garden with the younger ones chatting to the neighbours. I remember it was two in and two out in double quick time today. Downstairs I ran in my towel to get my pyjamas and there I saw it – the worst thing that could have ever happened. Our special Noddy Clock was lying on the floor smashed to pieces.

Panic overtook me. 'No painting today, that's for sure.' Who did it? How did it happen? Well, for me the sunny day soon became a dull one. We were all rounded up together on the settee. 'Who did it?' We all in turn answered, 'Not me,' and the response was a smack for each of us, and so on until there were four or five tearful faces all with the same thing on their minds. Nobody owned up. I had the feeling, small as I was, that everyone was telling the truth. But the truth of the matter was the clock was broken and somehow something had caused Noddy and Bigears to be on the floor instead of in the clock face.

After seeing all the kids like this I had a thought. If I admitted breaking the clock perhaps the punishment would cease and we'd be able to paint, so I said to mum and dad, 'I did it'. The other kids were sent into the dining room and the paper and paints were put on the table for them. I was taken upstairs and taught that day that I wasn't being punished for breaking the clock but for lying. I understood all this, but I felt awful because I had not lied. I'd lied in the fact that I had owned up to something I had not done. My punishment was to go to bed without any tea.

My feelings.
I learned so much by this day:
(a)   Being the eldest girl feeling the pain of the younger children and not wanting them to suffer;
(b)   Wanting the peace of the family and the sunny

day to carry on;
(c)   The feeling of guilt for lying in the end.

All of you who experience yourself as essentially bad, evil, unacceptable to yourself and others have, as children, been put in situations like the one Jackie describes, a situation from which there is no escape (young children cannot leave home) and out of which there is no peaceful and happy solution. You dealt with these situations as best you could, but you were left with a feeling of guilt and a sense that you could atone and somehow put matters to rights by sacrificing yourself and taking on the burden of suffering. You may not even remember the original situation, but so strong were the emotions that you felt and so impressive the conclusions you drew from it that they became part of the foundation of the structure you call your life. You might have decided that you would devote your life to helping others, and so strictly do you apply this rule by trying to ignore your own interests and well-being and to meet the needs of others that you create for yourself a great deal of suffering. You have set yourself the task of making the world perfect, to abolish all suffering and injustices, and when you fail you despair. Even when you do achieve something you find that people do not always show the proper appreciation and gratitude for your sacrifices, and you cannot help feeling sad and resentful. When people do try to help you or to give you things – love and sympathy as well as presents – you find that other people's generosity makes you frightened. You can give, but you cannot receive, and so you find the thought of illness and old age, when you would have to depend on other people, very frightening.

Another set of conclusions you might have drawn from the profound moral dilemmas of your childhood is that life, your life, is a tragedy. Not for you the humdrum mediocrity of happiness. You are a lone figure, singled out by Fate, or God, to play a significant but tragic part on life's stage. The heroes and heroines in the theatre of your imagination did not always end their adventures hand in hand with their lover to live happily ever after. You had alternative plots where you saw yourself as the heroic figure, after curing the sick and freeing the oppressed, riding off alone into the sunset, or in a

defiant stance before a firing squad, or mourned over by
chastened fellow countrymen who, at last, have recognised
your true worth. With this tragic role in mind you grow up
always expecting the worst, and find that your life is full of
disasters, so much so that you may come to feel that you are
damned. But, at least, if God has gone to the trouble of
damning you, it does mean that He has noticed you.

Seeing your life as a tragedy does have its advantages,
just as self-sacrifice has the advantage of making you feel
virtuous. But in your determination to see your life as a
tragedy you may do the things which actually make it a
tragedy (not pursue a career commensurate with your talents, marry the wrong person, take to drink to drown your
sorrows, etc., etc.); and in seeing your role in life as sacrificing
yourself for others, you may go beyond the practical things
that you can do for others and instead see your altruistic acts
as some form of ritualistic self-sacrifice by which you inflict
pain on yourself in order to secure the safety of others. You
might use self-sacrifice as the only way to solve *all* family
problems or as the way to resolve *all* family crises. Many of
the obsessional rituals which some depressed people feel
compelled to carry out have this as one of their meanings.[12]

So, in your guilt at your failure to be perfect, in your need
to sacrifice yourself to atone and to protect others, in your
identification of yourself with unhappiness rather than happiness you create for yourself a great deal of suffering. You
feel that such suffering gives your life a significance which a
happy, contented life would certainly lack. You did not consider that life, ordinary life, contains enough natural disasters, mishaps and losses without you creating any more.

But it is those natural, chancy, spontaneous mishaps,
disasters and losses which you fear. You prefer to create your
own disasters in the attempt to control them, while you avoid
the random disasters of the wide world by staying safe inside
your prison of depression.

7 Besides, it's safe inside the prison

Once, when I was talking to a group of psychologists about
depression and I had asked them to give their images of

depression, one psychologist said,

> The worst part is when I'm coming out of the
> depression. When I'm depressed I feel I'm in a
> bathysphere deep under the water. There I'm in
> complete darkness except for a small circle of light
> which must be coming from the surface. The
> bathysphere is floating in the deep water, so I have to be
> careful not to move about too much. If I did the
> bathysphere might plunge to the bottom and I would be
> done for. When the depression ends I suddenly go up to
> the surface, and that is terrible, because floating on the
> surface is the wreckage of my ship – all the things that
> have gone wrong while I've been depressed and now I
> have to put them right. I always think of it as a Spanish
> galleon that's blown up, and now I have to gather up the
> pieces and build it again. I hate that.

This is a powerful image of the dangers and the safety of depression. Terrible though the prison of depression is, it seems to be a refuge from still greater horrors. You are afraid that you could plunge further into bottomless depths of complete destruction, madness and death.

> Which way I fly is Hell; myself am Hell;
> And in the lowest deep a lower deep
> Still threat'ning to devour me opens wide,
> To which the Hell I suffer seems a Heaven.[13]

Dangers, perhaps even greater dangers, threaten you if you leave your prison of depression for the ordinary world. There you might have to change, and change always involves uncertainty. The good thing about being depressed is that you can make every day be the same. You can be sure of what is going to happen. You can ward off all those people and events that expect a response from you. Your prison life has a regular routine, and like any long-term prisoner, you grow accustomed to the gaol's security and predictability. The prison of depression may not be comfortable, but at least it is safe.

8 The Deadliest Sin

All of us, when we were children, created our personal myth, the story which we believed would be our life, not just so as to have a map to guide us through life, but to bolster up our pride in response to the insults the world had inflicted on our small person and to give us courage enough to attempt the journey. Unfortunately, we all grow up thinking that the map, our myth, *is* the reality, and so when our map proves to be inaccurate, as it must, since reality rarely conforms to myth, we all have to face the fearful task of recognising that our map is nothing but a map and that we need to change it, to bring it more in line with reality. To do this we have to admit that we are wrong, and for some of us, particularly you who get depressed, admitting that you are wrong is something that you find very hard to do. Given the choice, you would prefer to be *right and suffer* than *wrong and happy*.

As you well know, when we say we are wrong we create an area of uncertainty. If what I thought proves to be wrong, then a whole range of possibilities immediately opens up and it might be some considerable time before I can discover which of these possibilities is right. If you cannot tolerate uncertainty then you cannot afford to admit that you are wrong.

Absolute certainty may appear to you to be a wonderful thing, giving complete security, but have you ever considered that if you want absolute certainty you must give up freedom, love and hope?

Freedom means making choices and allowing other people to make choices.

Love arises spontaneously and is freely given. It cannot be coerced into being and produced on demand.

Hope can only exist where there is uncertainty. Absolute certainty means complete hopelessness.

If we want to live life fully we must have freedom, love and hope. So life must be an uncertain business. That is what makes it worth while.

But you want absolute certainty and you have too much pride to admit that you could be wrong. You take pride in seeing yourself as essentially bad; you take pride in not loving and accepting other people; pride in the starkness and harshness of your philosophy of life; pride in the sorrows of your past and the blackness of your future; pride in recognising the evil of anger; pride in not forgiving; pride in your humility; pride in your high standards; pride in your sensitivity; pride in your refusal to lose face by being rejected; pride in your pessimism; pride in your martyrdom; pride in your suffering.

Pride, so Christian theology teaches, is the deadliest of the seven sins since it prevents the person from recognising his sins and repenting and reforming. Sin or not, it is pride that keeps you locked in the prison of depression. It is pride that prevents you from changing and finding your way out of the prison.

Chapter 6

OUTSIDE THE WALL: LIVING WITH A DEPRESSED PERSON

When I first planned this book I put this chapter about living with a depressed person after the chapter on how to change, but as I worked on the first section and went on, as usual, talking with my clients, I realised that this chapter needed to go before the chapter on change. For if someone close to you is depressed, and if you want that person to cease being depressed, then you have to be prepared to let that person change, and thus you yourself must change. But just what you would have to do needs some careful thought.

When I have a teaching session about depression with a group of health professionals I usually begin by asking how they feel when they are with a depressed person and what images they have of this experience. One day I met a group of nursing auxiliaries whose job it was to visit old people in their own homes and to help them bathe regularly. Thus these women had to deal with a great deal of unhappiness and depression in their patients. As we talked of the feelings that looking after these old folk aroused one of the women mentioned that her husband had been depressed since he had retired. As she spoke it sounded very much like what many women say after their husband retires – how she cannot get her work done because he is around the house, how grumpy and difficult he is, wanting meals at particular times and expecting things to be done when he wanted them, and so on. The group continued talking, and later we came to the question of what images we had of being with a depressed person. Then this woman spoke again. She said,

'I feel that I'm in a boat in a heavy sea. Sometimes I feel

I'm at the top of a wave, and then I go down into a trough again.'

'What sort of a boat is it?' I asked.

'An open boat – a rowing boat – but there's no oars or sails or rudder.'

'Are you alone in the boat?'

'Yes.'

'When you're at the top of the wave, can you see land or another ship?'

⸴'No. There's nothing in sight. Just rough ocean.'

As she described her image we each became aware of how terrible her plight was. Her husband, in his depressed state, made her feel helpless and alone. The doctors, she said, gave confusing advice and no help. She could only react to things as they happened and could not change or control them. She was trapped in an isolation as terrible as that of her husband. She was sorry for her husband, but she also felt angry and frustrated – and then guilty because she knew it was not right to be angry with someone the doctors said was ill.

This is the curious thing about depression. People call it an illness, but if you live with it you know it is not like any other illness. If someone you care about has a physical illness or an injury – bronchitis or cancer or a broken leg – you feel simple concern and sympathy for that person. You might feel anger at the injustices of life or at the carelessness of other people who have inflicted this suffering, and you might occasionally feel impatient with your loved one who fails to rest properly or to take his medicine regularly, but you do not find yourself possessed of a terrible rage with your loved one. Sick people can be querulous and difficult, but they do not turn on you and say hurtful, cruel things just as you are giving them extra love and comfort. Sick people are not usually impervious to reason. They do not demand that you never leave the house while most of the time refusing to speak to you when you are there. Sick people do not rush upstairs and lock themselves in their bedroom when a neighbour drops in, nor do they sit in silence all day, brighten up and chat happily when visitors call, only to relapse into a hostile silence when the visitors leave. Having someone sick in the house can disrupt family routine, but sickness does not usually create a

continual atmosphere of anger, mistrust and uncertainty. No matter how serious an illness is, you can come to understand it, and even if you can do nothing but let the illness run its course, you can see the pattern and not feel as if you are the helpless victim of uncontrollable and dangerous forces. You might say to someone in the family, 'Don't come too close. I don't want to catch your cold', and if someone has a dangerous infection medical science will protect you, but how can you be protected from the danger you feel of having a great well of despair open up in you? Being with a depressed person can be a very difficult and dangerous business.

It is not just relatives who report a confusion of feelings, many of them bad, which arise when with a depressed person. I have talked with psychologists, nurses, doctors and social workers, and they all say how they begin by feeling great sympathy and concern for their depressed client, but soon find themselves feeling confused and helpless. Now if you are in the business of helping people and you think that you are quite good at it, then being made to feel helpless is very threatening. Some professional people, too, report the sense of danger, that being with a depressed person will awaken their own latent depression. It is no wonder that some professionals refuse to treat depressed people or bring consultations to a quick end by reaching for the prescription pad.

The images of being with a depressed person that professional people give are of two kinds. There are the images of wandering in a fog, not knowing where you are going, or being involved in some strange geometric pattern that cannot be completed in any satisfactory way. The other kind of image is that of being on the outside of a prison wall, knowing that the depressed person is inside the prison, wanting to help the depressed person but being unable to reach him. One image given by a psychologist was of being outside a circular brick prison. There were no windows, but the depressed person inside would remove one brick. The psychologist told me, 'When I see a brick being removed I try to put my hand through the hole to touch my client, but as I do he slams the brick back into place. Then he removes a brick on the other side of the prison, and I dash round there to try to get my hand through the hole, but as I reach there, he slams the brick back into place and I'm left on the other side of an impenetrable wall.' This image shows very clearly how the message that the depressed person gives is, 'Help me, help me – stay away', and how painful and confusing this is to the person outside the prison.

What can you do?

Ways of thinking about the problem

When something goes wrong in our relationships with other people there are three kinds of questions we can ask in order to discover what happened and what should be done to put it right.

1. Who is to blame for this?
2. Who is responsible for this?
3. What does this mean?

Each of these questions represents a different way of conceptualising the problem. Often in discussions about relationships we use all three kinds of concepts and so we get very muddled. If you are worried that I am going to blame you for your relative's depression then you must read this section very closely and make sure you understand it.

1 Laying blame

Something goes wrong and we look for the culprit. 'You dropped my best teapot', 'He backed the car into the gatepost', 'He took the car without permission', 'She spent the house-keeping money at bingo'. When we find the culprit we can say, 'It's your fault. What are you going to do about it?' We expect the person at fault to be contrite and to make repara-tion. If he or she does accept the blame and does make some reparation then all (or most) is forgiven and life proceeds smoothly again. But sometimes the person does not accept the blame and instead puts up arguments like, 'It's your fault I dropped the teapot. You gave me a fright when you shouted', 'If you had cut the hedge back I'd have been able to see where I was going', 'You said I could take the car – don't you remember?', 'If you took me out more I wouldn't need to go to bingo to give me a break from all this cooking and cleaning and looking after you and the children'. Then the argument starts and goes on for hours, weeks, and, in some families, for years.

Matters are not made any simpler by saying that the offence is a crime and calling in the police. The culprit may be found and brought to court, and, if found guilty, fined or sent to gaol. Just why people get fined or sent to gaol is not quite clear – is it to punish them or to teach them better ways of behaving? This whole question of crime and punishment is very complex, and I raise it here only to say that if we think in terms of blaming, feeling guilty and never forgiving, all we do is make our relationships worse and make even greater problems for ourselves. So, please, leave blame and guilt aside and think about these issues in terms of *responsibilities* and *connections*.

2 Being responsible

In the course of my work as the chief administrator of a department of clinical psychology I often have to draw up a job description for one of the posts in the department. The job description must show very clearly what the holder of the post is responsible *for* and whom the holder is responsible *to*. All this can be clearly defined and followed. If a problem arises about who is responsible for what we can resolve it through discussion and reference back to our job descriptions.

From this orderly way of defining and limiting responsibility I go and talk to my depressed clients and what do I find? They are responsible for everything! There isn't anything that can happen in the entire universe that they cannot see themselves as responsible for and feel guilty about. Usually they confine their responsibility to their family and their job. They are entirely responsible for the happiness of their spouse, children, parents, brothers and sisters, grandparents and, if they are so minded, to the entire range of their cousins and in-laws. None of these relatives is capable of being responsible for himself or herself. If my client is working, then no matter what his job is, he is responsible for the welfare of the entire organisation, no matter if it is an international business or a vast government department. My client sees himself as responsible for everything, and when he sees himself as failing in his responsibility he says, 'I feel so guilty. I should take mum and dad out more often/I should have made sure my son worked harder for his university exams/I should set an example to the others in the office/If I had given my sister more help her husband wouldn't have left her/It's my fault if any of my pupils fail their A levels' and so on.

The essence of a job description is the understanding that the holder of the post agrees to carry out certain tasks and to be responsible for himself in doing these tasks. He has to report to or be accountable to a senior colleague, but in his work he is responsible *for himself*. When I talk to my depressed clients I find that while they are prepared to be responsible for everything and everybody in the universe there is one exception. They are not prepared to be responsible for themselves. They see themselves as passive and helpless. Things happen to them. They don't choose to do anything. They are compelled to do things by forces out of their control. They see themselves as unable to avert disasters or to take positive steps to achieve success. The black cloud of depression descends without reason, without any choice or design on their part. They are compelled to meet other people's demands and they cannot choose to refuse. The world is the way it is and they have no choice but to live in it at its behest.

They are the people that they are and they have no choice but to suffer themselves, to be the cross which they have to bear.

When I sent the first part of this book to Jean for her comments she wrote back,

> One thing I have chewed over and over is the first part where you set out the six opinions. In nos 2 and 6 you use the word must. I have never felt the compulsion of must in holding these opinions, though they are two of my 'favourites'. I don't feel that I *must* fear people. I just do. I don't see anything about them that must be feared – they just *are* terrifying, and the same with forgiveness. I don't feel that I mustn't forgive myself – I just don't. I rather feel that the element of compulsion that 'must' gives these makes them seem more of a positive decision than I think they are. In adopting such hopeless attitudes I don't think there is a positive decision. It's really a small point, but I immediately thought, 'I don't feel that "must" '.

It is not a small point. It is the essence of living your life in a prison, and of finding your way out of that prison. There are more prisons than the prison of depression. Each of us builds our own prison when we decide upon the opinions which we want to regard as the solid, enduring truths of our world. Some of us build large, spacious prisons where we can roam with ease and where we feel free enough to change some of the boundaries of the prison when we wish. But some of us build narrow, dark prisons where we feel cramped and pressed upon and where we feel we cannot change any aspect of our prison. Our prison simply *is*. We do not even feel that we *must* behave in a certain way, because, as Jean said, 'must' contains a positive decision. Deciding that I must do this implies that there is an alternative, albeit one that appears impossible. A decision is the outcome of a choice. If we make decisions, then we are responsible for those decisions, but if the decisions which determine our lives are made by other people, then we are not responsible. If, when we build our prison, we deny that we have made any decisions and claim that all the decisions have been made by other people or powers beyond our control, then we can feel that we are not responsible for ourselves. If our prison is cramped and miserable, it is not our fault, and so we can come back to the sorry round of blame, guilt and not forgiving.

Freedom consists of recognising that we choose our own prison and of deciding to create a spacious, light, airy prison filled with delightful things, a place where change is created and welcomed. Freedom means recognising that everything we do is the outcome of a choice (bearing in mind that not all choices are made consciously, and that 'not deciding' means 'choosing not to decide'). Freedom means being responsible for yourself, and it also means looking very closely at your relationships and deciding to what degree and in what way you are responsible for the welfare of other people.

Within organisations it is fairly easy to decide what responsibility we have for other people. For instance, in our department I accept that it is my responsibility to provide the appropriate experience and opportunity for study for the psychologists who come there for training, but it is not my responsibility to make sure that they work hard enough to pass their examinations. That is their responsibility. But where loved ones are concerned it is much harder to set limits to our sense of responsibility. I want my son to have a happy life, so I find it hard sometimes to say nothing when I think he is making the wrong decision. It is not just a matter of wanting our loved ones to be happy. It is the pain we feel when we know they are not happy, or are weak or in danger. I remember, as quite a small child, feeling an overwhelming and exceedingly painful pity for my mother. To end this pain I had, in some way, to help her, but it was help she neither understood nor wanted. What she did want from me was something I could not give. When my depressed clients talk to me of their sensitivity in their relationships and when they say things like, 'As much as my mother annoys me, I couldn't ever say anything to upset her', or 'Dad can manage to look after himself, but I go round to see him every morning, just in case there's anything he needs', I know they are talking, at least in part, of their painful, loving pity and of how they try to deal with it. We try to protect our loved ones in order that we should not pity them.

But there are limits to what protection we can and

should give. When our children are babies we need to protect them, but once they start to move around and explore we have gradually to decrease our protection, for if we try to go on protecting them we prevent our children from growing up to be ordinary, confident adults, capable of looking after themselves. So many of the depressed people I have met have told me of loving parents who protected them and of how they find the world such a terrifying place (it must be – why else would their parents need to protect them?) and of how they lack the confidence to live their lives. As parents we must define the limits of our responsibility to our children, limits which change as the child grows older, until the child is an adult and our responsibility is that of a good friend. For the child, growing up means seeing our parents become older and in need, sometimes, of our help. But the relationship and responsibility should still be that of good friends – loving concern and interest, with minimal criticism and advice, help when asked, and allowing one another to make our own decisions since we are all grown up.

Without losing any of the virtuous aspects of pity and concern for our loved ones, it is both possible and necessary for us to define the degree of responsibility we have for each of our loved ones and so be able to say, 'Yes, I do want my mother to be happy, but I will not lie to her just because the truth is unpleasant', or, 'Dad doesn't need to see me every day. If I went there less it might encourage him to go out more.' Nothing is to be gained by going over the events of the past years and feeling guilty or blaming others. There are really very, very few parents who actually try to harm their children. Most parents love their children and try to do what is best for them. But as all parents know, when our children are small we are usually caught up in all sorts of difficulties so that we do things which later turn out to be mistakes, and we do things which turn out to be very much for our children's benefit. The trouble is, at the time we have no way of knowing what will be a mistake and what will be a success. So often what we thought was good parenting turned out to have bad effects on our children, and what we thought we had done wrong and what we regretted turned out to benefit our children. So, waste no time going over the past searching for blame and guilt. What needs to be done now is to look at what is happening *in the present* and to try to understand it. *Understanding* means *seeing connections*.

3 Seeing connections

The other day Jack came to talk to me. For the past five years his wife Fay has been depressed, sometimes very badly, and she has been given many pills and some ECT. Only recently has she started coming to see me, and Jack found this confusing, since all along the doctors have been telling him that Fay was suffering from endogenous depression whose cause was unknown. So he came to talk to me, and, in the course of the conversation, we talked about Fay's parents. Jack said that Fay tried to do too much for her parents when they were quite capable of looking after themselves and they did not show much concern for Fay when she was ill. 'Fay's mother visits Fay's sister every week,' said Jack, 'We go and see them but they visit us no more than once a month, and when Fay was in hospital and very ill, they didn't visit her at all.'

'When someone gets depressed it's always difficult for the parents,' I said, 'You know yourself, when the doctors were saying that Fay had endogenous depression, a kind of physical illness, while it was all very worrying for you, you didn't have to feel guilty about it because it wasn't your fault. But now Fay's coming here and we're talking about how she lives her life, and this involves you, since you have to ask yourself about what you're doing that's helping to make her depressed and what you should do to change. Now if you think about it, it's much harder for parents. If they think, 'Fay's like this now because of what happened in her childhood', they feel very guilty, and helpless as well. You might feel guilty about what's happened in your marriage over the past ten years, but you and Fay are still together and still young, and you both can put things to rights and have a good life, but Fay's parents can't go back twenty, thirty years and change things. That's why many parents whose adult children get depressed like to insist that the depression is a physical illness, or that the child should pull himself together and get out of it – that way they don't have to feel guilty.

That's why, too, Fay's parents didn't want to see her when she was in hospital.'

Jack found my explanation very illuminating. He still thought that Fay's parents should visit her, but now he could see a connection between Fay being depressed and what her parents were doing, and this connection, this meaning, made the whole painful business slightly easier to live with.

A person may do something which seems strange or wrong to us, but if we are able to talk to that person and find out how that person sees the situation we shall find, first, that the person sees the situation differently from us, and, second, there is a connection between the meaning that the person has given to the situation and what he does. Of course, the meaning that the person has created is not an *excuse*. You may steal, or riot, or murder, or argue with your spouse because you feel that you had a deprived childhood and you have never forgiven your father. Your reasons do not excuse your bad behaviour, but they do provide an *explanation* which can become the starting point for change.

Unfortunately, we are not very skilled at finding another person's meaning. It is often much more satisfying to say, 'Wouldn't you think she'd look after her mother/dress better/put her children's welfare before her own' and so on, rather than to think carefully about why a person does what she does. In families people often ask for explanations, but don't phrase their questions very well. 'What do you think you're doing, bringing your bike in here?' 'Mrs Smith's little girl wears pretty dresses and she brushes her hair every day. Now why aren't you like that?' 'Why do you have to play golf *every* Saturday?' 'Why do you get upset just because I forgot your birthday?' Such questions do not inspire thoughtful answers, rich in explanation. Again, in families people do give explanations, but no one actually *hears* what they say. Finding explanations means asking careful questions and listening to the answers.

We give our world meaning and we act in accordance with that meaning. All our acts, all we say and do, have consequences. To live wisely we need to be aware of the consequences of our acts. We teach our children to look for the consequences of running headlong on to a busy road, or not obeying their teachers, or not cleaning their teeth every day. But we are not very good at teaching children to be aware of the effect of their actions on other people. Perhaps this is because so many adults are not very expert at seeing the effect of their actions on other people. The most glaring example of this is of those people who believe that by being violent to young people you can teach them not to be violent to other people. Beating children certainly punishes them, but what they learn from that beating is likely to be something that the person inflicting the beating neither wanted nor predicted. Within families can be found many examples where one person does not see the consequences of his actions, the connections between what he does and what these actions mean to other people and how these people then act. For instance, a father may feel that he is not very successful and that he would feel more satisfied with himself if his son had a successful career. So as soon as the boy starts school the father encourages him to work hard and do well. At least, the father calls what he does 'encouraging'. His son calls it 'nagging', and comes to dread his father's interest in his schooling. The boy loses his joy in learning and looks for ways of escaping from school and from his father. The father's actions have more consequences than just upon his son. His wife sees the effect the father's passion for his son's success has on the son and she tries to protect the boy. This divides the boy even more from his father, but the person in the family who feels the loneliest and most isolated is the daughter who sees her father and mother so involved with her brother that they have no time for her. The father does not see what effects his actions have on his family, the mother does not see that she is alienating her daughter, the son does not see that he is set upon a life of escapes and failures, and the daughter does not see that on the basis of her experience of her father and brother she has concluded that all men are selfish and unlikely to be interested in her. Thus the father's actions, like a stone thrown in a pool, have consequences in all directions.

However, while the father's actions have *connections* with the actions of the other members of the family, it is not correct to say he is *responsible* for those actions. Each member of the family is responsible for his or her own actions. They each make their own decisions and they are not *compelled* by their father's actions to behave as they do. (When someone harasses you, it is always possible to deal with that harassment, at least in part, by being indifferent to it and by laughing at it. Alternatives can always be found through discussion, but not if you practise Not Speaking and Keeping Things to Yourself.) We are free to make any number of choices, including the choice to see ourselves as not being free to make a choice. We create problems for ourselves and the people around us when we refuse to take responsibility for ourselves but expect other people to take responsibility for us (as in this family, the father expected the son to do for him what he would not do for himself – be successful), when we deny that we are free to choose but insist that we are compelled to behave as we do, and when we refuse to see the consequences of our actions.

Of course, the consequences of our actions are limitless, since everything in this world is connected to everything else (a family is part of society and in our small world every society is connected to every other society), so we can never be aware of all the consequences of our actions, but it is a good idea to be aware of the consequences of our actions which may rebound on us. I have come across some psychologists who have been convinced, rightly, that they are not responsible for their colleagues, but who fail to see the connections between what they do and what their colleagues do. Such lack of wisdom makes problems for people in groups, either working groups or families.

Seeing connections is part of wisdom, and living wisely means living harmoniously. Living harmoniously means avoiding the painful dead-ends of blame, fault-finding, guilt, revenge and not forgiving; it means being responsible for yourself, limiting and defining your responsibility for others, and seeing the connections between your actions and the actions of others.

So now let's go back to this question of living with someone who is depressed.

Mothers

The mothers of people who get depressed are extraordinary people – or, at least, so my clients would have me believe. My depressed clients sit in my room and tell me about their mothers, and, as they do, I realise that if any of these remarkable women came to visit me none of them would actually enter the room by the door. Instead I might hear the sound of golden trumpets as the room filled with a heavenly light and up above I would see the mother slowly descending, her angel wings gently moving, and the glow of her halo revealing her compassionate, loving, beautiful face. Some mothers would enter like this. The rest would swish through the window on a broomstick. Having a mother who is an angel or a witch is very difficult, but some poor people have mothers who alternate, unexpectedly, between being angels and being witches, and that is even more difficult.

So I sit with my depressed client and we talk about this angel ('She'd do anything for me. I'd never do anything to upset her') or this witch ('I've only got to hear her voice on the phone and I'm upset'). Then one day I happen to be shopping in town and I run into my client, accompanied by an ordinary, middle-aged or elderly woman who is introduced to me as 'My mother'. As we chat about the weather and other trivial matters, I try to be unobserved as I peer at her to see if that carefully waved hair conceals a halo, whether there are huge feathered wings folded under her modest coat, or whether there is a black cat at her heels and cloven hooves tucked inside her neat, sensible shoes. Peer as I might, none of these signs is there, and I have to conclude that my client's mother is just an ordinary woman.

Now it is not a good idea for me to say to my client, the next time we meet, that I thought his mother was an ordinary woman. That will never do, because he does not want his mother to be ordinary. Ordinary people make mistakes, and he wants his mother to be perfect. So he insists that his mother is a Perfect Angel and All Criticism is Forbidden. If his mother's deficiencies are too glaring to be denied, he expresses his disappointment that she is not a Perfect Angel by insisting that she is the Perfect Witch. But only he is allowed to criticise her. If you agree with his criticisms of his mother he gets very resentful ('How dare you criticise my mother') and if you try to point out her virtues he knows that you are siding with her against him. ('You don't understand. You don't know her like I do.') Spouses will be as familiar with these arguments as I am.

So being the mother of someone who is depressed is very, very difficult. You know that you are an ordinary person. You wouldn't mind being a Perfect Angel, but you know that you've made mistakes, especially when your child was young and life for you had quite a few difficulties. You know that your child does not understand about these things, and you find it hard to talk about such matters. You know that you care about your child, and you always did your best in difficult circumstances, and still do, but somehow you can't get through to your child. He (or she) seems to hang on to you, and yet every time you think the two of you could be close, he pushes you away. Sometimes he might hurt you terribly by saying cruel things to you, but even if he says nothing and is always polite to you, you know that he has a lot of resentment against you. You feel shut out, confused, helpless and misunderstood.

Val would tell me how much she feared her mother coming to visit, how everything her mother said or did upset her, how she was sure that gifts from her mother were offered not because her mother loved her but because she wanted to put Val under an obligation to her. Yet Val could not detach herself from her mother and treat her with that polite indifference we use for people we do not like but have to meet. Just why she could not do this can be seen in the poem which Val had written when she was twenty and so deeply depressed that she had been admitted to a psychiatric clinic.

Mother, Mother, why don't you come?
Can't you hear me crying for you?
I'm frightened and I'm alone.
I want to be comforted.
I want you to take me into your arms, like a child.
I want to cry myself asleep on your shoulder,
And relax warm and secure.

But nobody comes.
The pillow soaks up the tears,
The hostile darkness embraces me.
The blanket supplies impersonal warmth.
Only the spattering of icy snow on the window
Lulls me to sleep.

A year later and still depressed she wrote,

SOLITARY CONFINEMENT

You laughed at my weaknesses
 – so I feared to show them.
You trampled on my dreams
 – so I dreamed alone.
You were too busy to listen
 – so I never spoke.
You handled my secrets indiscreetly
 – so I ceased to share them.
You were insensitive to my needs
 – so I hid them from you.
You never seemed to understand
 – so I stopped trying to communicate.
You hurt me by your indifference
 – so I bled inwardly.
You wouldn't let me near you
 – so I kept my distance.
You cared for my physical needs
 – so my soul became impoverished.
You drove me into myself
 – so now I am imprisoned!

If you are the mother of someone who is depressed
perhaps, as you read these poems, you felt, not just the shock
of such passion and the fear that your child feels like that
about you, but also some memories of your own mother and
how you got along with her. If you have read the first part of
this book you have found some things that apply to you, and
to your mother. Beliefs such as that anger is bad and that you
should never forgive get handed down from one generation to
another like the family jewels. There is one woman whom I
have known for ten years, who has been depressed for longer,

and who would tell me how, whenever she and her mother fell out over something, they would not speak for months and months. Neither would forgive the other. Setting such an example to the children, the grandmother and mother ensured that the three daughters never got on well together. Even at their father's funeral two of the girls would not speak to one another, and now one of the girls is completely estranged from the family. All this is to be expected in any family where the rule is 'Never Forgive'.

But of course it is not just mothers alone who make up these rules and see that they are obeyed. There are always fathers.

Fathers

Fathers, like mothers, become the victims of their depressed child's determination to have as parents Perfect Angels and not ordinary, fallible human beings. Of course, some fathers (and mothers) go along with this. They like the idea of being Wonderful Daddy, always there, caring for and protecting his little child, or being Famous Father, to be admired and emulated. But most fathers are aware of the wall between themselves and their child, and they feel baffled and confused. In the confusion is the realisation, sometimes dimly perceived, sometimes known with startling clarity, that what is happening to your depressed child is connected with your own marriage. And your marriage has never been an easy, uncomplicated and simple relationship. Neither is the marriage of your depressed child.

Spouses

My father, who was a commercial traveller and who spent much of his time listening to his friends and customers telling him about their problems, always said, 'Never interfere between husband and wife.' What he meant was that it was a dangerous business to get involved in any argument between a married couple. I often think how right he was as I try to find my way through the angers, fears, jealousies, resentments, loves and loyalties in order to discover the meaningful connections, not just in my client's marriage but the marriage of his parents. There are rules in every family about what can be said about each person in the family, and if I carelessly infringe these rules I am in trouble.

But marriage must be talked about since depression is not some *thing* inside a person but it is the way that person relates to himself and the people around him. A spouse is just as much involved in the depression as the person who is depressed. So when a depressed person who is married comes to see me I ask if the three of us can get together, at least occasionally, for a discussion. Through this request I have discovered that I have had as clients wives of the most important men in Lincolnshire. I know this because when I ask if a husband could come along with his depressed wife, the wife has relayed to me the message that, much as he wished he could do this, if he absented himself from work for as much as an hour or two, thousands of acres of the best Lincolnshire potatoes would stop growing, wilt and die, or British industry would grind to a halt, or the spiritual lives of all Christians would be put in jeopardy, or the Nato forces of Western Europe would be rendered defenceless, or international banking would be brought to the verge of bankruptcy. I cannot help but be so impressed with this that I may forget that saying in which so many family therapists believe, 'The craziest member of the family is the one who refuses to turn up for therapy sessions.'

So it is with all these Very Important Men, and with some of the wives of depressed husbands. It is not that they do not want to help their spouse, but they are afraid that their own depression will be revealed, or what they see as their murderous anger held in check by a smiling mask of kindly reasonableness will burst forth in disintegrating madness. They cannot see that their depression or anger is no more than the pain of being an ordinary human being, since they do not want to be an ordinary, fallible human being. They want to be, and to be seen as being a Perfect, Wonderful Person who looks after a spouse who is ill. Such a posture fits neatly with the medical model of depression, where the depressed person is told that he is suffering from a mental illness, that he is a patient, not a person, and that pills and

ECT will cure his illness. Spouses who do not wish to inspect their own way of living believe in the medical model of depression.

But not all spouses are like this. They may not see a connection between their partner's being depressed and their own behaviour, but they are prepared to do anything which could help their partner. When this means coming along to talk to me they do this, and some of them make a few discoveries about themselves. Ron would bring Jackie to see me, and when I first invited him into my office along with Jackie he thought he was being asked to talk about Jackie in the way that relatives are asked to talk to the doctor about the patient. But he soon found that it was not so. Ron said, 'When I came here I thought I was an onlooker, but now I know I'm part of it.'

One set of connections which needs to be looked at is how aspects of our relationship with our parents become part of the meaning we give to the relationships within our marriage. Sometimes we can see quite clearly that our wife is like our mother, or our husband is like our father, but it is not always easy to realise that our husband reminds us of our mother or our wife reminds us of our father, usually because we have conflictual feelings about these similarities. A man may be pleased that his wife keeps him in order in the way that his father kept him in order, but he may secretly resent her domination just as he secretly resented his father's. A woman may be pleased that her husband cossets her in the way that her mother cossetted her, but she may secretly resent the way he limits her independence in the same way as she resented her mother's restrictions. Sometimes we find ourselves re-enacting in our marriage scenes from our childhood. If such scenes made us happy, then such re-enactments can be quite joyful and pleasant, but if such scenes in childhood made us feel frightened, helpless, angry, jealous or resentful, then replaying such scenes in married life can only create greater unhappiness. Sometimes we do not perceive the similarity between the scenes from married life and those from childhood. When Fay and I were working out what were some of the things that made her feel down, she told me how nervous she felt when her mother visited her since 'an atmosphere' could develop between her mother and her husband, and so she had to try to prevent this and to keep everything smooth and peaceful. In another conversation she told me how, as a child, she had to act as a mediator between her mother and father whenever they quarrelled. Until I pointed it out she had not seen how she had been interpreting any difference of opinion between her mother and husband as being the same as the arguments between her parents. I went on to comment that probably her reaction to 'an atmosphere' between her husband and mother was stronger than need be because she brought to the present the fears of her childhood. Quarrels between parents are always frightening to a child, since the child knows that he is dependent on his parents and that, if they fight, one or both of them might desert him. But an argument between a woman's mother and her husband should not imperil a wife's security – not unless she sees herself as dependent upon her mother and husband as she was upon her mother and father when a child.

Just who is dependent on whom is another connection which must be looked at very carefully. In a culture where 'masculine' means 'strong and independent' and 'feminine' means 'weak and dependent' many married women have to keep up the excruciating position of trying to support a weak man while making sure he appears to the world as strong and independent. Any woman who has a marriage containing such a pretence knows how exhausting keeping up this pretence is. Not wishing to hurt her husband by exposing his weakness, the woman may collapse into a depression from which escape is impossible until she and her husband are able to face together the questions of weakness and dependency.

Sometimes a man, or a woman, needs the partner to be weak and dependent for reasons other than appearing strong to the outside world. Sometimes what the 'well' spouse needs is to be needed, and the 'ill' spouse obligingly meets this need. (Some mothers, fearing the desolation of no longer being needed, can need their child to be ill, and the child, loving his mother, obliges.) When we need a person as well as love that person we can let our need influence us more than our love. We can say, 'I worry about you. I don't want you to be hurt', and mean 'Don't do anything I don't want you to do.'

Now I'm going to tell you a story and, as you read it, put yourself in the position of the princess.

In the days of ancient Rome there was once an Emperor who had a beautiful daughter. Just as beautiful princesses are wont to do, she fell in love with a handsome man, and, just as powerful fathers are wont to do, the Emperor did not approve of her lover. So the Emperor's soldiers came and seized the man and threw him in the dungeon under the Colosseum.

During this emperor's reign the most popular game that was played in the Colosseum was called 'The Lady or the Tiger'. In this game one prisoner, usually a wicked and admired villain or a noble who had offended the Emperor, was put in the arena alone and facing two locked doors. He was told that behind one door was a tiger and behind the other a beautiful lady, but he was not told which door was which. All he had to do was to choose the door to be opened. If, when he had chosen, the door was opened and out came the beautiful lady, the Emperor would pardon him and give him a farm far from Rome, and he would marry the lady and retire to his farm midst much rejoicing. But if the hungry tiger came out, he would die a horrible death.

When the princess heard that her lover had been seized and would be playing the Lady or the Tiger game she went secretly to the gaoler and bribed him to tell her behind which door would be the lady and behind which the tiger. When the day of the game arrived she sat in the royal box and when her lover entered the arena and looked at her she signaled to him which door he should choose to have opened.

Now if you were in the princess's position and your lover/spouse were in the arena, which would you choose.

The Lady or the Tiger?

For some people the choice is easy. Some choose the tiger, on the principle that 'If I can't have what I want then nobody else is going to have it'. Some people choose the lady on the principle that 'Much as I want my loved one near me, so long

as I know that he/she is somewhere in the world, alive and happy I am content'. But some people find the choice impossible because as much as they want their loved one to be well and happy, they cannot bear the thought of facing life without their loved one.

Now if you fear that you could not face life without your spouse then you will be inclined to do things to keep your spouse with you and not let him or her wander. If husbands are allowed to go out to pubs and clubs, to spend their time in ways that you do not know about, then they could meet all kinds of people and they could lose interest in their wives and homes. If wives are allowed to go out to work, or to go out with other women, then they could meet all kinds of people and they could lose interest in their husbands and homes. So some of you feel it is much, much better if your spouse is safely at home where you can keep an eye on him or her. And what better way to keep your spouse safe than for him or her to be depressed.

Now for some of you (most, I hope) this is an extremely shocking and wrong thing to say. You don't want your spouse to be depressed. You want to see your spouse leading a happy normal life. But for this to come about you both need to look at your marriage to see how much you both relate to one another as adults in an equal relationship and how much you are both involved in a struggle for control of the other and of family life. If your marriage is more of a battle for power than a co-operative of equals, then being depressed can be part of the struggle for power, a way of one person controlling the other and preventing any change. Terrible though depression is, at least you know where you are with it. Your depressed spouse will not be out and about, doing things and meeting people in situations out of your control; your devoted partner will not leave you, ill and depressed, while you need looking after.

Sometimes, when I am talking with a married couple, I say, 'Now there is no one single thing that you can do which will suddenly stop you being depressed, so what I am going to ask you is a purely hypothetical question. I would like you to tell me what you would say if I said to you that if you and your wife/husband stay together she/he will go on being depressed and if you separate she/he will be well.' Not every 'well' spouse says, 'We'd separate.' When I put this question to one couple the husband who had been telling me how much his wife's deep and lasting depression and massive anxiety terrified him, said, 'If someone in authority said she would get better if I left then logically – straight away – I'd say I'd go – but then I'd wake up in the night, and I'd know I wouldn't go.' At the end of our discussion he thanked me for giving him the opportunity to talk things over at such length – 'I've been asking the psychiatrist for ages if we could have some psychotherapy' – and two days later I had a letter from him to say that his wife would no longer be coming to see me.

In the course of my work I have met many people who are suffering from terrible disabilities – mentally handicapped people who know they are not as clever as most people, people whose brains and spines have been damaged beyond repair in accidents, people who are dying slowly of multiple sclerosis or cancer – and who have not despaired. They know the implications of their disability, but they are able, in a sense, to escape from the prison of their damaged body, to separate themselves from their physical pain, and so to be interested in life, to care for other people and to enjoy their company, to take an interest in many things, to enjoy wit and humour and to laugh. But in depression no such separation of the suffering body and the free mind is possible. Body and mind are imprisoned, and the pain and suffering cannot be transcended. This is why depression is such a terrible infliction, and why doing anything to keep a person in the prison of depression is the utmost cruelty.

Before all you depressed people cast yourselves in the role of the virtuous, helpless victim in the hands of a powerful, ruthless spouse, please consider the words of Sheldon Kopp,[1] whose many words I would recommend to you for thoughtful reading.

> The victim is far more dangerous than the powerful, responsibility-burdened caretaker. Beware the helplessness gambit of the chronic victim! Some people typically get out from under their own responsibilities (in which they would otherwise have to take care of themselves) by acting helpless and weak in order to invite others to do for them. If the other person does not respond, then he is accused of being cruel and unfeeling. But should he arrogantly take on the role of caretaker, then the helpless one will soon hold him in contempt as being a weak fool, and what he offers will be returned as somehow not good enough. In the long run the helper is made to feel helpless. Finally the victim is in the power position (though he has won nothing but the degrading imposition of his will by playing through weakness) or failing that, he settles for the spiteful sense of having been able to keep the other from having his way.

So the victim can imprison the gaoler just as much as the gaoler can imprison the victim, and the result is stalemate. To find your way out of such an impasse you have to be prepared to inspect your marriage, not in the usual way of mutual recriminations, but by defining responsibilities and seeing connections.

When I am working on this with a couple I often ask each why he or she married the other. By then I have heard a great many complaints. Now I want to hear of the virtues that each found attractive in the other, and what do I find? That the virtues, seen so attractive in one light, can be experienced as pain-inflicting attributes in another, the very attributes about which the greatest complaints are made. Chalky married Rachel because she was strong, realistic, practical and organised (as well as pretty), but when he is depressed and she is encouraging him to be out and about and not let things get him down, he feels that she is unsympathetic. Jackie married Ron because he was so gentle and calm, and now, when she gets anxious and needs to talk and rush about, he infuriates her because he says nothing. 'Ron never worries,' she says. Chalky cannot see that Rachel is expressing her love and concern in the ways that she knows best, and Jackie cannot see that Ron is a silent worrier.

Sometimes the 'well' spouse, hating to see the changes that depression has brought to his partner says, 'I want you to go back to what you were.' A wish impossible to fulfil, for none of us can go back to what we were. The only way out of depression is to change, and this sometimes means that your partner has to make changes in things that you value. Like many depressed people, Tony despised 'ordinariness', but he knew that his wife did too, and that she loved him and clung to him because she saw him as extraordinary, even though she found much of his extraordinary behaviour quite painful. Later when Tony had decided that it was not worth spending his life locked in battle with his wife, he wrote the couplet,

> If you hadn't loved my devils so
> I might have sooner let them go.[2]

Sometimes we cannot bring ourselves to make any changes in our marriage because we cannot bear to admit that our marriage is not everything that we want it to be. Most of us enter into marriage with romantic ideas that mean living happily ever after, and when this proves not to be the case we can feel cheated and angry, but we may hang on to the marriage and try to keep it as it is in the desperate hope that one day all our romantic dreams will come true. The trouble is that men and women can have such different ideas of what is romantic. Men who dream of coming home to a woman who is a lovely wife and mother find it hard to accept that a woman can feel that looking after a home and family is boring, frustrating and unfulfilling. For many women the most important way of expressing love is not in sexual intercourse but in all those delightful, romantic gestures that anyone who watches the advertisements on television or reads women's magazines and romantic novels must know.

Yet so many husbands fail to realise this. Kay[3] used to describe how she dreamed of coming, dressed in a beautiful gown, into a room where her husband was standing, waiting for her. As music filled the room he would take her in his arms, kiss her, and then they would dance, slowly, beautifully, and so romantically. Fay would say to me, 'If only I didn't have to arrange all our outings. If only he'd come home one evening and say, "Go and get dressed. I've booked our theatre seats, and a table for supper afterwards." ' Nothing wrong with dreaming such dreams and hoping for them to be fulfilled, but unfortunately some husbands from whom such behaviour is expected could travel faster than a speeding bullet than they could be so sophisticated and romantic.

Now all these problems that I have mentioned, and many more, could be resolved, or at least minimised, through frank and open discussion. But unfortunately this is the one thing that none of you is any good at doing. You are all experts on Saying Nothing, Not Wanting to Upset Anyone, Keeping Things to Yourself, Feeling That He Should Know Without Me Telling Him, and so on. You are all experts on Not Talking.

Not talking

In her study of love in our society Jill Tweedie[4] wrote of the silences between mother and daughter and between husband and wife. When a girl is young, Jill argued,

> Out of insecurity and a wish to protect, the mother does her assiduous best to crush her little woman's selfhood and turn her into one in a safe line of female nobodies . . . She knows everything and tells us nothing or, worse, she pretends. In the name of loyalty to her husband, our father, in the name of our best interests, she will not breathe a word of what her life has been. Carefully she constructs a painting-by-numbers, helps our clumsy hands to fill the colours in. Fall in love – pink and red. Marry – shining white. Dear little babies – pink and blue. Happily ever after – silver and gold. Does she believe these are the proper colours? She

blurred them herself, of course, and got them wrong,
but is she hoping that we will be luckier? When she
comes round, years later, to cry over our kitchen table
smeared with the food spat out by our own infants,
sobbing of our father, what he has done, how she has
lived, what she has to put up with, what she really
wanted to be, it is too late. Why didn't you tell me,
mother? Why did you lie and lie?

Parents have good reason to lie to their children, and
wives to husbands and husbands to wives. Jill went on,

If you are to reveal yourself, warts and all, to another
human being – and this is an essential part of growth,
as well as being necessary for mental health –
self-preservation demands that that person has no
reason to use your vulnerabilities against you. Any
inequality provides an ulterior motive to do just that.
An 'inferior', whether by class, caste, employment or
simply in the world's eyes at the time, might be a true
friend and confidant unto death but there are many
reasons why he or she should not be; and if, for instance,
a livelihood is dependent upon a 'superior', the motives
for using that friendship are heightened.

Between 'superior' men and 'inferior women', the
same distrust occurs, foundation for the battle between
the sexes. Many a woman does not receive the full
confidence of her husband because he knows, however
much that knowledge be concealed, that the
relationship is a dependent one and that if a crunch
comes, her economic survival may oblige her to use her
knowledge against him. For the same reason, women
conceal things from their husbands – there is too much
at stake for them to afford such intimacies . . . In any
unequal relationship, the two concerned must devote a
precious amount of energy simply to jockeying for
position and the relationship devolves from a frank
exchange to a tiring and constricting conflict of
strategies. It is not easy to be honest with an equal who
has no reason to use your weaknesses. How much more
difficult when the motive is there.

So the more you see yourself as weak, bad, evil, unacceptable to yourself and to other people, the less you can confide in anyone who you fear might want to use your confidences against you. No wonder George Brown[5] in his survey of depressed women found that a significant factor in their lives was the lack of a 'confiding relationship'. It was not just that they had no one who would listen; it was that they had no one they could trust enough to confide in.

Those of you suffering outside the wall of depression are part of this silence, this not speaking. This is the first answer that I must give you when you ask, What shall I do?

What shall I do?

Listen and share.[6]

Sharing means being prepared to reveal your own weaknesses. Listening means accepting the other person's pain. Don't push it away, saying, 'No, no, it's not like that', or 'Don't worry about it. It's not as bad as you think. Everything will be all right. You'll soon be better.' Don't run away from the other person's pain by belittling it or denying that it exists. Accept the pain, stay with it, and offer, not advice, but a comforting hand or a shoulder to cry on.

Have the courage to face the pain and the courage to accept change. Have the courage not to be afraid of one another. Have the courage to accept the world as it is, and one another as you are, in all your strengths and weaknesses. For we must love our loved ones for their sins as well as their virtues, for their weaknesses as well as their strengths. We must love them as they *are*, and not as we want them to be. And we must hold them in love in the same way as we hold a rose – gently – for if you hold a rose tightly the thorns pierce you and the petals are crushed.

Now to say that all again in a little more detail.

Chapter 7

SUPPOSE I DID WANT TO LEAVE THE PRISON, WHAT SHOULD I DO?

1 Don't play the 'Yes, but . . .' game

For as long as you have been depressed, and probably for longer, you have been an expert in playing this game. This is how it goes:

You, to friend: 'I don't know what's wrong with me. I'm always tired, even when I wake up in the morning. I just drag myself through the day. I feel drained.'

Friend to you: 'Isn't it time you had your holidays? If you had a break right away from work you'd feel a lot better. Get away, have some sunshine and do nothing for a while.'

You to friend: 'Yes, you're right, I do need a holiday. But I can't get away. The new manager's only been with us a few weeks and he doesn't know his way around the place yet. He's always coming to me to ask how we do this and how we do that. And our secretary's off sick – usual vague sicknote from the doctor. Goodness only knows when she'll be back. And my eldest has got his finals coming up soon. I know he's not at home, but he rings us every week and I know he likes to know we're there, just in case something happens. Kids are like that, you know.'

Sometimes you play the 'Yes, but . . .' game silently.

You to doctor: 'I've been feeling down, doctor, ever since my mother died. I know that's a year ago and I should be over it by now. I try to pull myself together but it's so hard. I dread waking up in the morning, and I'm not sleeping. I go off all right, in fact I can't wait to get to bed, but then I have terrible dreams and I wake up and lie awake for hours.'

Doctor to you: 'Well, you have had quite a few worries over the past couple of years, haven't you? And it takes a long while to get over losing someone close to you. I'll give you something to make you feel a lot better. They take about a week or ten days to start working, but you'll soon find you're your old self again. And something to help you sleep.'

You to doctor: 'Thank you doctor.'

You to self, silently, 'The last time he gave me something to make me better I came out in a terrible rash. He said the rash had nothing to do with what he gave me, but I don't think he was telling me the truth. And those sleeping pills, they just make me feel dopey the next morning.'

Sometimes when you play the 'yes, but . . .' game the 'but . . .' is not even consciously thought, since it is one of those Eternal Truths on which you have built your life.

You to husband: 'Just look at the mess those kids have left. Clothes and dirty dishes all over the place. They think I've got nothing to do except pick up after them.'

Husband to you: 'Leave it. They're old enough to clean up their own rooms now. If they don't they can just live in their own mess. You do too much for them, making their beds, doing all their washing and ironing. You slave after them and they just don't appreciate it. They're nearly grown up. It's time they learned to look after themselves.'

You to husband: 'You're just as bad as them. That's where they get it from. You just drop your clothes where you take them off', and so on with the usual few words of domestic bliss. This is a diversionary tactic on your part so you do not have to present your 'but . . .' or even think it. For your unspoken 'but . . .' is your Eternal Truth that 'If I am not needed I cease to exist. I must do things for my family so they will go on needing me. If I make my children keep their rooms tidy they will go away and leave me and I shall be alone forever.' You don't have to say this to yourself. You just *know* it.

We all play the 'yes, but . . .' game when someone foists advice on us that we do not want. Sometimes we point out how the advice is unacceptable, and sometimes we answer politely and express our distrust and rejection of the advice silently to ourselves, and sometimes we just change the sub-

ject of the conversation without even noting consciously that
the advice runs counter to our Eternal Truths. We do all these
things as such ordinary and regular activities in our conversations that we do not take special note of our doing so. But
here I am asking you, as the first step in finding your way out
of the prison, to become aware of when you play the 'Yes, but
. . .' game. (One popular form of the 'Yes, but . . .' game is 'Yes,
I'm depressed, but I don't want anyone to know.' So long as
you are a closet depressive, hiding your state from yourself
and the rest of the world, you can never find your way out of
the prison.)

When you catch yourself playing the 'Yes, but . . .' game,
ask yourself why you are doing it. Are you rejecting advice
because it is of that useless and stupid 'Pull yourself together'
kind or are you rejecting the ideas in the advice because such
ideas threaten the edifice you have so carefully built around
you? Have you become so clever at playing the 'Yes, but . . .'
game that you play it with yourself and thus stop yourself
from doing anything new? When you do try something new,
like going to a Keep Fit class or taking extra vitamins, and
you do not feel better *immediately*, do you say to yourself,
'That's no good' and cease your efforts? Have you made a rule
of your life the well known precept 'If at first you don't
succeed, give up'?

One reason we all play the 'Yes, but . . .' game is that it
protects us from having to recognise and to think about new
ideas. New ideas are always upsetting. They suggest that we
might be wrong. They make the world a changing, uncertain
place instead of being anchored on our Eternal Truths. New
ideas are dangerous. That is why the pedlars of new ideas are
often silenced by being sent to gaol or murdered, and why
newspapers are closed and books burnt. The 'Yes, but . . .'
game is your form of censorship, and you use it all the time,
especially when you come looking for help to end your pain.

'Please,' you say, each in your own way, 'take the pain
away. Give me the magic pill or wave the magic wand or utter
the magic formula or give the magic explanation and take the
pain away, but don't change me.'

Some professional helpers actually accept this demand
and try to meet it. They may give you pills which dull the pain

or they may give you an explanation which you can use as an excuse for your depression. The professional helper tells you, you are as you are because you had a difficult childhood, and he fails to make clear to you that what matters is not what our parents did to us but what we do with what our parents did to us. Eagerly though you might seize the pills or the excuse, you soon find that though the pain may be dulled and you move more freely, the depression still lurks in a dark corner, like a sleeping tiger, and as much as you try to excuse your bad behaviour the memories of your childhood become even more painful.

There is no magic that will take away the pain and leave you to live your life *as you are*. You are a human being like the rest of us, and one of the facts of being a human being is that our actions have consequences and *we cannot escape the consequences*. (We may not be punished *for* our sins but we are certainly punished *by* them.) If you believe that you are essentially bad, evil, unacceptable to yourself and other people, if you fear other people, if your philosophy of life makes you fearful and pessimistic, if you are unreconciled to your past and you fear the future, if you believe that anger is bad and if you never forgive, then such beliefs and the actions that follow such beliefs will cause you pain. The *only* way to stop the pain is to change your beliefs. The only way to stop the pain of depression is for you to change.

One way or another, this is what I say to my clients the first time they meet me. Some clients leave and do not return but others stay and say, 'Okay, I accept I've got to change. But promise me that when I've changed I'll have no more problems and that I'll be happy.'

This request is based on two assumptions, namely:

1. Anyone who hasn't got my problems has no problems at all (therefore when my present problems disappear I shall have no problems);
2. Happiness is total certainty (therefore unless I know exactly what is going to happen I cannot be happy).

Both these assumptions are wrong. All human beings, rich and poor, young and old, wise and foolish, have problems and difficulties. As much as we might want to be secure and to be able to plan our future and see our plans come to fruition, no such security is possible since we are all members of a world-wide community and we are affected by matters far beyond our control. Here in Lincolnshire, we expected never to see a Vulcan bomber again since the squadrons based here were being disbanded and the planes broken up for scrap. No one would have predicted that in 1982 the Vulcans would be bombing the airstrip on the Falkland Islands. I would not have predicted that instead of trying to help Fay deal with the uncertainties of Jack leaving the Air Force I would be trying to help her deal with her fears that he would be sent to the South Atlantic.

So when my client says, 'I'm prepared to change provided you tell me beforehand *exactly* what will happen when I change,' I can only explain that I, being a mere human, cannot predict the future. Change creates possibilities, and every possibility more possibilities. Change is a journey of exploration into completely new territory. I cannot show you the way. I can only go with you, making my own discoveries as we go along.

Some clients are prepared to take this chance of risking change without guarantees. I guess if you have got this far through this book you are prepared to risk some changes. So we will proceed.

Having decided to give up playing the 'Yes, but . . .' game, you need now to look at what you habitually do when you feel you are in danger. Now when any of us are threatened there are only two things we can do. We can stay and fight or we can run away. Sometimes we act precipitately and sometimes we stay to assess what is the wisest thing to do. If our house catches fire, should we stay and fight the fire, or should we rush out of the house? When our boss criticises our work, should we argue with him or be silent? Most people are quite flexible about when they fight and when they take flight, but some habitually do one or the other. Some people will never argue over anything. At the hint of a confrontation, they are off. Now, in the process of change, of finding your way out of the prison, you will come across many new ideas and be offered the chance of having new experiences. What is your usual reaction to what you see as the danger of something new? Do you take off like a startled hare, fleeing to something that you know is safe, or do you dig yourself even deeper into your entrenched position and fight off all change from there?

Try to work out which is your habitual response to change which you see as dangerous, so that as you dare to explore you don't suddenly find yourself running away to the safety of the old ways, or resisting the new ideas with old prejudices. If flight is your preferred mode of dealing with danger then you probably believe that self-inspection is dangerous and you say things like, 'I think I inspect myself too much.' The fighter from entrenched positions would never say this, since you inspect yourself frequently. Trouble is, you always find the same things. You say, 'I know what I am like. I like to keep myself controlled and orderly – I can't change.' Meanwhile, I am trying to re-define the meaning of new ideas and new experiences.

New ideas and new experiences are not dangerous. They are *interesting, exciting, life-enhancing, good fun*, and *challenges to be mastered*. No fight, no flight. Just challenge and mastery.

Lao Tsu,[1] whose wisdom is as pertinent today as it was

two and a half thousand years ago, spoke of the sage, the person who lives wisely and harmoniously. Where problems are concerned, he said,

> Because a sage always confronts difficulties
> He never experiences them.

The way out of the prison of depression is the way of learning how to live wisely and harmoniously. Such wisdom has always been known, but each of us must rediscover it for ourselves. All that I am putting in this book has always been known, but as what I am saying strives to be *wisdom* and not just intellectual knowledge I have had to discover it myself and to know that I know it. Now I am trying to interpret and present it in a form which I hope people of the 1980s will understand and find useful. Soon my interpretation will be out of date. Other people will have to re-fashion and re-present for another society and a different time what human beings have always known about how to leave and to stay out of the prison of depression. When Vicky Rippere[2] looked back over what has been written about depression since the six-teenth century she found that it is only quite recently that depression has been thought of as an illness. Instead, depres-sion, or melancholia, has always been thought of as a lack of wisdom in living and a lack of self-knowledge. Over the cen-turies the cures for depression have always been the same. Vicky summarised them as,

> The basic notion of circumspect, temperate living, based on knowledge of one's own individual and constitutional susceptibilities, the focus on enhancing efficient biological functioning through attention to diet, sleep and exercise, the strategy of deliberately avoiding known physiological and psychological precipitants, the notion of the individual as a member of a supportive social network, the practice of systematically preparing to face adversity, and, finally, the concept of personal responsibility and initiative in choosing to live with care.

Discovering how these ideas apply to you and how you can use these ideas is the way out of the prison. There is no magic key that unlocks the door. The door is always open, could you but see it. So to find the open door you have to set out on a journey. It will not be an easy journey. It will be rough going in some places, and sometimes you might despair of ever finding your way but if you persevere you will reach your destination and recognise it when you are there. You may fear to start on a journey of unknown length to an unknown destination, but have courage. As Lao Tsu said,

A journey of a thousand miles starts under one's feet.

2 Treat yourself kindly

This is the hardest change to make. If you can manage this, the rest is easy.

Treating yourself kindly means looking after yourself. Yet this is the one thing you will not do. If you were physically ill, and not depressed at the same time, you would look after yourself. You would make sure that you did all the right things to get better. But here you are, enduring one of the most punishing experiences a body can take, and you do nothing to help your body to cope. Worse than that, you do the opposite. Instead of resting, you push yourself to do more and more. When you do lie down to rest, instead of deliberately thinking of pleasant things or indulging in a delightful fantasy, you lie there thinking horrible things and imagining the worst. Instead of making sure that, even though you aren't hungry, you eat nourishing and attractive food, you starve yourself, or else gorge yourself on cakes and sweets and then, instead of feeling pleasantly replete, you feel guilty and hate yourself for being so greedy and uncontrolled. If you were tired and overworked, and not depressed at the same time, you would make sure that you took the time to relax, to do something pleasant and entertaining, to have a holiday. Instead, you refuse to allow yourself to relax, to take time off and do something pleasant and, if you do find yourself doing something pleasant and relaxing, you make sure you do not enjoy it. If you were tired, ill, and overworked, or even just living a normal life, and at the same time you were not depressed, you would look after yourself.

Or would you?

Perhaps when you were not depressed you did sometimes cosset yourself, but most of the depressed people I have known have never been in the habit of looking after themselves, and treating themselves kindly. They feel they must do everything the hard way, and every present they buy themselves and every pleasure taken must be paid for by extra hard work or by some penance or by giving something to someone else. If they have a bad cold, they struggle to work rather than staying in bed. They ignore all the signals that the body gives to show that something is amiss and they keep on going until one day they collapse with a burst ulcer or a uterine haemorrhage. So many women who get depressed have struggled on, refusing to seek treatment for menstrual disorders, yet every woman knows how wearying and debilitating menstrual pain is. (Yes, I know there are many male doctors who do not understand this and who trivialise or refuse to treat such disorders, so if your doctor is like this, either educate him or go to a woman doctor.[3]) All this neglect of your body and the effort to consider everybody else before yourself stems from the way you see yourself as essentially bad, and therefore you must always strive to be good, never daring to rest and take things easy.

But being depressed is a profound emotional experience, and all emotional experiences, whether pleasant or unpleasant, happy or unhappy, are accompanied by physiological changes. When we have a profound emotional experience, we then need a period of quiet to recover. When you are laughing, you can feel the changes going on in your body, and, pleasant though these changes are, you finally have to stop laughing and let your breathing and your heart rate go back to normal. To be angry or frightened means having strong physiological changes taking place in your body, and so if these emotions go on and on, as they do in depression, then further physiological changes will take place and come into consciousness as tremors, headaches, stomach pains, constipation and those sorts of strange, unpleasant feelings which, if you are so minded, you become convinced are heralding a brain tumour or a heart attack or a lethal cancer. Such pessimistic interpretations of the symptoms of tension simply make you more tense, thus producing more tension and more symptoms. Great and prolonged tension makes anyone's body more vulnerable to the various viruses that plague us, so it is no wonder that depressed people are more likely to pick up colds and influenza and other such diseases than are people who are not depressed. The wear and tear on the body of being depressed is very great, and so, to get out of the prison of depression, you must cherish your body and treat it kindly.

When you were not depressed you probably had some hobbies, sports or interests which you quite enjoyed but now you are depressed you will not do anything that might give you the slightest smidgen of pleasure. Since nothing holds any interest or meaning for you, you will not attempt anything from which the smallest enjoyment might come. So when someone says, 'How about coming for a walk? It's a beautiful day,' you say, 'Yes, but I know I won't enjoy it. And walking could bring on that pain in my chest. If the neighbours see me out walking they'll say, "Well, there is nothing wrong with him. Why isn't he back at work?"' So you stay inside and turn your face to the wall, and that chance vision of beauty which might have lifted your heart and given you courage goes unseen, that blessed tiredness which follows physical effort is not experienced, and that chance encounter where you felt the wisdom and love of another person is missed. And all because you will not give yourself pleasure and open yourself to the possibility of new experiences.

(Later in the day in which I had written the above paragraph Mark came to see me after an interval of a fortnight. I had first met Mark when he was recovering in hospital after taking an overdose. He had not lived in Lincoln for very long and knew few people, so I suggested to him that he should attend a day centre run by the Social Services. Instead of saying something like 'Yes, I know that would be a good idea, but being with all those people would make my headaches worse/I'm too frightened to go on a bus and I can't expect my wife to take more time off work to take me/I'd meet other depressed people there and that would make me feel worse' etcetera, etcetera, Mark went along like, as he said, an obedient schoolboy doing a lesson which he disliked but which he knew he had to do to pass an exam. But the dull, unpleasant lesson turned into something else. At the centre he had met a voluntary worker, John, who was preparing to enter the ministry of the Anglican church, and in conversation with John, Mark was able to discuss his search for meaning in his life and his fear of death. John also introduced Mark to his church's Fellowship group, where Mark felt welcomed and at home. When Mark came to see me to tell me all this, he had not undergone a sudden conversion and all his depression disappeared. He was still a troubled young man, plagued by headaches and stomach pains, but what he had gained was a measure of trust which enabled him to say, 'I know I will get better one day – perhaps not for months, or years, perhaps never altogether, but I'll be all right.')

Perhaps part of your refusal to treat yourself kindly lies in your belief, acquired when you were a child and at the receiving end of the activities of parents who held this belief, that if you take notice of a child and give him things he will be spoilt. This word 'spoilt' was around me a lot when I was a child, since people, especially my mother, were always telling my father that he was spoiling me. Since I did not know what spoiling a child meant, I had to try to work it out. At first it seemed that people were saying that Dad gave me too many presents. Of course he was generous, but on what he earned there was little money left over for gifts. But what he did give me was time and attention. He told me stories, explained things to me, read books to me, showed me what a beautiful and interesting world I lived in. He listened to what I had to say and he took me seriously as a person. Whereas the people who believed that he was spoiling me let me know that I was of no importance at all, or, worse, a nuisance, a blot upon the landscape. My father was giving me the courage and optimism to face life, to be myself, to speak up for myself and what I believed in. The people who feared that I might be 'spoilt' were saying, 'Go away. Be quiet. Nobody's interested in what you are or what you have to say. You are not important. You are a nothing.' I was an adult before I worked out what 'spoiling a child' means. 'Not spoiling' a child means trying to break that child's spirit.

Well, your spirit has certainly been bent, if not broken,

so now is the time to start putting it together again. You must begin by being kind to yourself and by letting other people be kind to you.

Of course, you feel that you don't deserve the kindness and concern of other people. Very often my clients tell me how they are wasting my valuable time and that I should really be seeing some more deserving client. (I know full well that these same clients will at some other time fend off any kindness and concern on my part with, 'She's paid to say those things.') Nowadays when my clients claim not to be deserving of my valuable time I just say, 'Don't be silly.' I used to go into long explanations of how everybody is deserving of help and how it is not right for me to judge one person as being better than another, but only to judge whether I might be able to help this particular person. I stopped giving this explanation when I realised that my depressed client would not appreciate the argument that all the people who come seeking help are equal in their right to be helped. My depressed client assumes that I am constantly judging, criticising, condemning others, because that is what he is doing – what you are doing.

And in this continual process of judging others, rather than accepting them, you work out careful sums of giving and taking. If anyone gives you something – a present or love – you feel that you must give something back in at least an equal amount. Presents, or their equivalent, can be quickly returned with the excuse to yourself that you do not want to be beholden to anyone. You have what someone once said about Arthur Koestler[4] 'the vanity to give but not the generosity to take.' When someone offers you love, in any of the many forms that love can take, you are in trouble. You see relationships as a constant balancing of the books and you fear making a debt, the repayment of which is beyond you. But if you want to get out of the prison of depression you have to learn that a loving relationship is not an exercise in bookkeeping. A loving relationship is not one where each person says, 'If you love me then I shall love you. If you are good to me then I shall be good to you. How can you expect me to love you when you do things that I don't want you to do? If you don't do what I want I shall stop loving you.' Relationships where these remarks are made are ones of commerce and blackmail.

When you are depressed you feel that all the love and kindness you once had has vanished, and so when someone offers you even the smallest modicum of love and kindness you feel that you should not accept it since you cannot return it in equal amounts. But now is the time to practise receiving. Practise just saying 'Thank you' when someone gives you something without adding 'You shouldn't have'. People like giving presents. Have the generosity to let them have the pleasure of giving. People like to be kind and helpful. Have the generosity to let them have the pleasure of being kind and helpful.

Practise, too, accepting compliments. Try to give up saying, 'This old dress, I've had it for years,' or 'I'm such a fool with figures. I coudn't have managed it without Jim's help' and so on. Try, even, paying yourself compliments. Now I know this is very hard. I well remember one night, years ago, when the Lincoln self-help Depressives Group had a visit from a psychologist who was interested in co-counselling. He talked to the group about this and then set them some co-counselling tasks. All went well until he asked them to say, one after another, something good about oneself. This request brought an embarrassed silence, and then the group leader burst into tears. Then there was much rushing to comfort her and much muttering about this psychologist who had upset everyone. He retreated, and nothing further was said about co-counselling for many months. Then, one evening when the group was together and feeling stronger, they decided to try this exercise again. Each person had to write down a list of his or her virtues. I was not there at the time but afterwards one of the members told me that out of a group of eight people only five virtues were acknowledged and one of these was 'playing chess'! They were still all enjoying the pride of humility!

Treating yourself kindly means looking after yourself and accepting yourself in all your humanness. You are not the most perfect, wonderful person that has ever graced this earth. Neither are you the worst, most imperfect, wicked person that has ever dared to draw breath. Like the rest of us, you are a mixture of good and bad, and all your good and bad are mixed up together and belong together. You are not as bad as you think and you are better than you acknowledge. Treat yourself kindly, and when this is hard to do, perhaps you might like to say to yourself the words of Gerard Manley Hopkins:

> My own heart let me more have pity on; let
> Me live to my sad self hereafter kind,
> Charitable; not live this tormented mind
> With this tormented mind tormenting yet.[5]

3 Put pills in your power

My mother always said that the reason doctors don't tell you things is that if they did you would soon know as much as they did. I think she was partly right. The other reason why doctors do not tell patients what they know is because they do not like admitting that they do not know. The extent of medical ignorance is far greater than the extent of medical knowledge, and this applies to all branches of medicine. However, one of the good things in medicine today is that fewer and fewer doctors are adopting the pose of the unapproachable autocrat who knows everything and says little, and then only to those closest to him in the medical hierarchy, barely acknowledging and rarely speaking to the humble, grateful and obedient patient, the lowest of the low, who receives his words like Moses receiving the Commandments. Thank goodness there are many more doctors around today who accept themselves as fallible human beings, of modest knowledge and skills, who share their knowledge and skills with their patients, since they know that they are like their patients, engaged upon mastering life's problems and that such problems are mastered through the search for truth and self-knowledge and not by lies, posing and posturing. Such doctors take the time to listen and to explain so that the patient remains in control of his life, helped by the doctor to make informed decisions.

Nevertheless, I still find many depressed people who accept what pills the doctor prescribes and obediently take them. They feel guilty if the pills do not work, and they apologise to the doctor as he writes out another prescription. There are people who will lie to the doctor, rather than see his disappointed face, or to get out of the surgery never to return. There are people who dutifully take the prescribed pills while silently worrying about harmful side effects and long-term addiction. There are people who have been taking pills for so long that they have come to believe that the daily ritual of taking pills is the only thing that stands between them and madness and death. Thus whenever a doctor tries to reduce the amount of tranquillisers, anti-depressants and sedatives absorbed every day, the person, fearing the loss of his ritual, immediately becomes more anxious and more depressed, often dramatically so, and so the doctor has to desist and let the ritual go on. Thus the pills are in control of the patient rather than the patient being in control of the pills.

So, if you are taking pills for depression, anxiety and insomnia, make sure you know enough about the pills to feel in control of them, knowing what kind of pills they are, what effects they are expected to have, and what effects they are having on you. To find out about the different kinds of pills you will probably need to do some reading. No doubt your doctor told you something about them when he prescribed them, but however adequate an explanation is in the surgery, it is impossible to take it all in and of course you cannot refer back to it to check something. Fortunately nowadays there are a number of useful publications about the drugs used in psychiatry. Malcolm Lader,[6] the Professor of Pharmacology at the Institute of Psychiatry, London, has written a brief, informative booklet for the National Association for Mental Health. In it he says, 'Not much is understood about the biochemistry of depression and its treatment, except in general terms.' In discussing the response of depressed patients to tricyclic anti-depressants, the most commonly used anti-depressant, Lader remarked, 'This suggests that the therapeutic action of anti-depressants is not to *cure* the depression itself but to hold the symptoms in check until the illness lifts of its own accord.' Thus anti-depressants and tranquillisers are like aspirin. They do not remove the cause of the pain but simply reduce the amount of pain, thus allowing you to get on with your life and to work out what has gone wrong with your life and what you need to do to put things to rights.

In the chapter 'Drug treatments for depression' in his book *Overcoming Depression*, Andrew Stanway[7] includes in his list of the side-effects of the tricyclic anti-depressants something called 'fuzzy thinking'. My depressed clients who are on large doses of anti-depressants, sedatives and tranquillisers often complain that they cannot think clearly. This makes it very difficult for them to go through the work of reviewing and reassessing which is the essence of the psychotherapeutic process. The 'fuzzy thinking' is part of the pain-killing effects of the medication, with pain-arousing thoughts no longer coming so clearly into consciousness. This

is where you need to be in control of your drugs, so you can decide how clearly you want to be able to think and to interact with your environment, and how much you want the pain to be dulled. This is the principle which is followed now in the care of people with cancer. Such people used to be drugged into stupor to reduce their awareness of pain. Now each person is encouraged to make a judgment about how much pain can be tolerated to allow the person to go on living as ordinary and pleasant a life as possible. In this kind of medical care the patient is recognised as the expert on his own pain, the person who decides what is tolerable and desirable. The patient is responsible for his own pain.

This is what some depressed people manage to do for themselves. Some decide not to take any medication, preferring to stay with the pain and work through it. Some people get to know their medication and so discover what drugs actually reduce the pain without too many unpleasant side-effects and when it is useful to take them. They make judgments like, 'I can manage staff meetings but when it's my turn to take school assembly I get very anxious. So I take a librium half an hour before I'm due on the stage' or 'It's not worth taking those anti-depressants where I have to watch what I eat – no cheese, or Marmite, or alcohol. It just makes too many complications in the family meals.'

Strong anxiety impedes clear thinking, and when medication makes clear thinking even more difficult, it is no wonder that some people fear that something has gone wrong with their brain and that their memory no longer functions properly. If as well they have had ECT, which does interrupt the memory processes, their anxiety about their memory becomes even greater. If their experience of ECT has been followed by a feeling of greater liveliness and happiness then the interference with memory is not a problem, but if there has been no change or if the person has been living fairly easily for a while and then plunged into another state of depression and the doctor suggests another course of ECT the question of how the person's memory has been affected becomes pressing. My depressed clients often ask me what I think about ECT and whether I would advise them to have it. My answer is simply that ordinarily I would not approve of a person having his chest cut open or being thumped heavily and persistently on his chest, but when these are the ways of getting the person's heart to start functioning again, then of course I approve. ECT has an equally dramatic and usually successful life-saving effect on a person who has become so depressed that he is immobile and starving or agitated to the point of exhaustion. But if you have a heart that threatens to stop, you cannot live your life hoping that every time it does there will be someone close by to thump you in the right way to get it going again. Instead you have to alter your way of living so as to create the conditions which will keep your heart going of its own accord. Similarly, you cannot live your life hoping that every time you get depressed someone will give you ECT which, like a magic wand, will drive out all your bad thoughts, leaving only good thoughts and a happy mood. Instead you have to alter your way of living so as to create the conditions which enable you to live wisely and harmoniously, not dependent on pills and ECT.

If you are worried about your memory and fear that it may be damaged beyond repair then give some thought to something you know quite well – remembering is one of those processes where the more you try the less you can. Trying to remember is always a fruitless process. If someone says to you, 'What kind of refrigerator do you have?' the answer either comes to you or it does not. If it does not, trying to remember will produce nothing. You have to wait until the answer comes suddenly and spontaneously into your mind. Memory is a spontaneous process. It is not something you can control.

Of course you can discover some ways of encouraging the spontaneous ideas to appear. Witness that common exchange between mother and child.

'Where's my school bag?'

'Where did you have it last?'

The wise child soon realises that the mother is not being obstructive and difficult but is encouraging the child to think about the places and activities associated with the bag and then the memory and perhaps the bag may reappear. We cannot force a memory out of our mind like an inch of tooth-paste out of a tube, but we can create the conditions in which the memory may spontaneously appear.

Many of my depressed clients are not greatly pleased when I point out to them that, depression quite apart, their ability to remember recent events is decreasing because they are getting older. But of course this is what happens to all of us, and most of us adapt to this change by finding systematic ways of reminding ourselves of things that we need to remember. I organise my work by using a thick diary where I note down all the things I have to do and all the information that in earlier years I would have remembered without difficulty. I also write lists of work to be prepared and oh, the pleasure of crossing items off the list. I never go shopping without a list, and if I find that there is something at home which I need to bring to work I put a note in my make-up bag to remind me when I am getting dressed the next morning. As well as helping my memory, all this list writing helps me feel that I have my life well organised and well controlled.

But sometimes all this organisation is threatened by events over which I have no control. Then I start to worry, and it is then that I have to find, yet again, that peaceful place within myself.

4 Create a peaceful place within yourself

When Chalky first came to see me he told me of the pains he had in his chest and arms – sometimes a dull ache, sometimes a sudden stabbing pain in his chest or a darting pain down his arm. I asked him what he thought was causing the pain.

He looked even more anxious. 'I think it's – it's my heart. The doctor just dismisses it. Says it's just tension. He might be just telling me that so I won't worry.'

He sat stiffly, forward in his seat, hands clenched on his knees. I tried to get him to relax. You could have cracked walnuts on his chest and arms. He smiled apologetically at his failure to follow my instructions to relax and, as I explained how prolonged tension in the muscles produces pain and other strange sensations, he looked politely disbelieving. Nothing I could say would take his suffering away from him.

So we talked of other symptoms of his depressed state –

how he could not think clearly, how he dreaded every day, how meaningless life had become, how he struggled to keep going for if, for a moment, he faltered, he would plunge into a far greater, deeper depression.

'The bottomless pit of chaos, madness and death?' I asked.

'Yes,' he said.

So much for my attempts to get him to relax.

This is why depressed people cannot manage to relax. It is not that they are in some mysterious way prevented from relaxing but that they fear that if they do stop struggling and let themselves relax something far worse will happen to them.

But it will not. If you stop struggling, if you seek ways of relaxing and finding an area of peace within yourself, you will *not* fall down into the pit of depression. You will not become mad or die.

Being depressed is like being thrown into a pool of deep water. If you struggle and splash around helplessly you keep going under the water, the water gets in your eyes and nose and mouth, and you get tired and feel sick. But if you stay still, the water itself holds you up and you gently float. If you want to get out of the prison of depression you need to let your own natural resources buoy you up. Stop struggling and you will be all right. This may sound crazy, but no more so than that advice about what to do when your car goes into a skid. Turn the steering wheel in the direction of the skid. That advice always sounds wrong to a novice driver, but experienced drivers know that it is true.

So how do you learn to stop struggling and to create a peaceful place within yourself?

First, learn the techniques of relaxation and practise them regularly. The basic principle is simply to choose a set of muscles in any part of the body, clench these muscles and then let go. You can work systematically through every part of your body, and finish in a state of complete relaxation, or you can become aware of an area of tension – the muscles of your face set into a frown, or shallow breathing and a tightness in your chest – and consciously you tighten and let go and take some slow, deep breaths. It is a good idea to have some skilled instruction first. You can join a relaxation or yoga class, or buy one of the many relaxation tapes that are readily available now. If possible listen to the tape before you acquire it. Check that the voice on the tape sounds pleasant to you and, if the full relaxation is accompanied by a guided fantasy, that the picture you are expected to imagine suits you. In my yoga class our teacher during full relaxation will take us for an imaginary walk beside a lake and through a forest. All goes well for me until he mentions fir trees. All my forests contain eucalyptus.

It is a good idea to have some lessons with an experienced teacher of relaxation methods because you are probably so tense in some parts of your body that you have lost all awareness that those parts of your body can be relaxed. When I first started yoga my teacher would say, 'Now relax your shoulders,' and I would think, 'How stupid. How can you relax your shoulders? Your shoulders are just there.' It took me a while to discover that I was holding my shoulders 'just there' and that I could relax them. Then I came to realise how stiff my shoulders were and how tight the tendons were around my armpits, shoulder blades and upper spine. One friend, greatly experienced in yoga theory as well as practice, pointed out that I was holding myself in a 'flinching away from pain' posture, even though life was no longer dealing me the blows which required such a reaction. I practised my yoga diligently, and now I flinch only at the appropriate times, and when I do I practise relaxing my shoulders.

Once you learn the knack of relaxing your body you can practise it quietly when you have a spare half hour or when you are faced with a difficult situation and you can feel the tension rising. But relaxing the body does not always relax the mind. The old worrying thoughts can keep scurrying about there like noisesome rats. You have to find ways of quietening, relaxing your mind.

Richard is a young man who has had a very difficult life. One evening at the Lincoln Depressives' Group, when we were playing our favourite records, Richard told me that he had brought along his record of the Toccata from Widor's Fifth Organ Symphony. 'Every time I hear it,' he said, 'it fetches me out of depression.' This is what you must discover

– what sights or sounds take you out of the worrying round of immediate reality and into something more real, more beautiful, more important and more than yourself. I look at the sky, or trees, or birds, or usually all three together. I chose to live in a house which, though full of many imperfections, gives an immediate vista from each window of sky, trees and grass. I find that my garden calms and sustains me. At work my usual chair faces the window where I can see a row of poplar trees and the sky beyond.

When we take the time to look at nature, or to listen to music, or to read a poem we move into that quiet and concentrated state which is the essence of meditation, and meditation is all about finding that peaceful place within yourself and using it as a source of courage and strength. Meditation is not about sitting cross-legged for days and going into a trance and becoming very strange. Meditation is about discovering for yourself something that has been known by all peoples, all cultures and all religions. Le Shan,[9] whose excellent book on meditation is well worth reading, wrote,

> We meditate to find, to recover, to come back to
> something of ourselves we once dimly and unknowingly
> had and have lost without knowing what it was or
> where or when we lost it.

This is in effect what Krishnamurti teaches, 'There is nowhere to go. You are already there.' He said,

> Wander by the seashore and let this meditative quality
> come upon you. If it does, don't pursue it. What you
> pursue will be the memory of what it was and what was
> is the death of what is. Or when you wander among the
> hills, let everything tell you the beauty and the pain of
> life, so that you awaken to your own sorrow and to the
> ending of it.[10]

Meditation has a long Christian tradition,[11] beginning with Jesus' vigil in the wilderness. The early Christian monks who withdrew to solitude in the desert meditated by using the repetition of the prayer, 'Lord Jesus Christ, Son of God have mercy on me, a miserable sinner.' St Augustine taught that contemplation was essential for the soul to find

God. The religious houses which grew up in the Middle Ages provided a retreat for meditation, and such retreats are still available today, not only for those men and women who join a religious order but for those people who wish to withdraw for just a few days. A friend of mine went to a Quaker retreat for several weeks after her husband had died suddenly. There, she later told me, she had time to be alone, to sit in her room or to walk in the garden, or to be with people when she needed to be with people. If you want to find within the context of your Christian beliefs your way out of the prison of depression, you should consider making a retreat or joining one of the informal groups who get together for a few hours' meditation and communion.

If you would like to make a retreat but not necessarily a Christian one, there are now in Britain and America a number of communities of followers of the Eastern philosophies which offer the experience of a retreat and meditation. Such an experience can be very much like psychotherapy, since the ways of life in Buddhism, Taoism, Vedanta and Yoga very much resemble psychotherapy.[12]

Yoga has become so popular now that there should be a class close by to you which you could join. If you are worried about looking funny in a leotard and tights (everyone looks funny in leotard and tights) get a track suit or loose fitting trousers and top. You will also need a piece of carpet about as long and as wide as you are and a small cushion. In class there is no competition. Each person works at her or his own pace and own level. As my teacher always says, 'Go as far as you can – and then a little bit further.' You learn to stretch and bend your body, to control your breathing, to relax, to pay attention to yourself in the here and now (what is called centring) and to meditate.

Whether or not you join a meditation class, learning to meditate is something you have to do for yourself. You have to find what is the right way to meditate *for you*. Other people will make different suggestions and you can try each one out to see what works for you, but, whatever meditative path you follow, it must be your own.

To start, you have to find or create some space and time for yourself. This may mean ignoring the state of the kitchen floor or telling the family to leave you alone for an hour. Then you need to work out what is the most comfortable way for you to sit. Lying down is not recommended, since you tend to go off to sleep instead of keeping watchful attention. You can sit cross-legged on the floor (a small cushion under your buttocks helps to maintain a more comfortable posture) or you can sit in a chair which supports you comfortably. Some people cover their heads with a shawl; some people close their eyes; some people focus on a small object like a stone or a flower. Then you begin the process of centring, of bringing your thoughts back into yourself and becoming aware of where you are, how you are sitting, how your body is feeling. You breathe deeply and slowly, and as you do you attend to one thing. It may be your breath which you observe going in and out. You may count your breaths, and each time you find your attention wandering, you go back to one. You may think of a colour, and watch it with your inner eye. Or you may take a word or phrase and say it over and over with complete attention. It might be a mantra taken from Eastern literature, or a phrase which carries special meaning for you, like 'Love and hope', or 'Peace and light', or a verse whose meaning grows with familiarity like Julian of Norwich's

All shall be well and all shall be well and all manner of things shall be well.

As you do this, other thoughts will come into your mind. You just let them come and go while you pay attention to your breath, or your colour, or your mantra or your verse. At first you may find this very difficult, but you must persevere. At first you may manage to sit for only a few minutes, but as you come to discover that not only is sitting in meditation pleasant, but it leaves you with a continuing sense of peace and relaxation, and so you will naturally lengthen the time that you sit. Of course there are bad days when worrying thoughts will intrude and distract you from the immediate present, but do not give up. Let those bad days come and go too.

When you come to realise that nothing, not even the blackest, most terrible day of your life, goes on forever, then you are able to let things come and go and to pay attention to the present. In meditation we are practising the art of *mind-*

fulness, of *paying attention to one thing at a time in the here
and now*. Like looking at a small child's face and thinking
how beautiful she is, instead of regretting the circumstances
of her birth, or fearing that you are too inadequate to be a
parent, or envying her security as a child, or dreading what
may happen to her in the years to come. Like preparing a
meal and paying attention to the food itself and what you are
doing, instead of worrying about whether it will turn out all
right, or whether your family will like it, or being angry
because no one appreciates you, or thinking about what job
you must do next and the one after that and how on earth will
you get it all done. Mindfulness means paying attention to
the here and now and not worrying about results, paying
attention to what is and not to what might be. Learning how
to be mindful is learning how to be. The Zen arts[13] have
specialised in teaching how to be mindful and how to discover
the beauty of your own spontaneity. You may decide to study
one of these arts in order to learn how to live in the present,
the only place where we can live.

But to relax, meditate, be mindful and spontaneous, you
have to learn to trust yourself, and that means trusting
others.

5 Risk putting some trust in yourself and others

If you see yourself as bad, evil, unacceptable to yourself and
to other people, then you cannot trust yourself. If you fear,
hate and envy other people, you certainly cannot trust them.
If your religious or philosophical beliefs render you fearful
and pessimistic, then you cannot trust God or whatever you
see as the powerful forces which contain the universe. Trusting nobody, you must be constantly afraid.

There was a time when you trusted others and the world
you lived in. But then other people abused your trust, and the
world dealt you some unexpected and terrible blows. Some of
these things will have happened in your adult life and some
in your childhood.

In depression you are defending a position which you
adopted as a child when you were under very great threat. We
like to think that children are innocent in the sense that they

are not responsible for their opinions and actions but produce their opinions and actions as a result of the treatment they receive from the adults around them. Yet, what happens to all of us in childhood is that we are placed in moral dilemmas which offer us several courses of action. Being young and uninformed we may see only two possibilities when, in fact, other choices are available. Nevertheless, as children we have a choice and we make a choice. Jackie's story of the Noddy Clock shows a child being placed in a moral dilemma no different from that which many adults have to face — whether to tell the truth and to go on suffering and to allow others to suffer, or to lie to prevent the suffering of others and risk being found out as a liar.

A stark choice between two grim alternatives leaves the child with the question of how much courage he can summon to his aid. Faced with the choice between seeing your parents as wicked or yourself as wicked, one child might decide to be brave, to recognise that the people on whom he depends are incompetent or malicious, and so he has to look after himself, while another child might be too frightened to depend on himself and so decides that he must be the wicked one and his parents good. Thus in the same family with the same parents, one child may grow up rebellious and independent, and another child conforming and dependent. As children we made certain choices. As adults we are free to change these choices. Let me repeat, what matters is not what our parents did to us but what we do with what our parents did to us.

Children who decide to be independent grow up trusting themselves. Children who decide to conform to the demands of the adults around them develop very little trust in themselves. They always persuade themselves that other people know best, that other people are better and wiser than they can ever be. Conforming children whose parents are more often than not wise and good do not have to alter their perception of reality to make it fit their dream that the people around them love them and will protect them. But conforming children whose parents fail to be sufficiently wise and good often have to alter their perception of reality very drastically to make it fit their dream of perfect parents protecting them from all dangers. They cannot bear to see their parents as weak, inadequate, cruel or uncaring. So they have to lie to themselves, and lying to yourself always leads to trouble. A wife who insists to herself that her alcoholic husband 'really does care' usually ends up sacrificing her children for her husband. A man who tells himself that his competitive devotion to his work is 'really all for the family's sake' closes his eyes to his wife's distress and his children's anger. If we lie to ourselves long enough we lose the ability to distinguish between truth and falsity. When we cannot tell what is true for us we lose touch with who we are. One depressed person will say, 'I feel as though I don't exist.' Another will say, 'I am not in control of my mind.'

This, one way or another, is the path you have taken into the prison of depression. Not trusting yourself has rendered you helpless. Lying to yourself has made you lose touch with yourself. Both conditions are terrible but not irreversible. You can choose to trust yourself and to take responsibility for yourself. You can find yourself simply by accepting yourself. You have not gone away or ceased to exist. All you have to do is to *be yourself*.

When one of my clients tells me that he has decided to be himself I know that our meetings will soon come to an end. Val announced one day that she had decided to give up worrying that she was not the perfect mother, wife and daughter. She had decided to be herself. 'They will all have to accept me as I am,' she said, 'I'm not going to stay in just because the children think I ought to be there to wait on them. I'm not going to expect that my husband and I should have the same interests. If I want to garden or work on my photography I'll do it. And I'll try to accept mother as she is. If she wants to give us presents, I'll let her.' On her next visit to me she said, 'What I'd like is to have a three month break from seeing you. I'd like to see if I can get on all right on my own.' I knew she would be all right, just as I discovered Nick would be.

Nick was a very handsome, witty young man, and I found his company a delight, but he considered himself the most boring person in the world, a blight on any company. It was important, he said, to make a

worthwhile contribution in a social group. His
childhood experiences had taught him that this was the
way his parents judged people and he accepted this as
an axiomatic truth which he applied to himself and
others. The trouble was that he did not feel that he
could make a proper contribution to the group. The
social life of his family and friends centred on a pub
where they would meet regularly on a Friday and
Saturday night. Nick would spend a long time getting
himself properly dressed for these occasions and he
would become increasingly tense as he tried to prepare
himself to have plenty of witty things to say to his
friends. Once there, he felt himself to be grossly
awkward and tongue-tied, and the misery set in. But he
could neither avoid these social evenings nor devalue
their implications. So he stayed depressed, until one
day he arrived in my office beaming with happiness. He
said that on the previous Friday when he was getting
ready to go to the pub, he suddenly decided that, 'I was
going to relax and try and be myself. I did this – I didn't
try to crack any witties and get in with the group, and
as I did this I started to enjoy it. Funnily enough,
something did come to me that I really wanted to say,
when I didn't try to. When I tried to say something,
force myself, I'd say something that was alien – it didn't
make sense. But at the weekend things started coming
to me that I wanted to say and people were listening. It
was Friday night and I went through the same things –
the washing hair routine, all that jazz, and it came to
me in a flash that I could stop if I wanted to. I was
dreading going out, and I thought, why, if this makes
me feel that bad, why should I worry about other people.
I'll just go out and make sure I enjoy myself, and as soon
as I did that I wasn't worried. I felt like a different
person in a way. I was like a different person to myself.
With my parents, I've always felt that if I wanted to say
anything to offend my parents I shouldn't say it, and in
the end you don't have anything to say. It was like a
sudden enlightenment. We went to the same pub we
normally go to on a Friday night, but it seemed like a

different place to me, it seemed fresher, seemed to be more exciting, everything was great.' Such a discovery rendered me superfluous, and Nick no longer came to brighten my Monday mornings.[14]

Not trusting other people can come out in our behaviour in all sorts of ways. It can be in a fear of flying, because you cannot put your safety totally into the hands of other people. It may be an inability to use a public toilet or even a toilet in a friend's house because you do not trust another person to keep a toilet really clean. Or it may be in the complications of distrusting oneself and others that Jean described in one of her letters to me.

I find myself in states of raw red rage for days on end. I can find all sorts of reasons for my rage – the main one being my childish inability to accept the fact that the world is not perfect, and I realise it is going to take an awfully long time before acceptance of that fact is totally absorbed. Now the question is – what the Hell do I do with all that anger in the meantime? I think I know the answer. Jack pointed out that Anger is emerging and can be channelled, but I have been finding it tricky, because I have to keep my life paced to meet a lot of Emily's demands, which means containing a great deal of anger until I can find an appropriate outlet – tricky to release blind fury in a controlled manner whilst playing picture dominoes. I can hear you saying, 'Who said it would be easy?' . . . Where did all this anger spring from? It's been going on and building up for weeks – since the beginning of the invasion of our house by all sorts of friends and relations. I find it hard to relate to people honestly because of the Should and Ought in my head. Until I married my mother criticised out of existence every friend I ever had, consequently I prejudged all people I met by her standards, and of course never found anyone to like at all! I still suffer from this, and find it hard not to over-react and allow the free run of my heart and home to everyone. Or to find out what my true feelings about people are.

Sometimes not trusting others means expecting gratitude. You cannot take your family's and friends' love on trust. If you give them anything – presents, affection or your time and effort – you expect them to make their gratitude quite explicit, on the principle that seeing is believing. When such gratitude is not forthcoming you feel neglected and you complain. 'After all I've done for you' has alienated more children from their parents than any act of parental cruelty.

Usually not trusting others means keeping secrets and not confiding in others. That way you can both protect yourself and control other people since they can act only on limited information about you. You feel that you must try to control people, especially the people you love and depend on, and thus you create a power struggle where there should be love freely given and received.

Trusting other people should not be an either/or situation – either you trust someone or you don't. Each of us can be trusted in different ways and in different situations. To work out whether you can trust another person to behave in a certain way, we need to understand that person to the best of our ability. Sometimes a person appears to be untrustworthy but is, in reality, responding to the demands of a situation of which we are ignorant. A mother may be horrified to discover that her son is stealing money from her purse and spending it on sweets. What she does not know is that he feels that he has to purchase his popularity at school and he does not trust her enough to tell her.

Risking trusting others means learning more about other people and more about yourself. Then your acts of trust and mistrust are informed decisions and not the outcome of blind prejudice. Remember, trusting means hoping, and hoping means uncertainty. Trusting yourself and others means accepting uncertainty.

Rather than accepting uncertainty, when you were a child you constructed a simple view of the world, possibly with a predictable God, where virtue was rewarded and vice punished. When you discovered that the world does not work in this just and fair way you felt betrayed. My friend Jeffrey Russell who, as a mediaeval historian and a devout Christian, has studied the concepts of evil down the ages,[15] wrote to me recently to comment on my book *The Construction of Life and Death* and said,

> Another aspect of facing death is the sense that it's not
> fair if we've been nice girls and boys. Do you recall one
> of the most striking pictures to come out of the Warsaw
> ghetto? It's a small boy, perhaps ten years old, cowering
> against a wall as four heavily-armed Nazis approach
> him. The look on his face might as well be in writing:
> 'But Mummy told me that nothing would happen to me
> if I was a good boy.' So long as we hold to the illusion
> that God, or the cosmos, or whatever, will not harm us if
> we are good little children, we will not be able to
> construct death (and therefore, as you show so clearly,
> life either) in any meaningful way.[16]

Your lack of trust in God, or the cosmos, is the mistrust of someone who has been betrayed, and not the acceptance that life is a chancy, unpredictable business. You are trying, still, to hang on to your belief that if you are good everything will be all right. Sheldon Kopp calls this state 'pseudo-innocence'.[17]

> Unwilling to tolerate life's ambiguity, its
> unresolvability, its inevitability, we search for
> certainty, demanding that someone provide it.
> Stubbornly, relentlessly, we seek the wise man, the
> wizard, the good parent, someone else who will show us
> the way.
> Surely *someone* must know. It simply cannot be that
> life is just what it appears to be, that there are no
> hidden warnings, that this is it, just this and nothing
> more. It's not fair, not enough! We cannot possibly bear
> having to live life as it is, without reassurance, without
> being special, without even being offered some
> comforting explanations. Come on now! Come across!
> You've got to give us something to make it all right. The
> medicine tastes lousy. Why should we have to swallow
> it just because it's the only thing we *can* do? Can't you
> at least promise that we will have to take it just once,
> that it won't taste *that* bad, that we will be just fine

immediately afterward, that we will be glad we took it?
No? Well then, surely, at least you have to give us a
lollipop for being good.

But what if we are talking to ourselves? What if there
is no-one out there listening? What if for each of us the
only wise man, the only wizard, the only good parent we
will ever have is our own helpless vulnerable self? What
then?

What then indeed. Are you going to spend your life
looking for someone to protect you? Are you going to go on
hanging on to your parents, trying to make them into good
parents? Are you going to go on trying to make your spouse
into the perfect partner? Are you going to go on expecting God
to answer your prayers and to reward you when you are good?
(Some people say that God always answers our prayers, but
that sometimes His answer is No.) Are you going to go on
looking for the doctor who will take away your pain with a
magic pill? Are you going to go on looking for the therapist
who, with a magic word, will abolish all your misery?
Perhaps there is a guru who can do the trick. If only you could
find him. But then when you do meet a guru, this is what he is
likely to say,

> He who is in search of a guru should first seek the guru
> within himself. If he seeks a guru outside without
> seeking the guru within, then he is consciously and
> unconsciously stupefying himself. He who has no faith
> or confidence in his own inner guru and is trying to
> have faith and confidence in an outer guru, such a
> person may enjoy his illusions for a while, but
> ultimately he is forced to be disillusioned.
>
> Guru consists of two syllables *gu* and *ru*; gu
> (darkness) and ru (remover). He who removes darkness
> from our understanding is the real guru, and such a
> guru and his 'office' are always open in our hearts . . . if
> one cannot contact directly with the inner guru, then
> one must seek for an outer guru. The outer guru is he
> who guides the true seeker into this inner journey for
> the intimate contact with the inner guru.[18]

So, to find your way out of the prison of depression you have to trust yourself. But how can I do that, you ask, when I am so helpless and despairing? Just the right state to be in, says the philosopher Joseph Needleman.

> It's in weakness there's strength. If we can stay weak and keep open, keep moving around and come to the point where we just give up and know that what we are doing, where we are going is hopeless, really hopeless, and not grab on to something else and try to build a structure out of it, then we reach a state which in the traditions of the West is called Despair. Another word for this Despair in this sense is Deep Openness. When you're in Despair, when you come to the end of the rope, only then can help come.[19]

6 Find someone to talk things over with

Help comes in two ways – from yourself and from other people. But help cannot come from other people unless you are prepared to find it and to accept it. You have to find the people to confide in, and you have to overcome your habit of keeping things to yourself. Perhaps you are ready to confide in someone, but there is no one available. Your family will not listen, and your doctor prefers to write you a prescription rather than give you his listening attention.

So you need to find someone who will listen. Someone outside the family and, possibly, outside work, is usually best – someone who has no vested interest in keeping you as you are or who has no reason to feel guilty about what you might disclose. It need not necessarily be just one person. On your journey out of your prison you will meet many different gurus, people who throw light on your darkness. A nurse might listen to your fears about your health and the drugs you take, and may find the words to calm your fears. A friend may share with you the burden of family responsibilities. A parson or priest might listen and acknowledge your religious doubts and fears and impart the courage and trust which enables you to deal with these. Of course, not everyone you hope to confide in will respond in a helpful way. Many nurses will tell you that doctor knows best and hurry up and take your medicine. Friends may have so many concerns of their own that they do not want to know about yours, while some parsons and priests have all the sensitivity and understanding of an old boot and so always resort to their 'religious' language whenever they have to face real suffering. Nevertheless, 'Seek and ye shall find' or 'when the pupil is ready the master appears'. When you are prepared to set out on your journey without maps, you will find some friends who will listen and accompany you for part of the way.

You might like to consult a professional listener of some sort. You may find someone in the Health Service, or you might go to a private therapist. Talking to people who have been depressed and are now coping is tremendously helpful. Tony Lewis in his articles in the *Guardian* on his experience of depression during which he tried to kill himself, said,

> I would like to make a few suggestions for those finding themselves in my situation. First, accept and believe in the fact that you will recover, however hopeless everything seems. Secondly, make sure that your food is good and wholesome. Emotional problems use up a lot of energy, and if you don't eat properly you feel tired. Again, the stomach reacts quickly and sensitively to stress (this is exemplified by the sensation produced there when someone sees a horrific sight) and if you are anxious your stomach produces a lot of acid which should be neutralized.
>
> Equally important, try to keep fit. I always feel better after exercise, and therefore take part in yoga, walk a lot and swim a great deal. (It was only this year, by the way, that I overcame my ten-year phobia about water.)
>
> Another useful factor was the creation of a daily routine. Without some kind of time-table the day may seem endless and even the smallest decisions become difficult. So when you get up write out on a piece of paper all you intend to do and keep to it. This helped me. I was also grateful to have a lifeline with other people in the form of a club I belonged to. In that friendly, support atmosphere I felt relatively safe.

Talking to people was a great help. I found it especially comforting to have the counsel of people who had been through the same kinds of experiences I suffered.[20]

The club Tony Lewis spoke of could have been one organised by the Social Services, or by a voluntary organisation, or by a group of people who have decided to help themselves. Unless you live in the depths of the country, there will be group like one of these near by that you could join. If there isn't, start a group yourself. (More of this later.)

In looking for someone to talk to, inspect your friends and acquaintances. Something I have often noticed with my depressed clients is that many of them, when they first come to see me, give me the impression that they have not a friend in the world. They speak only of their families. Then one day my client tells me about a conversation with an acquaintance, and lo and behold it turns out that this acquaintance has been depressed and has got over it, and this acquaintance says such helpful, courage-strengthening things. My client is greatly impressed and sees more of the acquaintance who rapidly becomes a friend. It seems to me that this acquaintance has always been available as a friend, but my client has never seen it until now.

Friends are wonderful people. I always regret that I do not devote more time to my friends – write them longer letters more frequently, visit them more often, invite them here more often – but in my mental map of my world my friends stand like giant statues of themselves. My friends are the people with whom I have a continuing conversation. There may be long gaps between exchanges, since many of them live in Australia or America, but the conversation is never interrupted or concluded.

To turn an acquaintance into a friend you have to give that person time and attention. If you have no friends it is because you are so wrapped up in yourself that you do not give other people your time and attention. One part of not giving time and attention to other people is fearing that if you do they will reject you. The other part is feeling that other people are boring and you have better things to do than talk to them. But if you want to find your way out of the prison of depression, you need friends.

Carol Parris[21] recently interviewed a group of forty women who live in Lambeth, London, and asked them about their health and about their friends. She found that out of the forty women only thirteen had not 'visited the doctor and received a prescription for tranquillizers or anti-depressants at some stage in time as wives and mothers.' To the question, 'Do you have any friends that you are particularly close to?', she found that ten of them had no close friends at all, while most had only one close friend. She found that many women had strong relationships with their families. One said, 'We do a lot around the family, all of us. We don't do anything without phoning each other. We speak to each other every day on the phone. I can confide in my sister almost anything. But Mum still rules the roost and we don't do anything without telling her.'

Another woman said, 'When my mother was alive she was with me every day. I suppose that I didn't think I needed anyone else. I was very hurt when my mum died. I could talk to my mum about anything and I don't think even my husband and I have such a close relationship. A lot of men, I don't think they have the closeness, somehow.'

The value of a friendship with another woman was seen as being linked to shared experience. A woman said, 'If I stopped seeing my friends I'd be back on the lonely trail, wouldn't I? If we all stopped being friends, I'd be back how I was before, back to the depression stage. I find talking to my friends can be a lot easier than talking to my husband. Let's face it, he's a smashing bloke but he can't understand. He can't understand. He's at work all day so he can't understand the situation. Where if you speak to the girls they're more sympathetic. They're in the same boat as me. They've all got young children at home, and if I feel a bit down about something I can talk to them about it and I find I feel a lot better.' Carol Parris commented, 'The women I interviewed spoke enthusiastically of the way in which friendships with other women eased personal worries and frequently became substitutes for visits to the doctor.' One woman said, 'My relationship with my friend Jean is probably the strongest one because we can discuss anything with each other, you know, and if I've got any worries I'd come and talk to her and get it off my chest. I suppose it's why I don't go to the doctors so much. Things are not so bad once you have spoken about them, and we laugh about them and in a couple of days' time it's all right.'

A friend is someone whom we know and love and who knows and loves us. Even though you fear that if someone knows you that person must certainly reject you, you must risk rejection (not everyone will reject you, really) since, as Sheldon Kopp said, 'Who can love me if no one knows me?'[22]

In confiding in another person we are, in effect, telling our tale. Each of us has a story, the story of our life, and as we tell that story, or just part of it, we know that our life has significance, at least in our eyes and the eyes of the person who listens. One of the saddest things I find again and again in my work, is that so many of the troubled people who come to see me have never had the chance to tell their story. No one in their family has listened. In the person's sorry round from doctor to doctor, in and out of hospital, no one has ever sat down with the person and let him tell his tale in his own way. Of course case histories have been taken, but in those the doctor or the social worker have asked about what they thought was important. And you cannot tell your story to someone who can only spare you a few minutes of his precious time. So when the person finally gets to me and realises that I am prepared to listen (Prepared! My idea of heaven is being in a garden with people who tell me stories), the relief of telling the story is sometimes all the person needs to find his way out of his troubles.

In listening to another person's story we are, in effect, bearing witness to that person's existence, courage, suffering and pain. We open ourselves to the anguish of witnessing another person's suffering. Sometimes we can relieve our own anguish by hastening to cure the person's pain and to put right what has gone wrong, but so often there is nothing we can do. Then we have to be able to face our own helplessness and not preserve a glorified image of ourselves and reduce our pain by denying the other person's truth. For if we do this we wound the sufferer even more. As Jill Tweedie wrote,[23]

Ex-depressive as I am, with only the occasional lapse, I

cannot dismiss the idea that the vision of life seen in depression has the truth in it, the bare-boned skeletal truth, and an intrinsic part of depression is knowing this and being told that it is not so. Reality, however terrible, is bearable if others allow its reality. When they refuse you that, when they skip around you pretending you've got it wrong, that's rock-bottom time.

7 Discover that there's nothing wrong with seeing the funny side of things

What's funny about being depressed, you might ask. Of course, some depressed people do laugh. Some of you keep up a smile and a joke so no one will know how you really feel. Some of you laugh and feel what T.S. Eliot called

> the conscious impotence of rage
> At human folly, and the laceration
> Of laughter at what ceases to amuse[24]

Some of you never laugh and joke, not because you have no sense of humour (everyone has a sense of humour) but because you believe that life is a serious matter and to be a good person you must always take things seriously. You would never dream of laughing at anyone, because if you laugh at anyone that means that you don't love that person.

What rubbish! As anyone who manages to cope in any way with his life will tell you, one thing that makes life bearable is that it is funny, and that when we laugh at people we love we are showing that we love them for what they are, that we accept them as they are. When we laugh at ourselves we show that we accept ourselves. We all have our pretensions to exceptional greatness and goodness, and we will not give them up, but we know that they are pretensions, and therefore ridiculous, and we laugh at them, not in bitterness but in love. Laughter puts sensible limits on our pride.

One of the reasons that your parents, especially your mother, looms so large in your life, is that you dare not laugh at them. You want to see them as super-human, larger than life and you do not want to risk upsetting them. All children laugh at their parents, but some parents punish their

children severely for this and insist that the child must
accept the parent's evaluation of himself or herself as a
dignified, important person. Some parents want to insist that
their way of seeing the world is the only true one, so of course
they must forbid their children to laugh at them. What humour shows is that there is *always* another way of seeing things.

Yet, what else can you do about your parents, but laugh
at them? Most parents, by the time their children are grown
up, are too old and set in their ways to change very much, and
most of what they do which upsets you, upsets you simply
because you see it that way. Laughter is your way of seeing
things differently. Laughter means that you can love your
parents for what they are, that you can accept them and no
longer be afraid of them. Laughter casts out fear.

Harry Williams said of laughter,

> God, we believe, accepts us, accepts all men,
> unconditionally, warts and all. Laughter is the purest
> form of our response to God's acceptance of us. For when
> I laugh at myself I accept myself and when I laugh at
> other people in genuine mirth I accept them.
> Self-acceptance in laughter is the very opposite of
> self-accusation or pride. For in laughter I accept myself
> not because I'm some sort of super-person, but precisely
> because I'm not. There is nothing funny about a
> super-person. There is everything funny about a man
> who thinks he is. In laughing at my own claims to
> importance or regard I receive myself in a sort of loving
> forgiveness which is an echo of God's forgiveness of me.
> In much conventional contrition there is a selfishness
> and pride which are scarcely hidden. In our desperate
> self-concern we blame ourselves for not being the super
> persons we think we really are. But in laughter we sit
> light to ourselves. That is why laughter is the purest
> form of our response to God. Whether or not the great
> saints were capable of levitation, I have not the
> evidence to decide. What I do know is that a
> characteristic of the great saints is their power of levity.
> For to sit light to yourself is true humility. Pride cannot
> rise to levity. As G.K. Chesterton said, pride is the

downward drag of all things into an easy solemnity. It would seem that a heavy seriousness is natural to man as falling. 'It was by the force of gravity that Satan fell.' Laughter, on the other hand, is a sign of grace.[25]

Whether or not we believe in God, we know that laughter brings the grace of peace and sharing with others. It also brings courage.

8 Dare to explore new ways of thinking and doing

It is all very well for me to talk about courage and exploring, but if you feel so down and hopeless that you can barely get through each day you are not in any state to go rushing about and doing all sorts of new things. Perhaps the only new thing you can contemplate doing is going into hospital. *Deciding to go into hospital* is one of the biggest decisions you can take (don't tell me other people make that decision – you decide to let other people make that decision for you) since it means transferring yourself into an environment very different from your own.

The problem about deciding whether or not to go into hospital is that it is like buying a pig in a poke. It is very hard to find out what you will be getting. If you decide to buy a house, you can do the rounds of the estate agents, and if you decide to buy a car, you can read about the results of road tests in the car magazines, but if you decide to buy a stay in hospital (in the UK you've already paid for it out of your taxes, whether or not you want the added luxury of a private bed) finding someone who can give you the necessary information can be very difficult. (Why doesn't *Which?* do a survey of wards and hospitals?) Usually you consult your general practitioner and he suggests that you go to hospital. Most GPs refer regularly to just one or two of the consultant psychiatrists out of the eight or so who work in one psychiatric hospital, or there may be four or so consultant psychiatrists working at the general hospital where there are psychiatric wards. Few GPs have had spells as psychiatric patients in their own local hospitals. When a doctor is admitted to hospital it is usually at some place a decent distance from his home – thus supporting the still prevalent belief that it is a shameful thing to be a psychiatric patient.

So all your GP may know about the psychiatrist he is sending you to is that he is a good chap – very helpful (takes troublesome patients off his hands) and very reliable (will visit the patient in a crisis). The GP may know very little of just how each psychiatrist practises psychiatry.

Now psychiatrists come in many shapes and forms. I can refer to them as 'he' because there are in Britain few women psychiatrists, especially at consultant level. Each has his own idiosyncratic way of working, and so I can list only some of the varieties here. Some are wonderful – kind, understanding, sympathetic, wise, supportive and patient. Some are very strange, and leave you wondering who is the crazy one here. Some hold strictly to the medical model of depression and will give you pills and ECT and expect you to get better. Some try to give as little medication as possible and always have time to listen. Some visit their wards regularly and see their patients frequently while others make fleeting, irregular visits to the wards and appear to have abandoned their patients there. Some are trained therapists and some think psychotherapy is a waste of time. Some are skilled behaviour therapists while others think that if you reward a patient for anything you are only encouraging him to be manipulative and demanding. Some have a profound empathy with fellow human beings while others think that psychiatric patients are weak, inferior and stupid people. This last kind of psychiatrist often divides his patients into the 'deserving' and the 'undeserving' or frequently expounds his belief in 'penis therapy', i.e. 'All she needs is a good fuck' or 'What he needs is a woman.'

Still, you can ask your GP which psychiatrist he recommends. He may offer you a choice and he may even be able to tell you something about the psychiatrist. But if you come into hospital as a result of a crisis (usually a suicide attempt or a family row) you have no choice about which psychiatrist whose patient you become.

So, you enter hospital and you are given a bed on a particular ward. Now not only does one psychiatric hospital differ from another, but within a hospital one ward will differ from another. You are not likely to be put on a long-stay ward or a geriatric ward but on some kind of admission ward. There may be several admission wards in one hospital and each may be run differently from the others since different psychiatrists are in charge of different wards. Some wards may have just one consultant in charge while two or three consultants might admit patients to another ward. One ward may be a very quiet place, where patients are arranged in still-life poses around the walls, while another is all hustle and bustle where patients and staff (indistinguishable through the lack of uniforms) are busy doing all sorts of things. Some wards keep men and women strictly apart, while in others, like in real life, men and women mix together. On some wards all the patients are around about the same age, or at least not younger than eighteen or older than sixty, and they all have similar sorts of difficulties to overcome, while on other wards people of any age and with any disability can be found. If you are lucky you find yourself on a good ward.

What, then, is a good ward?
First of all, it has a consultant in charge who takes the time to listen. Before you come into hospital you should have a long talk with him so you can feel reasonably sure that he understands, at least in outline, if not in depth, what you are feeling and that you can trust him enough to put yourself in his care. Once in hospital you should see your consultant regularly, and not just in case conferences. You may be told that case conferences are for the patient's benefit, but really it is a benefit once removed. Staff have case conferences so they can communicate with one another, and occasionally the communication will be about you. The only immediate benefit you can get from a case conference is to be able to ask for weekend leave. Case conferences can be very upsetting for you if you have to go into a roomful of people where the only familiar faces are those of your doctor and nurse. But on a good ward you will know all the people at the case conference and thus it will not be too bad. So to help the staff you attend a case conference when asked, but you reserve your important interchanges with your consultant for when you see him on

your own or with your family. Beware the consultant who sees your family separately from you to gather 'facts' about you and your illness. (Apart from facts like your date of birth and educational achievements, there are no facts, just different interpretations by different people, some of whom are very biased.) This only serves to mark you out as the 'ill' one in the family and lets the other family members congratulate themselves on how well and sane they are. Beware, too, of the psychiatrist who likes to see your husband on his own so they can be two chaps together talking about what a problem the little woman is, and aren't all women like that, especially at that time of the month or when they reach a certain age, ha ha ha. A good psychiatrist has studied the methods of family therapy and marital therapy, as well as individual psychotherapy, and though you are the one in hospital he knows that there are problems in the home to which every family member contributes and which must be made explicit and, if possible, solved, if you are to cease to be depressed.

Perhaps your good psychiatrist may decide to hold no more than a watching brief over you and to arrange for you to see his junior doctor regularly. You may have to make some adjustments to your own way of thinking and speaking when you are with your junior doctor since in the UK now a great many of the junior posts in psychiatry are held by doctors for whom English is not their first language or, even if it is, come from countries very different from Britain. Such men (and a few women) are usually devoted and hard-working doctors, but they are at a disadvantage in a medical specialty which relies on language and an intimate knowledge of the society from which the patient comes. The diagnosis of depression depends so much on cultural values. If 'endogenous depression' means a depression for which no cause in the patient's life can be found, and if the doctor doing the diagnosing believes that all a woman needs to make her happy is a husband, a home and children, then a depressed married woman is likely to be diagnosed as having an endogenous depression and treated accordingly, which means a greater likelihood of receiving only drugs and ECT and little psychotherapy.

Still, your good consultant psychiatrist will be educating

his junior doctor along the right lines, and some junior doctors are already skilled therapists.

Next, on the ward will be a group of nurses who know that their role is to be therapists and not Florence Nightingales. Education in therapeutic skills, which always means greater self-understanding, is now the policy of the British General Nursing Council. Of course there are still psychiatric nurses around who fear to talk to a patient and so waste time, but these are becoming fewer. Thus on your good ward you will have lots of conversations with the nurses, sometimes informal chats, or longer, serious talks in private or in groups. On some wards each patient is assigned a member of staff – doctor, nurse, social worker, psychologist, occupational therapist – as that person's special therapist. The member of staff who becomes your special therapist is someone you can relate to easily, or as easily as you can manage, and your special therapist is responsible for arranging your therapeutic programme and seeing that it is carried out.

On a good ward your therapeutic programme is drawn up soon after you are admitted. It lays down all the activities in which you will be involved. As you progress you work out with the staff how your programme should change. As well as having discussions with a doctor and, if this is the system on the ward, your special therapist, you will attend the ward group which is held regularly. This is a meeting of all staff and patients on the ward and it is intended to improve the way the ward functions as a community. Some of the things discussed are practical ('Whose turn is it to do the washing up rota?') and some of the things discussed are personal but affect the community as a whole ('Why does Bill disappear every time he has promised to organise a table-tennis tournament?' 'Why is Dr Smith always late for the ward meeting?'). Then there are other, smaller groups, led by one of the staff where the members of the group are encouraged to help one another. Every patient belongs to a small group and is required to attend. As well as the small groups there will be relaxation classes, art therapy classes, occupational therapy classes, perhaps music and drama therapy classes, and a variety of recreational activities. At some stage in your stay on the ward you will be involved in most of these as part of your therapeutic programme. No chance to sit and moulder in a corner on this sort of ward.

But suppose you do find yourself on a ward where the only sound is the rattle of the drugs trolley? If you are in a terribly run down and ill state or if you are exhausted and need a break away from your family, then a short stay on such a ward can be helpful while you regain your strength. But once you do regain your strength a ward which offers no more than pills, ECT and nursing care will do nothing for you. There is no therapeutic miasma which seeps out of the walls and makes you better. If you want to get better you have to act on your own behalf.

Suppose you feel very ill but you do not want to go into hospital. Your GP can arrange for you to see a psychiatrist in his outpatient clinic. Again there are outpatients clinics and outpatients clinics. Some psychiatrists run clinics where each patient has a good hour to talk to the psychiatrist, who is always punctual. But there are outpatient clinics where a patient sees the doctor (not necessarily the consultant) for only a few minutes and then after a wait of an hour or two in a crowded, dreary waiting room. Such an experience only makes you feel worse.

Another alternative is to ask your GP to refer you to the *community nurse* for your district. There may be a community nurse attached to the health centre where your GP works or there may be a group of community nurses attached to the local psychiatric hospital. If your GP does not know about community nurses, telephone your psychiatric hospital (or the psychiatric wards of the general hospital) and ask to speak to the nursing officer in charge of community nursing. You will find a community nurse to be a great comfort and support.

Then there are the *clinical psychologists*. They will be doing all sorts of different things, but you can just ring them up and find out. In most parts of the UK they are organised into district departments whose head may be called 'District Psychologist' or 'Top Grade' or 'Principal Psychologist'. You can find where they are and who they are by phoning the District Health Authority and asking. If the person on the switchboard cannot give you this information ask to be put through to District Personnel. Someone there will know.

So, you track down the clinical psychologists. Next you want to find out what sort of things they do, so you just ask. If you find that they do offer a kind of therapy which you would like to try you can ask the psychologist concerned to take you on as a client or you can ask your GP to refer you. Usually, when a person refers himself the psychologist lets the GP know, especially if the person is taking some kind of medication.

What kind of therapy can a psychology department offer? There may be individual psychotherapy, group therapy, social skills groups, problem-solving groups, behaviour therapy or cognitive therapy. Each of these can take many different forms depending on the psychologist organising it and the people involved, but the last, cognitive therapy, is a method created specifically for the treatment of depression by Aaron Beck[26] whose book *Cognitive Therapy of Depression* sets out the method in great detail. If you want your journey out of depression to be as near as possible an orderly march, then this method should appeal to you. Practitioners of the cognitive therapy of depression are specially trained and, as yet, few in number, so you will have to ask around to find them. Failing this, you could read Beck's book for some very wise advice. You will find, too, that many of the psychologists who describe themselves as behaviour therapists use methods very similar to Beck's and just as effective. One very useful book on behavioural and cognitive methods is that by Lewisohn and Munoz, *Control Your Depression.*[27]

Your local clinical psychologists will be able to tell you about the different kinds of therapy available in the psychiatric hospital and to help you to decide whether you should come into hospital or perhaps attend the day hospital. (A good day hospital operates like a good ward). The psychologists will also be able to tell you about what private therapy is available locally. There will probably be some qualified psychotherapists who see people individually or there might be a private organisation which runs different kinds of therapeutic groups. There are not as many private therapists and organisations in Britain as there are in the

States, but their numbers here are increasing.

Most psychologists, while they will each give a preference for a particular theory, be it psychoanalysis, learning
theory, or personal construct theory, and for a particular
school of therapy, will say that, depending on the needs of
each individual client, every theory and kind of therapy can
be used to good effect. But don't expect that one psychologist
can tell you just what the trick is to get out of being depressed.
There is no trick, just hard work. Remember, too, that
psychologists are people and come in many kinds. Some will
be able to give you a great deal of help and some may give you
no help at all.

Remember that you will need different kinds of help at
different times. Jeremy Ross described how this was so in his
'painful and enlightening journey through breakdown and
therapy'.[28] He wrote,

At first I was very dazed and numbed by my collapse so
I tried to cope with the simple needs of life. These had to
be mechanically undertaken. Going to a day hospital
was supportive because it provided some routine and
helped maintain life. The feeling I experienced after the
numbness was just emptiness, a void and lack of energy.
I now see this insight as vital since it provided a base
line from which I was to proceed.

That void was composed of anger. My anger against
my father especially, also my sister, but primarily
against myself. This was blind; I did not know then why
I felt as I did. I have some idea some two years later. I
remember feeling the urgent need to vent this pressure
of rage and anger; just the act of raging was
therapeutic. Listening to a Bruckner symphony with its
climaxes helped, since it seemed to coincide with my
volcanic feelings. At the therapeutic community where
I lived, my Bruckner mania made me unpopular at first.
Later, my musical tastes were tolerated. Music has
always been a good way for me to release my feelings.

The simple fact at that time was that I had very low
opinions of myself and found it hard simply to talk and
mix with people. So much of life consists of coping with

people in all manner of situations. My therapist, a clinical psychologist, and I planned a two prong attack: first, the learning of simple social skills; secondly, the dealing with those feelings of lack of worth.

Talking to people is a complex matter as is mixing in a group. Feeling at ease is the first step – a hard one which took me several sessions. I had to learn to be seen to be listening to another person and be interested in them. I found that looking at the person's face was vital since boredom and lack of interest is seen in that glazed eye look. Yes, it all had to be learned, in the same way as walking or swimming is a skill which has to be learned and is not given at birth. This was the beginning of seeing myself in a social context and not as an isolated individual.

At the same time, my therapist and I met for an hour a week to examine my feelings. I wrote letters to my father, mother and sister telling them how I now felt about them. We discussed them and thought about how they would answer my letters. This went on for months – gradually increasing my knowledge of what went on in the family, how it worked and how we acted on each other, also what our reactions were. I saw that our behaviour was designed to keep the family going; the whole family lived and suppressed in order to survive its unresolvable internal problems.

From May 1979 to 1980, I spent a year at St. Charles' House, a Richmond Fellowship therapeutic community. However, here I had to cope with living in a volatile community and learn to live through contact with others in a structured, therapeutic setting. The daily contact of residents and staff always opens old wounds and creates new ones, but the setting, once it is trusted, can heal once the idea of reality of the community of members is believed in.

I was still having my hourly sessions with my therapist going over my family feelings; insights were developing here.

Perhaps the next major development was my voluntary work. I was asked to open and manage a community and mental health project in North London until the full-time organiser was appointed. In January 1980, the organiser was appointed and I only attended twice weekly for day sessions, mainly in advisory work and administration. I was trusted and given great responsibility and I was forced to recognise – this came very slowly – my abilities as a manager and counsellor. This spilled over into St. Charles' House since I was more confident internally and more able to cope with the complexities of the house. My confidence at St. Charles' increased my confidence in the work I did at the project. Increased self-confidence enabled me to face my own sexual feelings, long buried; my over-dependence on my mother and the weakness of my father in his role as father. I am still working on this area – burrowing deep into my childhood with its joys and terrors. This area is always yielding new material.

Jeremy Ross went to work in the legal department of MIND (the National Association of Mental Health). This gave him greater confidence but he continued on his journey of self-understanding.

I am now having weekly psychotherapy sessions which will last two years. The group consists of seven people, men and women, all from a whole range of backgrounds. Their experiences are wide-ranging but we have one thing in common – we need help and support to cope with relationships. The group sits in a small conference room in armchairs for one and a half hours; before the session and for the week after it, each member lives his own life and agonies. All is focused on that weekly session.

Let me describe what the group does in the form of an analogy with billiards. The group is a closed one, so there is a feeling of confidence and security, but this feeling is tinged with doubt. The billiard cue symbolises those forces within the group that lead to actions, speeches and reactions within the group. During the session those balls crash, knock, glance off each other. That is to say that what is said, or not said, and how it is said, and the reactions of those who keep silent, are determined by the way the members react to each other at that moment. Sessions in the past also determine reactions. To give an example, a member talks about the loss of a mother – leading to others talking more generally perhaps about the subjects of loss, pain and bereavement. The more members or the more balls on the table, the greater likelihood of something someone else says releasing some long suppressed emotion.

I have only been going to this group for about two months. I find it helpful and supportive and yet there are more undiscovered feelings and angers just waiting below the surface. Does this process ever end? Very well, I now know more about myself than ever before and this process seems to continue with new revelations regularly occurring. That is very satisfactory, but I want to be able to feel well and to cope with everyday life without the crutch of therapy. I want an end to this episode of illness.

But all I can say is that I find no end to the process of understanding oneself, the past and how to cope with everyday problems. The therapeutic process goes on as everyday contacts and situations provide a useful and usual method of learning about oneself and about other people. Group psychotherapy provides a safe structure within which trust can develop; the intensive relationships which a group engenders, can offer an 'intensive course' on using one's own insight. Observing the reactions of others has enabled me to learn to live with myself and others. The group psychotherapy will end, but the therapeutic process of living continues right into old age; in this sense, total recovery is not possible.

What is possible is some accommodation with reality. By reality, I mean the uncertainty of life; relationships fluctuate, periods of joy occur as do bouts of loneliness and depression. My accommodation with reality is realising that these fluctuations in feeling must be faced and talked about and, hopefully, kept in proportion. That is a form of recovery, but no cure. Life is no joke – but it may be fun sometimes at least.

Jeremy Ross spoke of staying in one of the houses run by the Richmond Fellowship. There are now numerous community homes, some run by private foundations and some by the Social Services which not merely provide a refuge but a place where you can learn more about yourself and others, and improve your skills of living in a group. Your local Social Services Department can tell you what places like these are available in your district. Also, there will possibly be some kind of *day centre* near you where you will meet people who are in the business of helping one another to cope. Sometimes the day centre is the responsibility of the Health Services and sometimes of the Social Services, and some day centres, or 'drop-in' centres are run by voluntary or self-help organisations. Through contacting the Social Services you may meet a friendly social worker who has time to talk.

Then there are organisations which are there to help. If you feel that you and your spouse together need some counselling, get in touch with the *Marriage Guidance* centre in your town. Remember, always, that *Samaritans* is only a phone call away. If part of your problem is that you drink too much there is *Alcoholics Anonymous* and their organisation for relatives, *Al-Anon*. In some places there are volunteer counsellors working with people who call themselves 'problem drinkers'. *Cruse*, the organisation for widows and widowers, may have a branch in your town. One way of finding out about these and similar helping agencies is to contact your district Health Education office. This will be listed in the phone book under District Health Authority.

Then there are a vast range of self-help organisations. There are *Self-Help Clearing Houses* in both England and the States[29] and a letter or phone-call to them will enable you to discover what groups are in operation near you. If you have a problem like a specific physical illness or a handicapped child, membership of the appropriate self-help group can be a great support. There is *Anorexic Aid*, if you are frightened to eat and *Open Door* if you are too frightened to go out. There are two self-help organisations for people who get depressed, *Depressives Associated*[30] and *Depressives Anonymous*,[31] both of which offer membership of a group or contact by letter and telephone.

If there is no *self help group* available in your area, why
don't you put a notice in your local paper or on the notice
board of your health centre, asking interested people to contact you. You will soon have the nucleus of a group. If you let
the social workers, psychologists and community nurses at
your psychiatric hospital know what you are doing, they will
give you plenty of support. Not only will they send people to
join your group but they can help you find suitable rooms for
your meetings. The Social Services, the Health Service and
the Probation Department usually have space in their build-
ings available in the evenings for self-help groups. Churches,
too, often have a convenient room.

What should the self-help group do? Well, this is up to the
group to decide. Some groups decide to be a kind of friendship
club where people meet for a chat and to do social things
together. Some groups decide to run as a therapy group.
Self-help therapy is quite possible. You don't need a professional therapist to run a therapy group. If you would like to
try this, but do not know where to start, get hold of a very
useful book by Sheila Ernst and Lucy Goodison called *In Our
Own Hands*.[32] This book tells you, very clearly and simply,
how to set up and run a therapy group and what kinds of
therapeutic exercises can be undertaken. The jargon of
therapy (Gestalt, encounter, bioenergetics, psychodrama,
etc.) is explained in a simple but critical way. Joining a
self-help group will be one of the most valuable things you
can do. You will meet a group of people who know what it is to
be depressed. You don't have to explain it to them, or apologise, or pretend that you are happy when you are not. In a
self-help group you give and receive friendship, and in sharing the responsibility for the group you build up your confidence and self-respect.

Well, those are some ideas about where you can get help,
provided you are prepared to go out and find it and to work
hard with what you are offered. Spoon-feeding is no use to
you. You have to feed yourself.

What can you do quietly, on your own?
You can read. There are hundreds, perhaps thousands, of
books like this one where the writer gives advice. Some of this

advice you will find useful, but no one book has all the answers for you. A book can be a signpost, pointing you along the way. Some of the most helpful signposts are not in books of advice but in literature, in poetry, novels, plays and biographies. You are not the only person who has found life to be difficult. This is why people write. Of course, there is fame and money, but the main reason for writing is to master our life, somehow to take our experience and create something of it, and by taking it out of oneself and putting it on the page we change painful confusion into poignant clarity.

One person who understood this perhaps best of all was the poet Rilke. When a young friend, Wolf Graf von Kalckreuth, a poet, shot himself Rilke wrote a requiem, where he chided him, not just for being impatient,

> Why could you not have waited till the point
> where hardness grows unbearable: where it turns,
> being now so hard so real? Look,
> this might perhaps have come with your next moment;
> that moment, maybe, was already trimming
> its garland at the door you slammed for ever,

but for failing to use his art to save himself.

> O ancient curse of poets!
> Being sorry for themselves instead of saying,
> for ever passing judgment on their feeling
> instead of shaping it; for ever thinking
> that what is sad or joyful in themselves
> is what they know and what in poems may fitly
> be mourned or celebrated. Invalids,
> using a language full of woefulness
> to tell us where it hurts, instead of sternly
> transforming into words those selves of theirs,
> as imperturbable cathedral carvers
> transposed themselves into the constant stone.
> That would have been salvation. Had you once
> perceived how fate may pass into a verse
> and not come back, how, once in, it turns image,
> nothing but image, but an ancestor,
> who sometimes, when you watch him in his frame,

seems to be like you and again not like you: –
you would have persevered.[33]

So, what you must do is turn your fate into a verse – or
something similar. It does not have to be good poetry or prose.
Most, or all of it, is for your eyes only. Just how and when you
write you will decide. In the first year that I came to England,
in 1968, the second depressed patient I met was Jean Brump-
ton. It never occurred to me that I had said anything to Jean
which might have been of any use to her, but years later she
got in touch with me to let me know that life was going well
for her and she sent me this poem

> *To Dr. Dorothy*
> To me you suggested the written word,
> Just about ten years ago,
> And when the appropriate time occurred
> Seemingly without effort did the writing flow.
>
> Anytime during day or night,
> With jumbled thoughts that made no sense,
> On any scrap of paper within my sight,
> They were scribbled down and sorted hence.
>
> A very real effect your guidance bore
> Also your calm and gently humourous way
> So, using the written word once more
> May I, my gratitude to you convey.

You can do what Jean did, write on scraps of paper as the
thoughts occur to you, or you can do what Philip Toynbee did,
keep a diary, a sort of log of your spiritual journey. As well,
you can do some of the exercises that psychologists like
myself sometimes give our clients. If you wish, you could get
other members of the family to do these exercises so that you
can all see more clearly how your basic values differ and you
can then decide whether these differences can be brought into
a harmonious balance.

First there is writing what we call a *script*. This can be a
self description, or part of a biography. If you feel that you are
completely bad and useless, then write a descripton of yourself as if written by a sympathetic friend. This will make you
look at yourself in a different way. You could choose some

event in your life which you feel was a turning point and
write your biography going backwards and forwards from
that point, trying to get very clear what was significant about
that event and trying to capture the half-thought, usually
quickly repressed ideas, which that event symbolises. Again,
answer very quickly this question, 'How old will you be when
you die?' and then decide

(a)   why you chose that age, or why you dared not think of
      an age (that is, lied to yourself. We all have some
      notion of when we expect to die, even if it is only an
      average of the ages at which our parents or grand-
      parents died);

(b)   what you *hope* to do between now and then;

(c)   what you *expect* you will do between now and then;

(d)   why there are differences between what you hope and
      expect and how these differences can be overcome.

Another script to write is one for that relative who causes
you the most pain and concern. Only, instead of saying 'She is
like this' or 'He does that', say 'I am like this' or 'I do that'. You
write the script as if you were that person. If you and your
spouse are working on this you can write scripts for one
another and then compare results. Don't fight over it. Try to
help one another deal with the shock of discovering how little
you know of one another.

Then there is the *writing of letters*. These are letters that
you do not necessarily post. They may be letters to people
dead and gone but to whom you still have something important to say – 'I didn't have a chance to thank you,' 'I never told
you how much I love you,' 'I'm so angry that you went and
died and left me all alone.' Or they may be letters to people
about old, but still strong, angers, resentments, jealousies,
guilts and fears. There is no point in sending such letters to a
little old lady who was once a fierce giantess who terrfied you.
But writing to that ferocious figure who denied you what you
needed can turn that figure in your mind into an ordinary
human being, especially if, in return, you write yourself the
letter you wish you had received from her but didn't. You
need to write to both your parents, so that you can arrive at a
point where you can recall your parents in the way that

Sheldon Kopp recalled his in the dedication of his book.[34]

> For my dead parents, whom I often miss.
> My Mother whose strength and ferocity nurtured me,
> almost did me in, and taught me how to survive.
> And my Father whose gentleness and passivity showed
> me how to love, let me down often, and freed me to find
> my own way.

Now we come to *laddering* which shows how the simplest, most prosaic decision we make is linked to the way in which we experience and value our existence. This exercise seems like a party game, but I must ask you not to use it as such. Many people find it very distressing, for even if they do not give you truthful answers to your questions, the answers that do come into their minds can be unexpectedly revealing. I do this laddering exercise only in workshops with people who have had some experience of self-exploration, and even they sometimes find it a shock. I would not give this exercise to a client, although I do frequently ask the question, 'Why is it important that . . .?'

So, the laddering exercise. Take any three things – three makes of car, three kinds of food, three types of music, three famous people – and ask, 'In what way are two of these the same and the other different?'

Suppose we took three kinds of food, say, cream cakes, apple pie, grilled steak.

In what way are two of these the same and the other different?

We could answer,

'Cream cakes and apple pie are the same because they are comforting foods and steak isn't.'

or

'Cream cakes and apple pie are soft and mushy and steak isn't.'

or

'Cream cakes and steak are because they are luxurious and apple pie isn't.'

or

'Cream cakes and steak because they are extravagant and wasteful and apple pie isn't.'

or

'Apple pie and steak are because that is what my mother used to cook me.'

or

'Apple pie and steak are because that's what I used to eat when I was in the Army.'

You might be able to think of some more similarities and differences, but the one that is important is the one that applies to you. Decide what it is and follow it through here. Suppose we decide on

'Comforting foods as against non-comforting foods'.

Now ask,

'Which do you prefer, comforting food or non-comforting food?' and the answer comes

'Comforting food.'

The next question is

'Why is it important to have comforting food?'

The answer might be

'Because it makes me feel better and makes me feel comfortable.'

'Why is it important to be comfortable?'

'Because that's what's life's about. I don't like being uncomfortable.'

'Why is it important not to be uncomfortable?'

'I don't know. Nobody likes being uncomfortable. I don't like being uncomfortable – it makes me feel I don't belong.'

'Why is it important to belong?'

'To belong – to feel you're part of a group – you know, being with people who know and accept you.'

'What would happen to you if you could not be with people who know and accept you – if you were completely on your own?'

'I'd get myself with a group as quickly as possible.'

'But what if you couldn't do that – if you had to be totally alone.'

'That would be the end of me, I guess.'

Another person might say,

'Comforting as against non-comforting food' but choose 'non-comforting food' as his preference.

'Why is non-comforting food important?'

'It, well, makes you stronger. Comforting food, sort of, holds you back.'

'Why is it important to be stronger and not held back?'

'Well, to achieve, to make something of yourself – I don't mean become famous – I mean developing yourself.'

'Why is it important to develop yourself?'

'Because – well – I want to find out who I am – who I could become – kind of knowing myself.'

'What is the opposite of knowing yourself?'

'Not knowing yourself – living in a kind of chaos, I suppose.'

'What would happen to you if you had to live always in a kind of chaos?'

'I couldn't – that would be madness – I'd die.'

So from the choice of food we go by way of the question 'Why is it important?' to how each person experiences his existence and his annihilation as isolation, or existence as clarity and annihilation as chaos. Try to work out which it is for you.

Now there are some other exercises you can do to find out more about yourself. Some I have mentioned before, like *The Lady or the Tiger*. Which would you choose and why? Find out whether your need for your spouse is greater than your love. And there is the journey to *Planet A and Planet B*. Would you prefer a place where you were safe, but everyone ignored you, or a place where people took notice of you but only to be hostile? Discover how much you need your paranoia.

Find out, too, how you feel about being liked or respecting yourself. Ask yourself,

'Suppose I was placed in a situation where I could act in only one of two ways. First I acted one way, people would like me, but I would not respect myself. If I acted the other way, people would not like me but I would respect myself. Which would I choose, respecting myself or other people liking me?'

When you have answered, then ask 'Why is it important that . . .?'

What this exercise might reveal is an important conflict. Perhaps you want to be able to respect yourself but people whom you see as powerful (by seeing them as powerful you have given them this power) force you to do things you don't want to do, or perhaps you want people to like you but in your job you should make decisions which other people won't like, and so you try to sit on the fence (so everyone thinks you are weak) or you try to avoid making decisions (so everyone thinks you are indecisive) or you try to find solutions which suit everyone (thus proving the old adage 'Try to please all and you shall please none'). You will have to work this out if you are going to be able to live at peace with yourself.

Another exercise is to write down a list, in order of importance, of the virtues you most value and the vices you most despise. Then ask for each one, 'Why is this important?' and see where your enquiry leads. See how the answers to these questions link to your answers in the other exercises. If you and your spouse do this exercise together you will discover some more clues to what is unspoken in your disagreements.

Another question to ask yourself is, 'Which frightens me most, fear or anger?' Both frighten you, but one frightens you more than the other. You might find that you prefer fear, on the grounds that a little anxiety gets you going and makes you feel alive, while anger you find completely abhorrent. You might be married to someone who will never admit he is afraid but who uses his anger to try to make his world into what he wants it to be.

Suppose there is some event looming and you are frightened of what is going to happen. Your mother may be coming to stay or you are required to go to the firm's ball, or your daughter expects you to go to her graduation or your son wants you to take him fishing – all fearfully dangerous events, of course – and you can't see any way of avoiding them other than by being very depressed. Try something else. Write down what it is you are expected to do and then say,

'If I do this, what is the very worst that could happen?'

Write down your answer and look at it in the cold light of day. If you have said, 'I'll die,' then rejoice, your troubles will soon be over.

If you have said, 'I'll make a fool of myself,' ask 'What is the opposite of making a fool of myself?' Then ask 'Why is this important?' See if you dare commit to paper just how vain you are.

Then go back to the original situation and say, 'How many different outcomes can I see?' List them all, the good ones as well as the bad ones, the fantastic ones as well as the prosaic. See if you can predict what then actually happens. (No cheating by using self-fulfilling prophecies like 'I'm sure I won't enjoy it.')

Then there are the things that you feel compelled to do. No strange force is compelling you, nor any person other than yourself. When you see your own values clearly you can ask,

'Do I do this because I believe it is right or do I do it because the parent in my head tells me to and I'm too scared to disobey?'

You are you; you are the parent in your head; you are the child who is scared to disobey. You can choose to spend the rest of your life going around as three squabbling people, or you can choose to make yourself into one whole person.

If you are a woman then you must spend some time thinking and writing about what it means to you to be a woman. The women's movement has produced an extensive literature. Whether or not you read some of this, or join a women's group (in some places there are Women's Therapy Centres) you must consider the fact that *two-thirds* of psychiatric patients are women, most of them with the diagnosis of depression. The diagnosing has been done by men. You must consider too that the days have long passed when all a woman could fit into her life span (no more than forty years) was marriage and children. Now, when a woman's children can take care of themselves, she still has half of her life or more to live. Home and family cannot be an occupation for a woman's full lifetime, not unless you want to devote your time to being an interfering mother-in-law or to being ill.

So you have to find something more to do. If you found when you did your laddering that your experience of existence is to be a member of a group, then join one of the helping professions or become a voluntary worker, alongside the helping professions, or join an acting group, or take up a team sport. If you found that your experience of existence is to seek clarity, then go back to studying, or take up one of the creative arts. Or perhaps you would prefer to create a balance. Having spent your life being part of a group, try something on your own, and find that solitariness is not so terrible after all. Or, seek clarity by learning to tolerate chaos and join a group of some kind. What you discover about yourself will be liberating.

When you think about taking up some new activity, and then feel frightened, you have to work out just what it is you feel frightened of. It may not be just fearing to make a fool of yourself. You are probably still carrying round in your head parental prohibitions like 'Don't mix with strangers,' 'Those kind of people are common,' 'No child of mine would ever do a thing like that' and, especially where sport is concerned, 'Don't do that, you'll hurt yourself'. Such prohibitions put a barrier between you and the rest of the world. You need to identify these prohibitions and decide whether you want to go on obeying them or whether you would prefer to be free. When you do manage to overcome your prohibitions and try something new, don't say, 'That was a fluke. I'll never manage it again.' Think back over what you did and write down the things that you learned from it. Then next time you can decide how, if necessary, you will alter what you did.

The greatest fear of all that you must come to terms with is that of death. You cannot live at peace with yourself until, somehow, you come to accept your death. Running away from it is no solution. But remember, it is very difficult to accept our death when we feel not just that we have not lived but that we have no right to live. So long as you regard yourself as bad, evil, unacceptable to yourself and other people you will be unable to accept your death and the thought of death will frighten you. When you accept yourself you can accept your death. It is not until you possess yourself that you are able to face losing yourself.

Accepting yourself can mean resolving the grief left over from earlier years. Then you have lost somebody – or even something – and you were not able to show your grief, perhaps not even admit it to yourself. There is nothing brave or wise in denying grief, in pretending that you feel no pain or anger or sorrow. The road out of your prison must take you through this grief. Perhaps someone will help you through an experience so crudely called 'grief therapy', but so effective. Here you have to enact a scene, perhaps the funeral where you did not cry, and now you do cry, or perhaps you pretend that the person you have lost is back with you, and you can talk to that person and say what should have been said and hear in return (you say it yourself) what you should have heard. Grief therapy is deeply moving, so it does help if someone is with you, but you may prefer to do it on your own by talking and writing – and probably crying. Remember, tears are good for you. Tears wash the eyes.

Accepting yourself means giving up all that nonsense about self-sacrifice. Leap in front of a bus and save someone's life if you must, but don't devote your life to domestic sacrifice. No good ever comes of it. All you achieve is to encourage your family to behave badly – to be selfish and inconsiderate, to expect the world to be the way they want it to be, and to be unaware of the needs and feelings of others. If you wait upon your children and never expect them to do their own washing and get themselves a meal or to look after their own belongings, you rob them of the chance to learn as they grow up the skills of living and thus you undermine their confidence in themselves. If you are sacrificing yourself to your family so as to make them need you and so they will not go away and leave you, then your self-sacrifice is dishonest. You are looking after others for your own sake, not theirs. Your family will know if this is why you are being so self-sacrificing and they will resent and despise you for it. If you are sacrificing yourself because you expect love in return, then all you achieve is to make others feel guilty when they do not live up to your expectations and to win no more than affection for what you do rather than love for what you are.

So you must ask yourself, 'Am I sacrificing myself so as to overcome my feeling that I am a bad, worthless person?' 'Does being a self-sacrificing doormat do anything for me except confirm me in my belief that I am a bad, worthless person?' 'Do I do things for other people, not because I love them, but because it is my duty, that is, because I am too scared to refuse to do things for them?' 'Does my self-sacrifice encourage others to continue being badly behaved?' (Some people get away with the most outrageous behaviour all their lives because their children and spouses are too frightened to complain, much less to demand that an adult behave as a responsible adult.)

You must also ask yourself 'In my need to do things for other people, am I so busy doing things for them that I don't really know what they want?' 'Does my sensitivity blind me to what other people are really like?' 'Do I really know the people I love?' 'Can I truly love someone if I do not know who that person really is?'

Finding out about yourself always means finding out about other people. Accepting yourself for what you are means accepting others for what they are. Accepting yourself means forgiving yourself for being what you are. Accepting others means forgiving them for being what they are – or what they were. In forgiving ourselves and others we gain the courage and strength of true humility.

'Humility,' said Philip Toynbee, 'must mean trying to see ourselves as we really are. And pride is always a denial of the (painful yet exhilarating) truth about ourselves.'[35] Humility is not a constant harping on your faults and errors and general worthlessness. When you find yourself doing this (like being unable to say anything good about yourself, or constantly apologising, or feeling quite unable to do anything even moderately well) remember what Archbishop Fenelon wrote to one of his parishioners,

It is mere self-love to be inconsolable at seeing one's

own imperfections; but to stand face to face with them, neither flattering nor tolerating them, seeking to correct oneself without becoming pettish – this is to desire what is good for its own sake and for God's.[36]

Humility, self-acceptance and forgiveness are all aspects of the one process whereby we come to see ourselves as we are and other people as they are. Since we no longer have the pride and arrogance to try to control ourselves and our world so as to make ourselves and our world into something which they are not, we can now be spontaneous. Since we no longer have to hide ourselves from other people, to put a barrier between ourselves and our world, we can be open and vulnerable, and so feel ourselves to be alive. Since all desire leads to suffering, ceasing to desire perfection reduces our desires and so our suffering. We then know, along with Lao Tsu, that,

> It is more important
> To see the simplicity,
> To realise one's true nature,
> To cast off selfishness,
> And temper desire.[37]

Learning to accept yourself and others, to be courageous, loving, humble and forgiving, and to face death with equanimity is no small task. But this is what you must undertake if you are to find your way out of the prison of depression. This is what Philip Toynbee found. He wrote,

Partly through my reading and partly through some independent but slow and heavy process within my mind and heart, I gradually began to think of this depression in quite a new set of terms. Instead of looking for its causes and thinking about how to get rid of them, I began to look for its purposes and to wonder how I could fulfil them. I couldn't and still can't tell whether God sends us such acute afflictions to bring us to some new understanding through our pain. But I am now as sure as I can be that depression is often a sign, whether human or divine, that the life of the victim needs to be drastically changed; that acts of genuine contrition are called for; that the dark block within can be dissolved only by recognizing that something like an inner death and resurrection is demanded of the sufferer.[38]

Death and resurrection – or a journey without maps. Good luck!

Chapter 8

SUPPOSE I DECIDE NOT TO CHANGE?

As you work at understanding and accepting yourself and understanding and accepting other people, you may come to the conclusion that there are things about you that you cannot change. You may now see clearly that you are engaged upon work which has little meaning for you and that to leave the prison of depression behind you forever you need to find some other work which you would find interesting and important. But jobs are hard to get now, and you have a family to support. You may now see clearly that your spouse can never give you the marriage that you want, and that staying in this marriage will mean that you will often be lonely. But you do not want to abandon someone who loves and needs you. You may see clearly now that you had brought from your childhood a burden of anger, resentment, guilt and grief. You may have forgiven yourself and your family and resolved the anger, resentment and guilt, and allowed yourself to grieve, but the sadness remains. You know that on certain grey days ghosts of the old, bad feelings will return.

You have not achieved a life of undiluted happiness. What you have achieved is to change uncomprehending, guilty depression into wise and gentle melancholy. You are a survivor who has rid himself of all unncessary baggage. You know that depression is not something visited upon you, but is a moral dilemma, the terms of which you now comprehend.

For you the journey out of depression is never over. But you can count your successes, like Philip Toynbeé[1] counted his. One day he went for a walk, and later wrote,

A free and purposeful man!
And a changed world.

For years all visual beauty has been tangled up with
nostalgia. 'Tears at the heart of things'; poignancy:
carried back by a tree to some half-memory of a
childhood tree, so *freshly* seen so long ago. A florid and
deeply satisfying melancholy. Or the tree was a
memento mori; my melancholy softly expanding into a
future with no trees at all.

But now, on this walk, I stopped several times and
looked at a single tree as I haven't done for years. No; as
I have never done in my life before. The tree was there
and now, in its own immediate and peculiar right: *that*
tree and no other. And I was acutely here-and-now as I
stared at it, unhampered by past or future: faced from
the corruption of the ever-intrusive ME. Intense
happiness.

Later he wrote,

But it is important to get rid of the disastrous Christian
notion of 'merits' to be acquired; like so many good
conduct marks collected through a term at school. If
there are stages on this journey and if I have reached
even the first of them, then I know what whatever is
new seems much more like a gift than an achievement.

He concluded that

I recognise more and more that if I have any godly
function on earth – and of course I have; everybody has
– then it is to act as both a warning and an example on
the very lowest rung of the ladder. The present account
of my hopes and fears; large failures, small successes;
humiliations and perceptions (perceptions often from
the heart of humiliation) is meant from the spiritually
backward – who nevertheless know enough about the
Spirit to be in a state of often subdued but never
extinguished hope.

Hope, and an armoury of things to do when grey days
threaten are what you now possess. Jill Tweedie[2] recorded
what she does.

Now, when I glimpse depression shuffling in the wings, waiting to come on, I have tricks up my sleeve to forestall it. I think, for instance, of optical illusions. That box, drawn on paper, that seems to project its closed end towards you but, at a shifting of the mind's gears, becomes suddenly open, hollow, so that you can look inside. Those pencilled lines of identical length, one with arrows at its ends pointing outwards, the other with arrows pointing inwards, the first seeming half as long again as its apparently shrunken twin. Marks on paper that serve as reminders of some possibility of control over reality, if only in the mind's eye.

I have other remedies, too. I no longer allow the blanket to fall without a struggle – instead, I force myself to track that fall to its source. The mind veers away, reluctant to reveal the awesome pettiness, the huge egoism that often sparks mild depression, the bloated baby that screams in all of us and blackens our horizons with its bawling for attention. Once the baby is discovered, though, the blackness lifts. Also, I attend to my body, something I once thought far too undramatic and suburban a thing to do. My soul in upheaval and you talk of a tonic or Vitamin C? Cold showers? Walk round the block? Would anyone have dared suggest such cures to Byron? Still, the links between body and mind are indissoluble and the banal fact is that forcing oxygen through the lungs does, sometimes, set the mood afloat again. Other people have their own methods of rupturing the dark circle. One woman goes away, anywhere, if only for a day. Another, reasoning that while she feels like death she might as well do the deathiest chores, does so and recovers. Yet another, drained of all energy, reads *Moby Dick* for the umpteenth time and forgets herself in Ahab's chase.

Kay, whom I wrote about in *The Experience of Depression* works in a department store in town. So I see her fairly often. Sometimes we have a chat and sometimes there is only time to smile and say hello. She has her down days. I see the tired strain behind her immaculate make-up and quiet smile. But she has changed. She has good friends now, including her daughter, Penny, and her daughter-in-law, and a much loved grandchild. She has always been beautifully dressed and groomed, but before her way of dressing seemed to create a barrier behind which she could hide. Now the barrier has gone. She is open, gentle and wise.

It was during the Falklands crisis that Kay and I met for a chat. That was the week the Coventry was sunk off the Falklands. The Ministry of Defence had announced that a frigate had been sunk but it was over twelve hours, a long night, before we were told which frigate it was. We talked, and Kay said, 'Did I tell you that Penny's baby was stillborn? She had a terrible time. Steven's on a frigate, down there in the South Atlantic. Now I know what worrying really is.'

Chapter 9

THE PRISON VANISHES

> We shall not cease from exploration
> And the end of all our exploring
> Will be to arrive where we started
> And know the place for the first time.[1]

It is hard to find the right word for what it feels like when the prison vanishes – when, one day, you look around and find that the walls have gone, that the world is right there, near you, and you are part of the world. I use the word 'enlighten-ment', even though that can sound as if the person has disco-vered the secrets of the universe. Of course, some people do say that they have had an incredibly marvellous experience in which some Great Truth was suddenly revealed. Such things happen, or so I am told, but the kind of enlightenment I am talking about comes gradually and is never complete. You find yourself in the process of being enlightened, and it goes on and on until the day you die. Somewhere during the process you find that you have changed. Of course you can stop the process and return to the unenlightened state where you spent your time worrying about the future, resenting the past, feeling bored, angry and envious in the present, and believing that in the overall scheme of things you are bound to suffer. To stay on the path of enlightenment we must be mindful of what we are doing.

Being enlightened does not mean escaping into some great philosophical and religious way of life where you no longer have anything to do with the mundane world. On the contrary, you become more aware of the real world *in the present*. Instead of thinking about the present in terms of the past (how I was deprived, was cheated, have suffered) and of the future (how I must do this perfectly, won't get it right, shall be blamed, shall be punished) you pay attention to what is happening now – the flavour of the food you are eating, the sound of a bird outside your window, the story someone is telling you, the task you are doing now. And as you are mindful of the present you are also aware that you are part of a great Whole which, though it is mysterious and unknowable in an intellectual sense, can be comprehended and is not fearful, but supports and sustains you. This Whole we can name and describe in whatever way suits us best – as God, or the Life Force, Tao or Nature. Our comprehension of the Whole increases our understanding of our daily life, and our mindfulness of our daily life increases our understanding of the Whole. Thus enlightenment is not a sudden switching on of a light: it is a gradually increasing brightness.

We can look at our world and say, 'It's nothing but . . .', or we can say, 'It's not this, but something more,' or we can say, 'It is'. If we say that the world is nothing but politics or atoms, then we have made our world a barren, lifeless place and ourselves barren, lifeless people. If we say that this world is unimportant and that what matters is something that transcends it, then we are dissatisfied and irritated with our world, and so, at best, we ignore it, and, at worst, destroy it through thoughtlessness or malice. But if we say, 'It is', then our world comes to us fresh each day, full of abundant life and endless charm.

We all know that beyond and within ourselves and our mundane world lies a reality which is awesome, mysterious and unknowable except in those rare moments when it reveals itself to us. If we deny that it is there we deprive ourselves of a rich and vibrant nourishment, and so we become meagre and limited people, mere caricatures of what we might have been. If we recognise this reality but insist that we know exactly what it is, if we see it in terms of some fairy story where the good are invariably rewarded and protected and the bad punished, then we have to spend our lives denying our perceptions and lying to ourselves about our experiences, forever engaged in a game of make-believe. But if we can face and acknowledge the awesome mystery, then we shall know great fear and uncertainty, but we shall also know, in rare, life-sustaining moments, the greatest joy, wisdom and delight. These moments make the rest of life worth while.

NOTES

The prison

1 Dorothy Rowe, *The Experience of Depression*, Wiley, Chichester and New York, 1978.
2 Dorothy Rowe, *The Construction of Life and Death*, Wiley, Chichester and New York, 1982.

2 Inside the prison

1 D.H. Lawrence, 'The Hands of God' in *The Ship of Death and Other Poems*, Faber, London, 1952, p.60.
2 Fleur Adcock, 'Things' in *The Inner Harbour*, Oxford University Press, 1979.
3 G.M. Hopkins, *Poems*, Oxford University Press, 1948, p.110.
4 Gerald Priestland in *Listener*, October 1980, p.538.
5 Colin Smith, 'One-eyed gateman guards the tombs of El-Alamein dead', *Observer*, 8 November 1981, p.14.
6 Philip Toynbee, *Part of a Journey*, Collins, London, 1981, p.44.

3 How to build your prison

1 *The Experience of Depression*, Wiley, Chichester and New York, 1978, and *The Construction of Life and Death*, Wiley, Chichester and New York, 1982.
2 *The Experience of Depression*, p.241.
3 *Ibid*., p.237.
4 *Ibid*., p.238.
5 *Ibid*., p.239.
6 *The Construction of Life and Death*, p.33.
7 *Ibid*., p.65.
8 *The Experience of Depression*, p.217.
9 The radio play *The Stranger in My Head*, by Bill Lyons, concerns a woman finding her way out of depression. At the beginning of the play she recites a poem to herself,

If only I was perfect
Like the women on T.V.
But I'm not the shiney, silky one
Dull lifeless hair, that's me.
And my whites were never white enough
And my children fight and scream
And I wander through life's minefield
Like a zombie in a dream.
And they never notice what I cook
Or if they do they moan
And we live our lives quite separately
Together but alone.
Not like the happy children
That bubble on my screen
Who always rush to Mummy
To tell her what they've seen,
Nor like the rugged husband
With the soft and kindly face,
Who'll kiss away the raging day
'Til the pain's gone without trace.
It makes me feel inadequate
To watch the perfect wife
Stand serenely in her kitchen
And orchestrate her life,
While her family cluster round her
And flash their fluoride teeth
And dazzle with their pure white shirts
And pure white souls beneath.
I dread the glint of morning
Of each new demanding day,
And no tablets fizzing in my glass
Can dissolve that hurt away.
As each day follows yesterday
In a never ending chain,
It seems each day – I've tried and failed
Just to try and fail again.
'Til the failures don't matter
And I just forget to try
And I build a wall around me
And no one knows quite why
And no one understands that,
If they think of it at all,
I am waiting here for someone
To care enough to scale the wall.

                              (BBC, Radio 4, 13 May 1982)

10 See *The Guinness Book of Records*, Guinness Superlatives Ltd, Enfield, England, pp.234 and 218. Nigel Moore ate 1,823 cold baked beans in thirty minutes while at the P.O. Social Club in Manchester on 19 June 1974. Hormutt Stock flipped forty-two mats on 29 May 1974, in Mannheim, West Germany. Unfortunately 'lack of standardization of the size and weight of beer mats has bedevilled the chronicling of records in this international pursuit.'

11 Jules Feiffer, cartoon, *Observer* magazine, 20 February 1977.

12 George Bernard Shaw, *Major Barbara*, Constable, London, 1947, p.334.

13 Theodore Mischel (ed.), *Understanding Other Persons*, Basil Blackwell, Oxford, 1974.

14 George Gordon Byron, 'Don Juan', *Byron's Poems*, vol. 3, 13.6, Everyman Library, Dent, London, 1963, p.369.

15 See Alan Paton 'The Challenge of Fear', *Saturday Review*, 9 September 1967. 'In one sense, the opposite of fear is courage, but in the dynamic sense the opposite of fear is love, whether it be love of man or love of justice.'

16 William Wordsworth, 'The Affliction of Margaret' (1804), *The Poetical Works of Wordsworth*, Oxford University Press, London, 1960, p.93.

17 European Values Study Group Results quoted by Ted Gorton in 'Belief in Britain', *Listener*, 17 and 24 December 1981, p.742. 'Belief in God is high, at 76%, but regular church attendance, at 14%, is the lowest in Europe. In religious matters, belief in the adjuncts of Christianity is low, particularly in the unpleasant areas of faith. Thus 30% believe in the devil and in hell. This rises to a 45% belief in life after death, and to an optimistic 57% for the notion of heaven. One of the most amazing claims is that 27% of British people believe in reincarnation. Sin is accepted as a reality by 69%. Perhaps not surprisingly, the highest figure for this is in Northern Ireland (91%).'

18 M. Argyle, and B. Beit-Hallahmi, *The Social Psychology of Religion*, Routledge & Kegan Paul, London and Boston, 1975.

19 See Preface and Conclusions of *The Construction of Life and Death*.

20 E. Slater and M. Roth, *Clinical Psychiatry*, Baillière, Tindall & Cassell, London, p.247.

21 Gerald Priestland, personal communication quoted in *The Construction of Life and Death*, p.201.

22 A fuller account of this is given in *The Construction of Life and Death*.

23 Letter to *Observer*, Sunday 5 April 1981.

24 *The Construction of Life and Death*, p.110.

25 *Ibid.*, p.67.

26 *Ibid.*, p.14.

27 C.S. Lewis, *A Grief Observed*, Faber, London, 1961.

28 Gerard Manley Hopkins, *Poems*, Oxford University Press, 1948, p.113.

29 'Village mourns eight lost heroes', *Guardian*, Monday 21 December 1981.

30 Victoria Brittain, 'Next year seventeen million babies are doomed to die', *Guardian Third World Review*, Friday 18 December 1981, p.7.

31 Cf. the words of Bertrand Russell. 'Those whose lives are fruitful to themselves, to their friends, or to the world are inspired by hope and sustained by joy; they see in imagination the things that might be and the way in which they are to be brought into existence. In their private relations they are not preoccupied with anxiety lest they should lose such affection and respect as they receive: they are engaged in giving affection and respect freely, and the reward comes of itself without their seeking. In their work they are not haunted by jealousy of competitors, but are concerned with the actual matter that has to be done. In politics, they do not spend time and passion defending unjust privileges of their class or nation, but they aim at making the world as a whole happier, less cruel, less full of conflict between rival greeds, and more full of human beings whose growth has not been dwarfed and stunted by oppression.' *Proposed Roads to Freedom – Anarchy, Socialism and Syndicalism*, Henry Holt, New York, 1919, pp.186–7.

32 That science has now made it possible for the human race to destroy itself and most other forms of life on this planet is a well-publicised fact that should concern everyone. There are other scientific discoveries, less well publicised, which raise major moral issues – for instance the techniques for creating foetuses in the test-tube, for preserving such foetuses in a frozen state and for producing clones from single eggs (see Margaret Jay, 'Experimenting With Life', *Listener*, 17 and 24 December 1981, pp.739–41).

Science creates anxiety not only through its practical results but also through its theory. The idea that the universe's expansion and contraction will mean the eventual destruction of our planet does not make scientists feel happy (see Steven Weinberg, *The First Three Minutes: A Modern View of the Origin of the Universe*, Scientific Book Club, London, 1977) since such an end, even millions of years hence, means an end to all human achievement. Even the fundamental concept of an infinite as against a finite universe can be a cause of anxiety. Tony (*The Construction of Life and Death*, p.14) said, 'A Person is a Being capable of living the life of the universe, it would be difficult to get close to. We're talking in terms of infinity. I don't know what infinity is but it scares hell out of me. There's no way I can cope thinking about an infinite God. One of the virtues of death is that it will end it. Death actually has a lot of things going for it. I'm not trying to be perverse but I do find the thought of some people and infinity more than I can bear.'

Gareth B. Matthews, in his *Philosophy and the Young Child* (Harvard University Press, Massachusetts, 1980, pp.34–5) quotes Michael, aged seven, who had pondered on this problem of infinity. He said 'I don't like to [think] about the universe without an end. It gives me a funny feeling in my stomach. If the universe goes on forever there is no place for God to live who made it. . . . It's nice to know you're *here*. It is not nice to know about nothing. I hope (the universe) doesn't go on and on forever. I don't like the idea of it going on forever because it's obvious it can't be anywhere.'

33 European Values Study Group, op.cit.
34 *The Construction of Life and Death*, p.118.
35 'Once upon a time, I, Chuang Tsu, dreamed I was a butterfly flying here and there, enjoying life without knowing who I was. Suddenly I woke up and I was indeed Chuang Tsu. Did Chuang Tsu dream he was a butterfly, or did the butterfly dream he was Chuang Tsu?' Chuang Tsu, *Inner Chapters*, tr. Gia-Fu Teng and Jane English, Wildwood House, London, p.48.
36 See Mr G. in *The Construction of Life and Death*, p.143.
37 *Ibid.*, p.126ff.
38 *The Experience of Depression*, p.96.
39 *The Construction of Life and Death*, p.127.
40 *Ibid.*, pp.86,84.
41 Jacky Gillott, 'Depression', *Cosmopolitan*, May 1976, pp.116, 118.
42 Epictetus, *Discourses as reported by Arrian*, tr. W.A. Oldfeather, Loeb Library.
43 G. Brown and T. Harris, *Social Origins of Depression*, Tavistock, London, 1978.
44 Alan Watts, *The Way of Zen*, Penguin Books, Harmondsworth, 1978, p.26.
45 Connie Bensley, 'April', in *Progress Report*, Harry Chambers/Peterloo Poets, Cornwall, 1981, p.10.
46 Connie Bensley, 'Technique', *ibid*.
47 Robert Lowell, *Day by Day*, Faber, 1978.
48 Philip Toynbee, *Part of a Journey*, Collins, London, 1981, pp.72, 238, 247, 257.
49 Alan Watts, op.cit.
50 *The Experience of Depression*, p.230.

51 As the psychoanalysts would say, every fear contains a wish.

52 Philip Toynbee, *Part of a Journey*, Collins, London, 1981, pp.87, 88, 90, 91, 99, 100, 101.

53 *Ibid.*, p.85.

54 *The Construction of Life and Death*, p.72.

55 *Ibid.*, p.72.

56 'We do not see things as they are. We see them as we are.' The Talmud.

57 *The Experience of Depression*, p.223.

58 *The Construction of Life and Death*, p.122.

59 *Ibid.*, p.101.

60 *Ibid.*, p.160.

61 See Tony's story in *The Construction of Life and Death*, pp.1ff.

62 Matthew 7: 1, 2.

63 Matthew 18:22.

64 Matthew 5:44.

65 Matthew 18:21 to 35.

66 Matthew 6: 12, 14, 15.

67 Matthew 10:34.

68 'All manner of sin and blasphemy shall be forgiven unto men; but the blasphemy against the Holy Ghost shall not be forgiven unto men.'
'And whosoever speaketh a word against the Son of Man, it shall be forgiven him, but whosoever speaketh against the Holy Ghost, it shall not be forgiven him, neither in this world, neither in the world to come.' Matthew 12: 31, 32.

69 *The Construction of Life and Death*, p.196.

70 *The Experience of Depression*, p.229.

71 *Ibid.*, p.38.

72 *Ibid.*, p.178.

73 *The Construction of Life and Death*, p.187.

74 See Ronald Eyre, *On the Long Search*, Collins, London, p.83. Eyre wrote, 'The most useful thumbnail definition of *dukkha* that I know came from a Buddhist monk in California (though it may not have started with him): "*Dukkha*," he said, "is the attempt to make reality repeatable." The sentence itself is very repeatable and each time I spin it round it seems to dig deeper and deeper.'

75 *The Experience of Depression*, p.235.

76 *Ibid.*, p.235.

4 Why not leave the prison?

1 D. Rowe, 'Poor prognosis in a case of depression as predicted by the repertory grid,' *British Journal of Psychiatry*, 118, 297–300, 1971.

2 See Sheldon Kopp, *The End of Innocence – Facing Life Without Illusions*, Bantam Books, New York, 1981.

5 Why I won't leave the prison

1 Melvyn Bragg, 'Writers of the Lost Ark,' *Punch*, November 1981, p.817.
2 C.G. Jung, 'Psychotherapy,' *Collected Works*, trans R.F.C. Hull, Routledge & Kegan Paul, London, 1960.
3 T.S. Eliot, *The Elder Statesman*, Faber, London, 1958.
4 *The Experience of Depression*, Wiley, Chichester and New York, 1978, p.225.
5 Alan Watts, *The Way of Zen*, Penguin, Harmondsworth, 1978, p.68.
6 If you want to find your way out of your depression and within a Christian context you may find the books by Harry Williams extremely helpful. See *Tensions, Necessary Conflicts in Life and Love*, Mitchell Beazley, London, 1976.
7 Louis MacNeice, 'Entirely', *Collected Works*, Faber, London, 1966.
8 Lao Tsu, *Tao Te Ching*, trans Gia-Fu and Jane English, Wildwood House, London, 1973.
9 See George Brown and Tirril Harris, *Social Origins of Depression*, Tavistock, London, 1978, on the lack of a confiding relationship.
10 Connie Bensley, *Willpower*, in *Progress Report*, Harry Chambers/Peterloo Poets, Cornwall, 1981.
11 See Chapter 8 'Suffering and Change' in *The Construction of Life and Death*, Wiley, Chichester and New York, 1982.
12 See Jill pp.132ff and Felicity, pp.116f, 176, in *The Construction of Life and Death*.
13 John Milton, *Paradise Lost*.

6 Outside the wall: living with a depressed person

1 Sheldon Kopp, *The End of Innocence – Facing Life Without Illusions*, Bantam Books, New York, 1981, p.60; see also his excellent *If You Meet Buddha on the Road, Kill Him* and *Mirror, Mask and Shadow*, Science and Behaviour Books, Palo Alto, 1972, 1978.
2 *The Construction of Life and Death*, Wiley, Chichester and New York, 1982, p.179.
3 *The Experience of Depression*, Wiley, Chichester and New York, 1978, p.179.
4 Jill Tweedie *In the Name of Love*, Jonathan Cape, 1979, pp.106,

159–60. This is recommended reading for anyone who wants to sort out his or her loving and sexual relationships. And any woman who has problems about being herself as well as a wife and mother should read Jill Tweedie's *Letters from a Faint Hearted Feminist* Robson Books, London, 1982, a collection of articles previously published in the *Guardian,*

5 George Brown and Tirril Harris, *Social Origins of Depression*, Tavistock, London, 1978.

6 To find out what people in 1982 think about love, sex and marriage the *Sunday Times* commissioned a major opinion survey. 'The survey was conducted by Market and Opinion Research International (MORI) on behalf of the *Sunday Times* among a representative quota sample of 1,069 adults, aged 18 and over in 51 constituency sampling points throughout Great Britain. Face-to-face interviews were conducted on 25–26 April 1982.' The results showed that people considered that 'Far and away the most important ingredient in a good marriage is the ability of husband and wife to talk freely to each other about their feelings (62%). Being 'in love' and maintaining a good sex relationship take a distinctly secondary place – in fact, women rated a shared sense of humour higher than either of them. And sexual fidelity has slipped almost to the bottom of the list (15%), lurking alongside that clearly outmoded concept known as "keeping romance alive" (16%)' *Sunday Times*, 2 May, 1982, pp.33–4.

7 Suppose I did want to leave the prison, what should I do?

1 Lao Tsu, *Tao Te Ching*, Gia-Fu and Jane English, Wildwood House, London.

2 Vicky Rippere, 'Behavioural Treatment of Depression in Historical Perspective', in S. Rachman (ed.), *Contributions to Medical Psychology*, vol. 2, Pergamon Press, Oxford and New York, 1980, pp.31–54.

3 Judith Gray in her study, 'The effect of the doctor's sex on the doctor–patient relationship', *Journal of the Royal College of General Practitioners*, 1982, vol.32, pp.167–9, found that 'Communication is easier, more time is given, drugs are less frequently dispensed and women patients are treated more seriously if the doctor is a woman.'

There is no doubt that some women have quite severe symptoms pre-menstrually and in the menopause. While most doctors agree that this is so, not all doctors agree on the appropriate treatment. Since being depressed never has one single cause but a whole complex of causes, pre-menstrual tension or the menopause cannot be the sole cause of a woman's depression but they can certainly make it a great deal worse, so if you are aware that you feel more depressed and irritable in the week before your period or that your depression and the menopause coincide, you must get your doctor to help you deal with these menstrual changes.

4 Arthur Koestler, *The Invisible Writing*, Collins, London, 1954.

5 Gerard Manley Hopkins, *Poems*, Oxford University Press, London, 1948, p.110.

6 Malcolm Lader, *The Mind Benders. The Use of Drugs in Psychiatry*, National Association for Mental Health, 22 Harley Street, London, 1981, p.19. Advice about how to get off the addictive benzodiazepam (Valium, Librium, Activan, Tranxene, Dalmane, Mogadon, Frisium, etc.) is given in *Trouble with Tranquillisers*, Release Publications Ltd, 1 Elgin Avenue, London, W9 3PR.

7 Andrew Stanway, *Overcoming Depression*, Hamlyn Paperbacks, London, 1981, pp.143–61.

8 See ibid., pp.178–87 for a clear account of why ECT is used in the treatment of depression, what the procedures and its side effects are.

9 Lawrence Le Shan, *How to Meditate: A Guide to Self Discovery*, Bantam Books, New York, 1974.

10 Krishnamurti, *The Second Penguin Krishnamurti Reader*, quoted by J.M. Cohen and J.F. Phipps in *The Common Experience*, Rider, London, 1979, p.19.

11 See Daniel Goleman, *The Varieties of the Meditative Experience*, Rider, London, 1977, for an account of the different 'Meditation Paths' developed from different religious traditions. Goleman shows that the similarities outweigh the differences, as did Aldous Huxley in *The Perennial Philosophy*, Chatto & Windus, London, 1946, and Cohen and Phipps, op.cit.

12 See Alan Watts *Psychotherapy East and West*, Ballantine Books, New York, 1968.

13 See Eugen Herrigel, *Zen and the Art of Archery*, and *Zen and the Art of Flower Arranging*, and David Brandon, *Zen in the Art of Helping*, all published by Routledge & Kegan Paul. There is a series of books entitled *Zen and the Art of . . .*, Zen practices adapted for sports like running and tennis have, from all reports, brought remarkable changes to the practitioners of these sports. The message of these books is 'Do not try; just be.'

14 *The Construction of Life and Death*, Wiley, Chichester and New York, 1982, pp.192–3.

15 Jeffrey Russell, *The Devil. Perceptions of Evil from Antiquity to Primitive Christianity* and *Satan. The Early Christian*

Tradition, Cornell University Press, Ithaca, 1977 and 1981.

16 Jeffrey Russell, personal communication, 1982.

17 Sheldon Kopp, *The End of Innocence – Facing Life Without Illusions*, Bantam Books, New York, 1981, p.45.

18 Sri-Ramamurti in *Seeking the Master* by Muz Murray, Neville Spearman, Jersey, 1980, p.12.

19 Joseph Needleman in *On the Long Search* (based on the BBC series on the world religions, 'The Long Search' by Ronald Eyre), Fount paperbacks, London, 1979, p.272.

20 Tony Lewis 'The struggle to keep the mind's eye open' and 'Down but not out', *Guardian*, 4 and 5 May, 1982.

21 Carol Parris, 'I find talking to my friends can be a lot easier than talking to my husband,' *Guardian*, 7 August 1982.

22 Sheldon Kopp, *If You Meet Buddha on the Road, Kill Him*, Science and Behaviour Books, Palo Alto, 1972, p.26.

23 Jill Tweedie, 'The vision of life seen in depression has the truth in it, the bare-boned skeletan truth,' *Guardian*, 17 April 1982.

24 T.S. Eliot, 'Little Gidding', in *Four Quartets*, Faber, London, 1974, p.54.

25 H.A. Williams, *Tensions, Necessary Conflicts in Life and Love*, Mitchell Beazley, London, 1976, pp.111–12.

26 Aaron Beck *et al.*, *Cognitive Therapy of Depression*, Wiley, New York and Chichester, 1980.

27 Peter M. Lewisohn, Ricardo F. Munoz, Mary Ann Youngren, Antoinette M. Zeiss, *Control Your Depression*, Prentice-Hall, Englewood Cliffs, New Jersey, 1978.

28 Jeremy Ross, 'Learning the Rules of the Fame', in *Mind Out*, the mental health magazine, No. 56, 1981, pp.19–21. (This bi-monthly mental health magazine is now called *Open Mind* and is available from 22 Harley Street, London W1N 2ED (01-637-0741).

29 Self-Help Clearing Houses: in the UK – Share Community Limited, 177 Battersea High Street, London, SW11 3JS, tel: 01-222-0924; in the USA – National Self Help Clearing House, Graduate School and University Center, CUNY, 33 West 42nd Street, Room 1227, New York, N.Y. 10036.

30 Depressives Associated, 19 Merley Ways, Wimborne Minster, Dorset, BW21 1QN, tel: 020 125 3957.

31 Depressives Anonymous, 36 Chestnut Avenue, Beverley, N. Humberside, HU17 9QU.

32 Sheila Ernst and Lucy Goodison, *In Our Own Hands, A book of self help therapy*, The Women's Press, London, 1981.

33 Rainer Marie Rilke, 'For Wolf Graf von Kalckreuth' in *Requiem and Other Poems*, trans. J.B. Leishman, Hogarth Press, London, 1957, pp.137–41.

34 Sheldon Kopp, dedication in *If You Meet Buddha on the Road,*

Kill Him, op.cit.

35 Philip Toynbee, *Part of a Journey*, Collins, London, 1981, p.66.
36 Fenenon, quoted by Aldous Huxley in *The Perennial Philosophy*, op.cit. p.292.
37 Lao Tsu, op. cit.
38 Philip Toynbee, op.cit. p.13.

8 Suppose I decide not to change?

1 Philip Toynbee, *Part of a Journey*, Collins, London, 1981, pp.56, 65, 337,
2 Jill Tweedie, *Guardian*, 12 April 1982. The optical illusions which Jill refers to are:

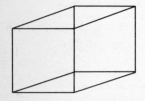 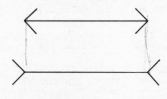

These show how we create our reality with our eyes, and how we can change reality. We can change reality, too, with our words. Is this glass half full or half empty?

9 The Prison Vanishes

1 T.S. Eliot, 'Little Gidding,' in *Four Quartets*, Faber, London, 1974.

INDEX

Mello